PROTECTING POWERS

WITHDRAWN

THE NSPCC/WILEY SERIES
in
PROTECTING CHILDREN

The multi-professional approach

Series Editor: Christopher Cloke,
NSPCC, 42 Curtain Road,
London EC2A 3NX

Jan Horwath,
Department of Sociological Studies,
University of Sheffield,
Sheffield S10 2TU

Peter Sidebotham,
Warwick Medical School,
University of Warwick
Coventry CV4 7AL

This NSPCC/Wiley series explores current issues relating to the prevention of child abuse and the protection of children. The series aims to publish titles that focus on professional practice and policy, and the practical application of research. The books are leading edge and innovative and reflect a multi-disciplinary and inter-agency approach to the prevention of child abuse and the protection of children.

All books have a policy or practice orientation with referenced information from theory and research. The series is essential reading for all professionals and researchers concerned with the prevention of child abuse and the protection of children.

PROTECTING POWERS

Emergency intervention for
children's protection

Judith Masson
With
Deborah McGovern
Kathy Pick
And
Maureen Winn Oakley

BICENTENNIAL
1807
WILEY
2007
BICENTENNIAL

John Wiley & Sons, Ltd

Other Wiley Editorial Offices

John Wiley & Sons Inc., 111 River Street, Hoboken, NJ 07030, USA

Jossey-Bass, 989 Market Street, San Francisco, CA 94103-1741, USA

Wiley-VCH Verlag GmbH, Boschstr. 12, D-69469 Weinheim, Germany

John Wiley & Sons Australia Ltd, 42 McDougall Street, Milton, Queensland 4064, Australia

John Wiley & Sons (Asia) Pte Ltd, 2 Clementi Loop #02-01, Jin Xing Distripark, Singapore 129809

John Wiley & Sons Canada Ltd, 6045 Freemont Blvd, Mississauga, ONT, L5R 4J3.

Wiley also publishes its books in a variety of electronic formats. Some content that appears
in print may not be available in electronic books.

Anniversary Logo Design: Richard J. Pacifico

Library of Congress Cataloguing-in-Publication Data

Masson, J. M. (Judith M.)
     Protecting powers : emergency intervention for children's protection / Judith Masson with Deborah
McGovern, Kathy Pick, and Maureen Winn Oakley.
       p. cm.
     Includes bibliographical references and index.
     ISBN 0-470-01603-5
     1. Children–Legal status, laws, etc.–Great Britain.   2. Child welfare–Great Britain.
     I. McGovern, Deborah.   II. Pick, Kathy.   III. Winn Oakley, Maureen.   IV. Title.

     KD3305.M37 2007
     344.4103′27—dc22   2006038738

A catalogue record for this book is available from the British Library

ISBN HB   9780470016022
ISBN PB   9780470016039

Typeset in 10/12pt Palatino by Aptara Inc., New Delhi, India
Printed and bound in Great Britain by TJ International Ltd, Padstow, Cornwall
This book is printed on acid-free paper responsibly manufactured from sustainable forestry
in which at least two trees are planted for each one used for paper production.

CONTENTS

LIST OF TABLES AND FIGURES

ABOUT THE AUTHORS

Judith Masson is Professor of Socio-legal Studies at the Bristol University, specialising in child law and socio-legal research and teaching courses on family law and international child law. She is co-author with Stephen Cretney and Rebecca Bailey-Harris of *Principles of Family Law* (7th edn, 2003, Sweet and Maxwell). She has been involved in empirical socio-legal research throughout her career, conducting studies on adoption by parents and step-parents (*Mine, Yours or Ours*, 1983, HMSO), the use of wardship proceedings by local authorities to protect children; kinship and inheritance (J. Finch *et al.*, *Wills Inheritance and Families*, 1996, OUP); social work partnerships with parents of children in long-term care (*Lost and Found*, 1999, Ashgate), and children's experience of being represented in care proceedings (*Out of Hearing*, 1999, Wiley). Judith is a member of the Judicial Studies Board and the Family Justice Council.

Deborah McGovern graduated from the University of Portsmouth with a BSc in Psychology and an MSc in Criminal Justice Studies. She spent nearly 10 years in public sector research, focusing initially on people with severe mental illness, and latterly on policing issues. She has been Deputy Clerk to the British Transport Police Authority since 2004. She was research fellow on the Police Protection Study and undertook the majority of the field work.

Kathy Pick was Research Fellow on the EPO Study and undertook the majority of the field work. She spent over 20 years in academic research, and has worked on five socio-legal research studies at different universities in the UK, including work on domestic violence in Wales, the Social Fund, credit unions and poverty, and homelessness and housing policy in Scotland. She was co-author with Tom Mullen and Tony Prosser of *Judicial Review in Scotland* (1996, Wiley).

Maureen Winn Oakley was Senior NSPCC research fellow at the School of Law Warwick University between 1995 and 2004. She is co-author with

Judith Masson of *Out of Hearing* (1999, Wiley) and worked on both the Police Protection and the EPO studies. Since leaving Warwick she has been involved in managing the Children's Rights Service in Birmingham and in September 2005 became Children's Rights Commissioner for Children and Young People in Sandwell.

ACKNOWLEDGEMENTS

The authors are indebted to the NSPCC and the Nuffield Foundation for the financial support, which made this research possible. Special thanks are due to Dr Pat Cawson, formerly Head of Research at the NSPCC and Sharon Witherspoon, Deputy Director of the Nuffield Foundation for their constant encouragement. Thanks are also due to the Tony Butler, who was Chief Constable for Gloucestershire and ACPO lead on child protection at the time of the Police Protection Study; to the Department of Constitutional Affairs; Her Majesty's Courts Service; the Association of Directors of Social Services for facilitating the EPO Study; and to the Departments of Health and Education and Skills, particularly Bruce Clark.

We wish to acknowledge the contribution of the members of the advisory groups for the two projects: Professor Lee Bridges of Warwick University, School of Law; Barbara Esam, lawyer, NSPCC Public Policy Department; Katherine Gieve, partner with Bindmans solicitors; Joan Hunt, Oxford University, Department of Social Policy and Social Work; Inspector Ian Clark, Gloucestershire Police; Mavis Maclean, Oxford University, Centre for Family Law and Policy and the Department of Constitutional Affairs; Arran Poyser, HM Inspectorate of Court's Administration; Paul Secker, Assistant Director for Social Services, London Borough of Wandsworth; Kevin Smith, CAFCASS Public Law Manager for Leicestershire; Philip Thomson, Head of Legal Services, Essex County Council.

We are particularly grateful to the police officers, local authority staff, solicitors, children's guardians, magistrates' legal advisors, magistrates and other court staff in the research areas who contributed by helping us to understand systems, find records and through sharing their views and experiences in interviews and discussions. Respect for confidentiality means that none of these crucial people can be named.

Many others contributed to the completion of this book: Dr Shilu Shah and Dr David Wright who assisted in transcription of interviews; Usra Iqbal and Sarah Reed who entered the data; and Nihid Iqbal and Lesley Morris who provided secretarial support. I am also grateful to the many colleagues who have commented on drafts, particularly Dave Cowan, Richard Young and Dendy Platt at Bristol University, Jonathan Dickens at UEA, Stephen Cretney, John Devaney of Queen's University, Belfast and Theresa Donaldson, formerly of the Northern Ireland Guardian ad Litem Agency.

PREFACE

Considerable concerns have been raised about the secrecy of the family courts; where decisions are made behind closed doors the courts are not fully accountable. The courts, in deciding whether children should be made the subject of emergency protection orders or care orders, etc., are intended to hold local authorities and their staff to account, but, when decisions are made in secret, the public can only trust that the actions are appropriate. However, allowing public or press access or even holding public inquiries does not provide an adequate basis for understanding how powers are used, the reasons actions are taken and whether organisations – the police, local authorities and the courts – use their powers appropriately. These approaches to providing public scrutiny focus on individual cases, and it is never possible to tell whether what happened in one case was the product of an unfortunate combination of events and individuals or reflects structural issues that apply elsewhere.

Public inquiries are only ever used where cases are thought to have gone very badly wrong, and these cases provide a poor basis for a wider understanding of problems and practices necessary for practice development or law reform. The understandings of emergency intervention gained through the *Cleveland*, *Orkney* and *Victoria Climbié* inquiries provided the public with a limited, one-dimensional, perspective of child protection social work and emergency intervention, which belies the variety and complexity of this work. Although inquiries may find a truth about a set of events, the financial cost of doing so is astronomical and the impact on individuals and services caught up in the process very heavy. The outcome is really only an exceptionally detailed anecdote and, as such, provides an inadequate basis for reform. Using individual cases as a mechanism for scrutinising practice also risks exposing those concerned, their distress and private tragedies to the extreme intrusion of the press and the prurient gaze of the public.

Socio-legal research provides a far better way of understanding systems and practices. By putting individual cases in the context of a sample of similar cases, identified on clear and consistent principles, it is possible to establish the patterns of practice and explore the reasons for them. Quantitative research makes it possible to establish influences and occurrences; qualitative research enables these to be linked to individuals' perspectives, interactions between those involved and the sequences of events. In the research discussed in this book, the picture constructed by linking both quantitative and qualitative material from the two separate studies enabled a complex set of interactions between the police, local authorities and the courts to be described and analysed. This provides the basis for considering the limitations of the courts, how to secure accountability in child protection social work and wider reform.

Researchers must be accountable for their findings; the methods used in the studies discussed here are explained in the Appendix A (see p. 225). The quotations in the text are taken verbatim from the transcripts of interviews, with only sufficient editing to remove identifying detail, repetitions and extraneous material. The analysis and the conclusions drawn are set out throughout the text and the wider implications are discussed in the final chapter. The principal author takes full responsibility for these; they should not be taken to represent the views of the organisations that funded or collaborated with the research.

This book has been written at a time when social services for children are undergoing major reorganisation (with the introduction of new terminology) following the implementation of the Children Act 2004. New departments are taking over responsibilities for both children's social services and education; local authorities are required to appoint a Director of Children's Services who will be professionally accountable for local authority functions for children in social care, education and health. These departments will remain the lead departments for child protection but will have many other responsibilities and include staff and senior managers without a social work background. The research was conducted before these changes were on the horizon. For the sake of consistency, the terms used by the interviewers and those interviewed 'social services' and 'local authority social services departments' have been retained in the text.

In order to fit with the accountability requirements placed on universities by government funding bodies, it has become customary for researchers on collaborative projects to explain who was responsible for each publication. This book and the research reports on which it was based were written almost exclusively by Judith Masson; Deborah McGovern and Maureen Winn Oakley wrote small parts of the report on the police protection study. Judith and Deborah worked together on the analysis for the police protection study; Maureen did the first analysis of the social workers' interviews in both studies. The remaining analysis and reanalysis of both the quantitative and qualitative material and the work on history, law and context in both studies was undertaken by Judith. None of this analysis and writing would have been possible without the meticulous fieldwork and the brilliant interviews on which it was based. Deborah McGovern had the main responsibility for the fieldwork in the police protection study and Kathy Pick took this role for the EPO study. Maureen Winn Oakley contributed much hard work and organisation to both studies.

1

EMERGENCY POWERS FOR CHILD PROTECTION

Parliament often makes family laws 'in the dark' – that is, without any clear picture of how the family justice system works, or the eventual impact of those laws once they are in place. (Department of Constitutional Affairs, 2006a)

INTRODUCTION

This is a book about child protection, the accountability of professionals using child protection powers and the effectiveness of the courts in controlling emergency child protection. It is based on, and discusses the findings from, two empirical studies into the use of emergency powers for child protection conducted between 1998 and 2004, and funded by the NSPCC and the Nuffield Foundation. These studies explored the way in which emergency powers were used to protect children. Who used them? Why? When? And in what circumstances? These studies sought to follow the socio-legal tradition of understanding the operation of the law in practice through the analysis of case records and interviews with practitioners, using the intentions of the legislators and the interpretations of judges only as reference points. The work explores the gap between the law in books, the Children Act 1989 and the law in practice (Abel, 1973) in order to explain the structural limitations that prevent practice from matching the intent of legislation and restrict the courts' ability to hold local authorities to account.

Child protection professionals work in a legal context doing 'statutory social work', but they also work within agencies and inter-agency structures where different professionals interpret their legal responsibilities differently, where law is not the only determinant of action, and where it is not always the dominant influence (Dickens, 2006; Braye & Preston-Shoot, 2006). Law is both a source of power and of control for social work action; social workers are also

In England and Wales, emergency powers allow children to be removed from danger without the need for either court proceedings involving parental participation or proof of significant harm. In doing so, they overcome the obstacles to child rescue created by highly formal court proceedings and deference to parents' rights. Emergency powers override the normal rules in care proceedings, which safeguard family privacy, to allow protective intervention but they place parents and children at greater risk of unrestrained action from child protection agencies, including the police. Moreover, where they are seen as avoiding unnecessary procedural complications, simplified emergency systems can become routine responses (Social Services Select Committee, 1983–4, para 123). Emergency child protection powers are restricted; their use is subject to conditions, procedures and time limits, but these are defined in such a way that the primary purpose, securing children's safety, is not frustrated. Not only do they ease children's entry to the child protection system they may also help to keep them there. The limited standards applied initially under emergency procedures may become determinative because all those charged with reviewing cases are influenced by the fact that such action was considered necessary (Cooper Davis & Barua, 1995; Chill, 2004).

Protecting children in emergencies necessitates a rapid response – *acting in time* (Ferguson, 2003). Government guidance on child protection, *Working Together*, includes a section on immediate protection, emphasising the importance of acting quickly 'where there is a risk to the life of the child or a likelihood of serious immediate harm' (Department of Health *et al.*, 1999, para 5.23; Department for Education and Skills, 2006, para 5.49). Immediate action creates the space for decisions to be taken about the child's future care. However, the focus on securing the child's safety, may lead attention away from balancing safety with the risks of intervention.

Child protection emergencies can arise from physical abuse where injuries require treatment. Long-term neglect is also recognised as significant harm, and may require an immediate response because of its damaging physical effects. Child protection emergencies are not defined entirely by the child's physical condition; the family context is crucial for the child's safety. The parents' response to a proposed intervention can create additional risks to the child through retaliation, self-harm or flight, and any of these may necessitate acting without warning parents. Emergencies may arise without warning but others can be predicted. *Working Together* refers to 'planned emergency action' on the basis that child protection interventions should, where possible, be based on interagency discussions not the views of a single agency alone (Department of Health *et al.*, 1999, para 5.50). Planned emergency response also occurs where the risk arises immediately an event occurs but it is unclear when this will be; for example, where a child will be born to a mother unable to provide safe care.

Like other aspects of child protection, identification of emergencies is a subjective matter where assumptions about how a situation will develop and perceptions about what is expected influence thresholds (Dartington Research Unit 1995, 17). Intervention is about both protection and prevention. Abuse is a predictor of further abuse; there are risks to children of not intervening once harm has been identified. Both victims and other children in the family may need to be separated from alleged perpetrators. The culture of blame means that workers are, or feel, at risk if they fail to prevent serious harm (Ferguson, 2003, 116; Scourfield, 2003;) and may therefore focus on making defensive decisions (Dingwall, Eekelaar & Murray, 1995; Fernandez, 1996, 178; Parton, 1996, 13). These considerations also apply to child protection generally; terms such as 'real emergency' or 'dire emergency' are used to distinguish cases justifying use of special powers from others where action needs to be taken but the ordinary powers can be used (Department of Health, 1991d) but it is not clear that there is agreement about what these mean or that it is possible when faced with an emergency to know whether it is (or will be) dire.

Just as nursing support can prevent the need for emergency medical admission, increased family support may enable parents to care for their children. For example, parents who are substance misusers may receive treatment for their addiction and be able to focus on their children's needs rather than their own. However, such a change is not simply about refocusing services from investigation and intervention to family support (Dartington Research Unit, 1995), it requires a change in the relationship between social workers and parents with increased levels of trust and respect. Local authorities have to make services available for families before a crisis has been reached, and parents and the community as a whole have to be willing to accept that health and social care professionals have a role in directing the way children are looked after by their parents.

PARTNERSHIP WITH PARENTS

The Children Act 1989 sought to rebalance relationships between families and the State by extending local authorities' responsibilities to support families and to set clear limits and procedures for intervention in family life. 'Partnership with parents and consultation with children on the basis of careful joint planning and agreement' was stated as the 'guiding principle' for the provision of services (Department of Health, 1991b, para 2.1). Rather than focusing on parental failings and seeing parents as disposable, the Act sought a change of emphasis, recognising the strengths of parents and their capacity to cope with their difficulties. The aim was to create positive relationships between families and local authorities so that parents would draw on their support when they needed this and local authorities would not have to resort to their powers of compulsion. Such co-operative working is more effective in securing children's well-being (Department of Health, 1995, 9), and reinforces both parental responsibility for children and the local authority role in supporting families.

Partnership with parents is not limited to circumstances where children are supported in their own homes, but includes arrangements where children are accommodated by local authorities. Accommodation (still sometimes referred to as 'voluntary care') was presented as a service to families without stigma (Parton, 1991, 155). Parents would remain fully involved in decisions about their children's care. In contrast to the previous law, parents retain the right to remove children from local authority accommodation, just as they would if their children were staying with relatives or friends. Parents do not have to give notice of their intention to remove their children; and if the local authority wants to continue to look after them it must obtain a court order. Changing the law in this way was controversial; concerns were expressed that foster carers would have to hand over children to parents who were obviously not in a fit state to look after them. However, Lord Mackay who piloted the Bill through the Lords, asserted that foster carers could keep children in such circumstances by relying on the general powers to safeguard children (Children Act 1989, s.3(5)). This explanation was not very convincing (Cretney, Masson & Bailey-Harris, 2003, 710), but it indicated that the government intended to hold onto the balance it had set in the Bill and to leave social workers and carers to manage the consequences as best they could.

Compulsory measures, requiring families to accept services or having children removed and placed in care, are only available where children are 'suffering or likely to suffer significant harm' (Children Act 1989, s.31(2)). The courts decide whether a case for compulsory measures has been established. Court orders are not routine; the 'minimum intervention' principle (Children Act 1989, s.1(5)) allows orders to be granted only where they are necessary for the child's welfare. This was intended to encourage local authorities to work with parents and gain their co-operation, rather than to resort to the courts. The Act recognised that children continued to need protection but sought to change the way protection was provided with greater reliance on protective agreements with parents and more limited use of the courts.

Partnership in Practice

Initially there was a decline in the number of care proceedings, but this may have reflected local authority uncertainty about bringing cases under the new provisions rather than major changes of approach. Early research on child protection cases brought to the courts suggested that proceedings were less likely to be crisis driven than they had been previously. Rather than rushing to court, local authorities made strenuous efforts to avoid compulsory powers and relied on providing accommodation or agreements for children to live with relatives. This change meant that fewer emergency orders were made than before the Act, but such orders were still used in cases of crisis where children were at home (Hunt, Macleod & Thomas, 1999, 67). Research on the use of accommodation also suggested that it had partly replaced proceedings. The majority of children who were being accommodated after the Act were very similar to those previously removed under court orders (Packman & Hall, 1998, 257). Emergency admissions to accommodation rather than planned arrangements were common; in one of the two authorities in Packman and Hall's study, two out of three admissions occurred with less than 24 hours warning, as did three out of five arrangements for 'difficult adolescents' over-all (Packman & Hall, 1998, 78, 121). As in the case of proceedings, a quick response was linked with viewing the provision of accommodation as a 'last resort'.

Partnership and Compulsion

The Children Act 1989 enables local authorities to protect children by work-ing with parents, or if this is not possible, to use their compulsory powers. Compulsory powers provide the context in which agreement is given or with-held. Parents' power to accept or reject proposals for their children's care is limited by social workers' powers. Packman and Hall identified cases where explicit threats had been made to parents to agree to accommodation. They questioned the voluntary nature of accommodation agreements where there were child protection concerns and commented that the use of threats of legal action meant agreements were just a sham. Also, if the response to a parental decision to remove a child from accommodation was court proceedings, this could feel little different from the previous law where they had to give notice and their parental rights could be taken away. Such an approach was contrary to the spirit of the Children Act, but made it possible to avoid court action as the Act intended (Packman & Hall, 1998, 95, 265).

From a lawyer's perspective, avoidance of proceeding poses further prob-lems, relating to the control of local authority power and the protection of the interests of parents and children. Legal proceedings are intended to ensure a fair hearing for all parties. If arrangements are made outside proceedings, the basis for intervention is not tested; threats may produce a response which the courts would not impose. The effect of the agreement and the duration of any arrangement may not be clear; there may even be uncertainty about what has been agreed. Agreements may be made which serve the interests of the parents and the local authority, but take little account of the child's wishes and feelings. Where there are court proceedings, a children's guardian puts forward the child's welfare interests, but outside the proceedings the child's interests are taken to be protected by the parents.

CHILD PROTECTION POWERS

As well as providing for agreements for accommodation and other services, the Children Act 1989 includes two methods of securing the protection of children in an emergency where the parents will not agree. Any person can apply to a magistrates' court under s.44 for an emergency protection order (EPO). Alternatively, all police officers have a power under s.46 to take children into 'police protection' without the need for any court proceedings. The grounds, procedures and effects of these provisions are considered below.

Emergency Protection Orders

An emergency protection order is a short-term court order to secure the child's immediate protection. Department of Health guidance states that the purpose of the order is to allow the child to be protected 'in a genuine emergency' and stresses that it should not be regarded as 'a routine response to allegations of child abuse or as a routine first step' for care proceedings (Department of Health, 1991a, paras 4.28, 4.30). Although the order is termed 'an emergency protection order' there is no specific requirement for an emergency, or for urgency, except in cases where child protection workers cannot get access to the child. The court must be satisfied that the order is necessary, which would not be the case where the parent could safely have charge of the child until care proceedings can be heard on notice, a period of three days.

The order requires anyone who can to produce the child if asked to do so; it gives the person with the order power to remove the child, or to prevent their removal, and parental responsibility. These powers are limited. The child can only be removed to safeguard their welfare and must be returned if it is safe to do so; the parental responsibility granted by the order only permits action that is 'reasonably required to safeguard and promote the child's welfare' (s.44(4),(5), (10)–(12)).

Emergency protection orders can be sought by anyone. In contrast to all other orders under the Children Act 1989, there are no restrictions on who can apply for them. Controlling EPOs is a matter for the courts. The court is responsible for ensuring that the conditions for making an order are satisfied:

> The court may make the order, if but only if, it is satisfied that there is reasonable cause to believe that the child is likely to suffer significant harm if –
>
> (i) he is not removed to accommodation provided by or on behalf of the applicant; or
> (ii) he does not remain in the place in which he is currently being accommodated. (s.44(1)(a))

The court assesses the evidence presented by the applicant, and will also hear from the parents if they have been notified, attend and want to make representations. The basis for the order is the court's acceptance that there is sufficient evidence to establish a serious risk to the child. The standard for intervention is on a par with the first part of the test for a care or supervision order but it is not necessary to prove significant harm, only that there is 'reasonable cause to believe' that it is likely. Alternative grounds apply to cases where a local authority (or the NSPCC) is making enquiries and these are being frustrated by an unreasonable refusal of access to the child. Refusal of access during child protection inquiries is a serious matter and has been an issue in a number of cases where children have been killed (Thomas, 1994, 77). In such cases, the local authority must seek a court order unless it is satisfied of the child's welfare (s.47(6)). The court considering any EPO application only needs to be satisfied that the applicant has 'reasonable cause to suspect' that the child is suffering or likely to suffer significant harm and 'reasonable cause to believe access to the child is required as a matter of urgency' (s.44(1)(b),(c)). In all cases, the court must also be satisfied that the order is necessary and in the child's best interests (s.1(1),(5)).

Procedures and Guidance

EPO applications are made to the Family Proceedings Court (the lowest level of court with jurisdiction in family matters) unless there are proceedings relating to the child underway in a higher court. Most applications are dealt with by 'lay' magistrates rather than professional judges. The Court Rules provide that applications should normally be made on one day's notice but allow applications *ex parte*, that is without notice to the parents, with the permission of the magistrates' clerk. Without notice applications can be heard by a single magistrate. *Volume 1* of the guidance on the Act (Department of Health, 1991a) appears to have assumed that orders would 'usually be heard ex parte' because the 'very fact that the situation is considered to be an emergency requiring immediate action will make [notification of the parents] inappropriate or impractical in most cases.' Also, '[i]t should be borne in mind that in certain instances to put the parents on notice of the application might place the child in greater danger' (Department of Health, 1991a, para. 4.46). However, *Volume 7* stresses the need for arrangements to be put in place for the immediate appointment of a children's guardian for EPO applications. It notes that *without notice* applications need the permission of the court, that a procedure for contacting a guardian at very short notice is required, and that the courts and guardian service should clarify their expectations about these appointments (Department of Health, 1991c, paras 2.69–70).

When granting the order, the court may include provision for the applicant to enter and search premises and/or a warrant to allow the police to assist them, using reasonable force if necessary (s.48). The Department of Health advises applicants to consider making such applications but points out that in 'dire emergencies' the police can use their powers under the Police and Criminal Evidence Act 1984 (s.17(1)(e)) to enter and search without a warrant (Department of Health, 1991a, para 4.57). The court may make directions about contact with the child or medical assessments so that it controls these aspects of the child's care. In addition, it has the power to exclude a person from the child's home if this would protect the child and avoid the need to move him or her, providing that there is someone else who is able and willing to care for the child there (s.44A).

The order lasts up to eight days; a local authority (or the NSPCC) can apply for it to be extended further for up to seven days. However, the Department of Health notes that even where the EPO has been obtained following a 'genuine emergency' it should be possible to make the application for a care order without seeking an extension (Department of Health, 1991a, para 4.66). Any challenges to the order should be made in the magistrates' court and not by judicial review (*Re M,* 2003). There is no appeal, but after 72 hours parents, carers and the child can apply for the order to be discharged if they were not notified of the original proceedings or were not present when the order was made (s.45). If the order is refused, the applicant cannot appeal but can apply again with further evidence (*Essex Count Council v. F,* 1993) or ask the police to use their powers of police protection.

Recently, three High Court judges have used their judgements in care cases to express anxieties about EPOs. Their views have been formulated at a considerable distance in time and space from the pressure to protect experienced by front line workers and without the experience of regularly making decisions in EPO cases. In response to specific examples, including one (*Re X,* 2006) of poor practice by all concerned, they have suggested a more restrictive approach to the use of such powers and greater emphasis on protecting parents' rights. Such statements are not binding interpretations of the legislation but they are expected to influence both local authority applications and magistrates' courts' willingness to grant orders.

Munby J, hearing a care case where children had been removed by EPO following a long history of concerns and lack of parental co-operation over the children's medical treatment, suggested that a child assessment order (CAO) should have been used rather than an EPO. The local authority had obtained an EPO without notice so that the children could be medically examined to establish whether the parents were following the children's drug therapy appropriately. It is unlikely that evidence would have been obtained had the parents been given seven days notice of the assessment which is required for a CAO (Masson, 2004b). Munby J acknowledged that EPOs were 'in principle' compatible with the European Convention on Human Rights, even where they were sought without notice to the parents but stressed the 'heavy burden of responsibility' on local authorities applying for, and courts granting, such orders (X County Council v B, 2005, para 34–5). He suggested that some practices, such as the use of eight-day orders, restriction on applications for discharge, the lack of appeal and the possibility of repeated removal, might not be fully compatible with the Convention. For this reason,

> it was all the more important that both the local authority and the justices in the Family Proceedings Court approach every application for an EPO with anxious awareness of the extreme gravity of the relief being sought and a scrupulous regard for the European Convention rights of the child and the parents. (para 41)

This approach was followed by Ryder J (who had acted for the local authority in X County Council). The local authority received information which suggested that a couple who were claiming to be the parents of a baby might have obtained him illegally in Africa and trafficked him to England. After discussion with social workers, the parents agreed to DNA tests. The day after the local authority obtained results indicating that the couple were not the child's parents, it obtained an EPO without notice and removed the baby. Ryder J was highly critical of this. Giving a short period of notice would have been adequate protection against the 'supposed risk' of the couple disappearing with the child and would have allowed them to participate in the proceedings (Haringey LBC v C, 2005, para 26). The fact that adults were claiming to be parents of an unrelated child did not justify removing the child without allowing them to take part in the proceedings.

Most recently, McFarlane J was extremely critical of the decision to seek an EPO, without notice and against the advice of the local authority lawyer. He said less about the obvious failures of the court to assess whether the order was justified. The case illustrates how weak accountability mechanisms can be. In the (unidentified) local authority an application could be made without legal or senior management approval; the court granted the order with little evidence giving 'totally inadequate' reasons in (Re X, 2006, para 97).

The application had been made immediately following a case conference where there had been no suggestion of any need to remove the nine-year-old girl from her parents. The action was not precipitated by a decision that an emergency response was required to protect the child but rather because the opportunity to intervene arose when the mother took her to the Accident and Emergency department of a local hospital and asked that she be examined for 'stomach pains'. Not only did the case identify defective decision making by the social workers and managers involved, it also indicated failures in the legal process. No children's guardian or solicitor was appointed to represent the child. The court never considered whether an application without notice to the parents was justified and did not assess the local authority's case adequately. It did not wait to hear evidence from the social worker who had most knowledge of the case but accepted, apparently without question, the assertions of the team leader. These failures of practice did not become apparent for many months; the child was separated from her family and placed in foster care for over a year before the local authority's care order application was rejected.

McFarlane J stated that cases of emotional abuse, non-specific sexual abuse or fabricated/induced illness where there is no medical evidence of imme-diate risk of physical harm 'will rarely warrant an EPO' (para 101*l*). EPOs should be limited to cases of 'genuine emergencies' and the court should con-sider separately whether there was a case for a hearing without notice. He questioned the wisdom of giving magistrates effectively the sole jurisdiction in EPO cases. In any event, magistrates needed to give more time and atten-tion to these cases even if this precluded them hearing other cases. He restated and expanded the guidance given by Munby J, with the aim of raising the standards of court proceedings for EPOs.

Police Protection

Police protection is a power that police officers can use where the requirements of the Children Act are met. The Act automatically grants the power to those who are police officers, just as other legislation gives the police powers to arrest suspects or enter premises without a warrant. The officer does not have to obtain authority from a court nor from a senior officer. However, social workers, lawyers, police officers and even Her Majesty's Inspectorate of Constabulary (HMIC, 1999, 25) refer to 'police protection orders' or 'PPOs' as if use of the power were subject to external control.

> Where a constable has reasonable cause to believe that a child would otherwise be likely to suffer significant harm, he may –
>
> (a) remove the child to suitable accommodation and keep him there; or
> (b) take such steps as are reasonable to ensure that the child's removal from any hospital, or other place, in which he is then being accommodated , is prevented. (Children Act 1989, s.46(1))

The basis for intervention is the police officer's belief about the risks to the child. Mere suspicion is not sufficient, the officer must have 'reasonable cause' for believing that the child is at risk. Not all risks justify the use of police protection; the officer must believe that child is 'likely to suffer significant harm'. As with an EPO, the standard for intervention reflects the first part of the test for a care or supervision order; but there is no need to establish the cause of the harm or that intervention is in the child's best interests. And nothing has to be proved to a court. The power allows control over where the child is accommodated for up to 72 hours so long as a 'designated officer considers that there is still reasonable cause for believing that the child would be likely to suffer significant harm if released.' The designated officer can also apply for an EPO on behalf of the local authority (s.46(7)). This allows the police to secure the child's protection beyond 72 hours even where the local authority is unable or unwilling to do so. The police do not gain parental responsibility for the child but have both a power and a duty to take reasonable action to safeguard and promote the child's welfare (ss.3(5) and 46(9)).

Once a child has been taken into police protection, the police have specific obligations to liaise with the local authority both where the child was found, and where the child usually lives. An officer who has removed a child from home or elsewhere must arrange for the child to be accommodated by a local authority or placed in a refuge. Local authorities are required to receive and provide accommodation for children in police protection (s.21(2)(a)). The officer must inform the child about what they have done and what else they propose to do, and must try to find out the child's wishes and feelings. He or she must also inform parents and carers about the immediate plans for the child and arrangements for contact. The officer's action is supervised by a 'designated officer' who is responsible for conducting inquiries and making further decisions about the child's care and contact with their family.

Supervision by the designated officer provides the only check on the proper use of police protection. There is no provision for external review, or for appeal, although in theory, misuse of the power could be challenged though a writ of habeas corpus or by seeking judicial review of the officer's decision. The short duration of the power makes it practically impossible to use court proceedings to secure release from it but if the power were abused, a child who was removed unlawfully might claim compensation.

Guidance on Police Protection

When the Children Act was implemented, the Home Office issued non-binding guidance to police forces in the form of a Circular. This largely re-peated to requirements of the statute, giving much less guidance than the Department of Health provided on other aspects of the Act (Barry, 1993, 9). Police protection was intended to be used when there was 'insufficient time' to apply for an EPO (Home Office, 1991, para 13). No further guidance was given about the circumstances when the power should be used but officers were directed to the definitions of harm in s.31(9) and alerted to the need to 'use a standard appropriate for the child' and take account of the child's particular characteristics (para 14). Guidance issued by the Department of

Health was slightly more expansive, acknowledging that police protection replaced the former police place of safety order 'which was used to hold children such as runaways and glue-sniffers or whose parents had abandoned them' (Department of Health, 1991a, para 4.71). Police protection was not only intended to provide an immediate response where the local authority intended to apply for an EPO, it was a general power for protecting any child at risk of significant harm who came to police attention, including children at risk from their own behaviour.

The Home Office guidance emphasised that children should not be brought to police stations, which had been defined as 'places of safety' under the previous legislation. Suitable accommodation for a child removed into police protection 'will clearly not be police premises except for a short period in exceptional circumstances.' Chief Constables were expected to liaise with local authorities to ensure there was provision for children who were removed (Home Office, 1991, para 15). They were also advised 'to consider designating officers of the rank of Inspector' to take on the role of designated officer (para 19). Designated officers were 'legally in charge' of children in police protection, even where they were accommodated elsewhere. The responsibilities they had for the child were equivalent to the limited parental responsibility conferred by an emergency protection order (para 23).

Following the inquiry into the death of Victoria Climbié (Laming, 2003), the 1991 Circular was replaced to provide 'greater clarity about when and how' to use the power (Home Office, 2003, para 1). The new Circular considered at much greater length what amounted to significant harm, indicating a range of circumstances when intervention might be required but stated,

> Police protection powers should only be used when necessary, the principle being that whenever possible the decision to remove a child from a parent or carer should be made by a court. All local authorities should have in place arrangements . . . whereby out of hours applications for EPOs . . . may be made speedily and without an excess of bureaucracy. Police protection powers should only be used where this is not possible. Save in exceptional circumstances (e.g. where there is an imminent threat to the child's welfare), no child is to be taken into police protection until the investigating officer has seen the child and assessed his or her circumstances. (paras 14–16)

The Circular repeated but expanded on points made in the earlier guidance about the role of the designated officer, providing suitable accommodation and liaising with the local authority. It stressed the separate roles of the officer who initiates police protection, the investigating officer, and the designated officer who provides 'an independent oversight' and should be 'at least of the rank of Inspector in all cases' (paras 8–9). Designated officers should regularly review the continued use of the power in respect of a child even though the child will normally be accommodated elsewhere (para 40). 'A police station is not suitable accommodation' but the Circular advised that where children were exceptionally brought to a police station 'every effort should be made to ensure that the child is physically safe [and] comfortable ... ' (paras 28–9). Arrangements could be made for children to stay with relatives but 'basic appropriate checks' should be made in relation to proposed carers (para 30). Police officers could apply for an EPO in their own right and the designated officer could do so on behalf of the local authority, whether the authority know of or agree to this. The police should 'make reasonable efforts to consult' the local authority before making such an application (para 53).

CONTROLLING THE POLICE VIA POLICE PROTECTION

Police officers are asked by the public for help in all sorts of situations which have nothing to do with law and order or the protection of life, limb or property, such as delivering babies and providing family advice and assistance (Punch & Naylor, 1973; Shapland & Vagg, 1988). These are part of community policing, and depend on mutual agreement rather than any exercise of power. The police are traditionally the temporary repository of lost and abandoned children (Thomas, 1994, 74) and occasionally come across children in distress in the course of their work. Police protection provides a way of policing such children who would be at risk if the police had no power to take charge of them. It sets limits; unless other powers are exercised, children can only be removed if they are at risk of significant harm. They cannot just be rounded up and taken from the streets. Unlike adults, young children cannot agree 'to help with police enquiries' nor to accompany an officer voluntarily; parents have the right to make these decisions, and even then, child suspects who are questioned are entitled to the support of an 'appropriate adult' to protect them from police authority (Hodgson, 1997). The existence of the statutory power to take a child into police protection avoids officers seeking to rely on discretion or natural authority and imposes controls on them. An officer who takes charge of a child in order to protect him or her becomes subject to a series of duties to inform the child, parent and local authority, and the supervision of the designated officer. These protect the child by ensuring there is oversight of the officer's actions and other people know where the child is.

EPOS AND POLICE PROTECTION COMPARED

The main differences between EPOs and police protection are the length of time they last and the way they are obtained. Although the parents of lost or abandoned children may be found quickly, and injuries which were thought to be inflicted may turn out to be accidental, there will be many circumstances where the problems are not resolved within 72 hours. In such cases, police protection must be followed by new arrangements to safeguard the child. The short duration of the power makes it impractical to move directly to care proceedings and so there must be an agreement with the parents or an application for EPO to cover the period between the end of police protection and the hearing of the interim care order (ICO) application. In such cases, the EPO can be seen as a way of extending the protection initiated through use of the police power.

Police protection is also a means of protecting a child before an EPO can be obtained. It is much simpler for police officers to decide to use their powers, than for a social worker to make an application to the court for an EPO, even though this can be done without notifying the parents or providing any written evidence. There are practical considerations such as the special arrangements that have to be made for legal advice or court proceedings out of normal working hours, whilst the police provide a service 24 hours a day. There are also questions of standards for intervention and the protection of human rights. Although the tests for an EPO and using police protection are almost the same, only an EPO is subject to external review before it is used. This is intended to provide some check against unjustifiable action, and some protection for the parents' and child's rights to family life. Evidence provided to the Climbié Inquiry suggested that, at least in London, there was general reliance on police protection in place of EPOs. Lord Laming recommended that legal advice should be available to local authorities 24 hours a day (Laming, 2003, rec 47), but this was not carried forward by the Government. However, the revised Home Office Circular, Department of Health Guidance and the new *Working Together* (Department of Health *et al.*, 1999) all indicate a stricter approach to the use of police protection.

> If it is necessary to remove a child, a local authority should wherever possible – and unless a child's safety is otherwise at immediate risk – apply for an emergency protection order. **Police powers should only be used in exceptional circumstances where there is insufficient time to seek an emergency protection order or for reasons of immediate safety of the child.** (Department for Education and Skills, 2006, para 5.51; Department of Health *et al.*, 2003, para 23.3 emphasis in original)

A recent claim by a child and his parents that their rights were infringed by the use of emergency powers required the courts to consider the interrelationship between police protection and EPOs. The Court of Appeal stated that the Children Act 'accorded primacy' to EPOs because they are 'sanctioned by the court' and involve 'a more elaborate, sophisticated and complete process' than police protection (*Langley v Liverpool City Council*, 2005, para 38). Reversing the lower court, it accepted that a police officer who knew an EPO has been obtained could still use the police power but such action was restricted to cases where there were 'compelling reasons' (para 46). Since there were no such compelling reasons, the police were liable for removing the child, even though a social worker could have done so under the EPO which had already been granted. It remains to be seen whether the additional test will raise the threshold for the exercise of the power.

THE USE OF EMERGENCY POWERS

Numbers can show trends but cannot indicate whether too much or too little use is made of these orders, or whether applications are being made in the right cases. The quality and usefulness of the data may be seen as reflecting the interest taken by agencies and government departments and suggest, at least in the case of police powers, significant neglect.

There are two main sources of data on emergency protection orders but neither provides a complete or accurate picture of their use. The *Judicial Statistics* (Department for Constitutional Affairs, 2003), published annually from a return completed by court staff, records the numbers of applications and orders for each calendar year. However, because returns are filed by only half of magistrates' courts the tables use imputed data. The Department for Education and Skills (and previously the Department of Health) publishes detailed statistics based on returns completed by local authorities in relation to each child who is looked after by a local authority (Department of Health, 2003a; Department for Education and Skills, 2004). This includes census information, a snapshot of the population of looked after children on 31 March each year, and information about children who enter or leave public care each year, using the standard financial year, April to March. In addition, it produced the annual *Children Act Report*, which included data on EPOs up to 2002.

There are two distinct ways of measuring the use of emergency powers, the numbers of applications and orders, or the proportion of care proceedings starting with emergency action. Table 1.1 reproduces the figures, from the *Judicial Statistics* (Department for Constitutional Affairs) for EPO applications and from the *Children Act Reports* (Department for Education and Skills) for orders made and extensions to EPOs. It also includes unpublished data on completed EPO cases from Her Majesty's Courts Service which were provided to the researchers, and calculations of the proportions of orders granted and extended. The number of applications shown in the *Judicial Statistics* is substantially lower than that in the Courts Service data; between 2000 and 2002 the published figures indicate a decline in use but the Court Service data show that the number of cases was stable or rising. Data from 1992 to 1996 make it possible to calculate the proportion of orders that were extended. Approximately one in eight orders were extended. The proportion of EPO

Table 1.1   Numbers of EPO applications and orders

Year	1992	1993	1994	1995	1996	1997	1998	1999	2000	2001	2002
EPO (HMCS)							3761	3494	2928	2942	3333
EPO app (*Judicial Statistics*)	2321	2505	3072	2959	2417	2821	2799	1750	2488	2121	1960
EPO DH; DfES	2064	2282	2754	2697	2237	2621	2612	1516	2232	1890	1728
EPO + ext (DH; DfES)	2423	2546	3144	3054	2565	2393	2473	1516	2232	2127	NA
extensions (DH; DfES)	359	264	390	357	328	–	–	–	–	–	–
% extended (DH)	12.5	11.6	14.2	13.2	14.7	–	–	–	–	–	–
% success (*Judicial Statistics*)	88.9	91.1	89.6	91.1	92.6	92.9	93.3	86.6	89.7	89.1	88.2

Sources: (DH) Department of Health, 2000, 2002; (DfES) Department for Education and Skills, 2003; Department of Constitutional Affairs, 2003 and unpublished data from Her Majesty's Court Service (HMCS).

applications resulting in emergency protection orders appears fairly constant at just under 90 per cent. More detailed information about the outcome of the EPO applications in the study is discussed in Chapter 7.

Table 1.2 reproduces figures from the *Looked after Children Statistics* (Department for Education and Skills, 2004) and provides information on children entering the care system under a care order, police protection, an EPO or by agreement under s.20. It indicates that the proportion of children entering through the use of emergency powers increased from nine to 12 per cent between 1994 and 2002; there was a slight increase in the use of emergency powers and a substantial decline in admissions under s.20, and overall. However, these figures do not provide the complete picture of the use of emergency powers. They record only the child's status on first entry to public care. Entry under an EPO appears low given the number of orders shown in Table 1.1 because many children would have entered under police protection with an EPO being made when the police power ended. The figures also omit children who are made subject to emergency measures in two different circumstances. First, children who are taken into police protection but do not enter the care system because they return home; second, children already looked after when emergency powers were used. These include children who run away from care and are returned by the police and those whose parents seek to remove them having previously agreed to their being accommodated under s.20.

Table 1.2 does not indicate what proportion of children with care orders first entered under emergency powers. The figures for care orders (which include interim care orders) relate to children who were not looked after before the care order was made and therefore were not subject to emergency measures. For information about the proportion of care proceedings initiated following use of emergency powers, it is necessary to look at research studies.

Table 1.3 outlines the proportion of care proceedings that were preceded by an emergency protection order in four separate studies. The first by Thomas and Hunt (nd) is the highest but probably reflects a substantial decline from the pre-Children Act position. Over 5000 children were removed under a place of safety order made by a magistrate in the year ending 31 March 1991, approximately twice the number of EPOs made in 1992 (Department of Health, 1994, para 3.10). The studies indicate considerable variation between authorities, and according to the ethnicity of the parents. The studies by Brandon *et al.* (1999) and Brophy *et al.* (2003) both show substantial use 'voluntary' accommodation (s.20) prior to care proceedings, and Hunt and colleagues comment that 'crises which would previously have attracted a place of safety order were being dealt with in other ways' (Hunt *et al.*, 1999, 68). High use of emergency powers was linked in these studies with agency culture, the involvement of the police and a lack of co-operation between parents and social workers.

Table 1.2 Looked after children and admissions to the care system 1994–2002

	1994	1995	1996	1997	1998	1999	2000	2001	2002
Children looked after	49100	49500	50600	51200	53300	55500	58100	58900	59700
Children who started being looked after	30400	32800	31900	31400	29700	28400	28600	25100	24600
Admitted under care order	2400	2950	3090	3180	4600	4300	4300	4300	4100
Admitted under PP	1100	1100	1200	1500	1400	1500	1600	1500	1600
Admitted under EPO	1600	1300	1600	1600	1600	1800	1700	1300	1400
Admitted under s.20	24600	25200	24800	22200	20500	19100	19500	17200	16700
% entering by emergency powers	9	8	8	10	11	12	12	11	12

Sources: Department of Health, 1998b; Department for Education and Skills, 2004.

Table 1.3   Use of emergency measures immediately before care proceedings

Study	% care applications with EPO	Comments
1991–1993 (Thomas and Hunt, nd)	45%	239/529 care applications preceded by an EPO
A quantitative sample from which Hunt and Macleod's more detailed study (1999) was drawn		81% of EPO applications in Y1 followed by a care order application; 85% in Y2
1991–1993 (Hunt *et al.*, 1999, 58)	43%	35/83 care applications preceded by EPO. 21/35 EPO preceded by police protection
1993–1994 (Brandon, Thoburn, Lewis & Way 1999, 140)	36%	9/25 care applications preceded by EPO. 7/25 preceded by s.20. 3/12 EPOs not followed by care proceedings
1998–2000 (1996–2000 for South Asian sample) (Brophy, Jhutti-Johal & Owen, 2003, 31)	35%	Higher proportion of cases in South Asian group started by EPO 60% 24/42; lower proportion for White group 19% 9/47. For 74/182 children care application preceded by s.20
2000–2002 (Masson, Winn Oakley & Pick, 2004, 17)	18%	Wide variation between 3 authorities and over the 3 years from high of 42% to a low of 5%

Limited comparative data is available for other jurisdictions but most only report the number of times emergency powers were used. In Sheehan's study of child protection in Melbourne, over 50 per cent of court cases started with apprehension, that is a compulsory removal of the child. She comments that child protection work was 'perceived as crisis intervention with children removed because of immediate risk or harm' (Sheehan, 2001, 81). This may reflect the reluctance of courts to make orders before a crisis is reached because of an unwillingness to accept social worker's concerns and the emphasis placed on family preservation (Campbell *et al.*, 2003, 130). In Manitoba, use of emergency intervention is reported to be much lower, averaging 14 per cent of the child protection agency's caseload. Apprehension is stated in the social work training manual to be 'a last resort' and plans are made with parents specifically to avoid the need for apprehension. Nevertheless, only half the apprehensions there were classified by the child protection agency as 'emergencies' (*KLW v Winnipeg*, 2000, para 83).

The Invisibility of Police Protection

There are no national statistics on police protection. The Home Office has never required these figures to be produced. Only a few police forces published information on their use of police protection or reported this to their Area Child Protection Committee (Barry, 1993, 14). Of the 16 forces surveyed for the first part of the police protection study, 13 kept records from which their use of police protection could be determined (see Table 3.1) but most of these did not routinely analyse their figures. Apart from the Act and the Circular, there are few references to police protection in government guidance, leaving the use and effect of the power obscure. There is no specific mention of children in police protection in the Codes of Practice issued under the Police and Criminal Evidence Act 1984. It is unclear whether Code C, *Detention, treatment and questioning of people by police officers*, applies to them. Children in police protection are not 'in custody' or 'detained' by the police, but neither are they at the police station voluntarily nor free to leave at any time. Although the power is briefly mentioned in the 1999 edition of *Working Together* (Department of Health *et al.*, 1999, 46, para 5.25), the new edition only specifically refers to it in an appendix (Department for Education and Skills, 2006, 202).

Discussion of the police power is also generally absent from child protection literature; Hunt and colleagues' study is a notable exception (Hunt *et al.*, 1999, 48, 56). Studies of court records and social services files miss it, and it is rarely referred to in accounts of child protection policing which tend to focus on the work of specialist Child Abuse Investigation Units (CAIUs) (Her Majesty's Inspectorate of Constabulary, 1999, 2005). Where the power is used to prevent a child being removed from hospital it is effectively invisible. Parents must be informed, but where it is used to prevent parents removing a new baby or an injured child from hospital they are likely to be so preoccupied by concerns for their child and themselves that the use of the power may seem irrelevant. Only where police actually remove children from them may parents become aware of the full effects of the power. Even this may be unclear where social workers are also involved and have indicated that they will obtain an EPO. The infrequent and transient use of the power, its use away from the police station, and the sensitivity of any research that relates to children have combined to leave police protection a largely unknown power. Police exercising police protection are a 'secret social service' (Punch, 1979) whose work is unrecorded.

However, the power is widely used. The authors estimated that, outside Greater London, the area covered by the Metropolitan Police, police protection is used in at least 4,500 incidents each year involving 6,000 children. Use in London, where figures are not collated, is believed to be substantially higher than elsewhere in England and Wales. Far more children are subject to this hidden power than to EPOs.

SYSTEMS OF ACCOUNTABILITY

Accountability requires individuals and organisations to be open about the decisions they take and the basis or evidence on which they take them (Simey, 1985, 24). Accountability may be secured through a third party, for example where the decision has to be endorsed by a manager or a court. Audit processes which check procedures have been followed or reporting and assessing against targets have increasingly been used to hold individuals and service providers to account (Power, 1997; Banks, 2004). All of these processes have been used since the mid-1980s to make social work more accountable, to parents and children, to the public and to central government. The Social Services Inspectorate has inspected social services in individual local authorities and also examined aspects of provision such as out of hours services more widely (Social Services Inspectorate, 1999). This work is now being undertaken by Ofsted and the Commission for Social Care Inspection (Poyser, 2005). Local authorities also have their own units which inspect and review the services they provide. Under the *Quality Protects* programme (Department of Health, 1998a, para 3.25) central government measured local authority performance against targets, for example on placement stability. The administration of the courts is inspected by Her Majesty's Courts Service Inspectorate, but this organisation has no remit in relation to judicial decisions. Inspections of police services are undertaken by Her Majesty's Inspectorate of Constabulary and data on specific police action has to be reported to the Home Office. These systems have not been used to make local authorities or the police accountable for emergency decisions but the use of police protection was scrutinized in the Climbié Inquiry (Laming, 2003).

The Children Act 1989 aimed to make social workers more accountable for their actions by clarifying the grounds for compulsory intervention and requiring court approval for all such action (Parton, 1991, 152, 194). It also made the courts more effective in holding social workers accountable to parents and children by ensuring parental participation with free legal representation and providing children's guardians to investigate and provide representation for children. The courts too were made more accountable; magistrates were required to provide written reasons for their decisions. The Act applied the same approach to emergency protection orders, but, as the research shows, there are practical and structural difficulties in controlling emergency decisions. EPOs are often granted without parents having an opportunity to participate in proceedings. There is no appeal; until recently magistrates and their legal advisers have obtained little guidance on the interpretation of these powers from senior judges.

Accountability for the use of police protection is provided through formal recording of decisions and their review by designated officers. This process allows for considerable discretion in terms of who has the role of designated officer and the form the review takes (see Chapter 3), but recent Home Office guidance indicates that officers at least of the rank of inspector should be given this role and stresses the need for forms to be available for inspection and audit (Home Office, 2003, paras 9–10). However, there has been no systematic attempt to monitor the ways in which the power is used nationally and, in many forces, this is not done locally.

THE EMERGENCY INTERVENTION STUDIES

In 1998, the NSPCC agreed to support a research programme on emergency intervention in child protection. A single study covering both police protection and EPOs was thought to be too complex; plans were made for a multimethod quantitative and qualitative study of the use of police protection to be followed by a complementary study of the use of EPOs. Information obtained in the police study would help identify issues for the later EPO study; as far as possible the two studies would be conducted in the same locations to facilitate access, allow maximum triangulation and develop a comprehensive picture of practice. The two studies were jointly funded by the NSPCC and the Nuffield Foundation.

The Police Protection Study 1998–2000

The aim of the police protection study was to establish how frequently and in what circumstances the power was used, the factors which led officers to take this action, the information recorded, and what happened to the children. Given the lack of previous research or accounts of practice, it was necessary to explore which officers used the power, how use was recorded and the balance of decision-making power between the officers involved in order to design systematic research to capture this. The first stage used telephone interviews conducted with officers with lead responsibility for child protection in 16 forces to survey policies and recording practices, and to identify where more detailed work, reading records and interviewing officers, would be practicable. It was assumed that geography and resources would be factors in the organisation of services, the pressures on the police and their responses. Therefore, the 16 forces included covered metropolitan, rural (sparsely populated) and mixed areas, were drawn from across the country and operated in areas with a single social services authority or with more than one. Eight forces were identified from these interviews for the second stage; this sample reflected the range of the first and additionally took account of forces' use of police protection. Both high and low user forces were included. All the forces included were in England.

The second stage involved collecting data from a sample of records of the use of police protection and interviews about specific cases with the officers involved, usually one officer who had initiated police protection and the supervising designated officer. Interviews were tape recorded, fully transcribed and analysed using Word; records were analysed using SPSS. The sample included 311 instances, involving 420 children, where police protection was used. Fifty-seven officers, 24 investigating officers and 33 designated officers were interviewed.

A third stage involved interviews with local authority social workers with responsibilities for child protection policy or management, or working in out-of-hours services (emergency duty teams). Interviewees were identified by CAIU officers and worked in authorities serving all or parts of the areas of six of the eight forces. These interviews were also recorded and transcribed. At the end of the project two focus groups were held with police officers who had taken part in the study to discuss the findings and get feedback on ideas for improving practice identified during the study.

The EPO Study 2001–2004

The aim was to establish the circumstances in which EPOs were used, who applied for them and for what reasons, how the courts dealt with applications, and the outcomes of the proceedings. The model for the structure and the selection of the sample was determined by the police protection study; there was a survey, a records-based study of recent cases and interviews with professionals in a small number of courts and local authorities. Three court areas (E, J and M), which are coterminous with the police forces were selected from the eight included in stage 2 of the police study.

The first stage was a national survey of court practice by structured telephone interviews with magistrates' legal advisers who had responsibility for public law Children Act proceedings. It covered 40 of the 42 magistrates' courts areas in England and Wales. These interviews focused on the practical arrangements for handling applications both during the day and out of hours; the appointment of children's guardians; and the influence of the Human Rights Act 1998. Where written protocols or guidance existed, copies were collected.

The second stage involved collecting data from court files for every application for an EPO and any subsequent care application made within the three selected court areas. These areas were all in England. Cases were identified from the court register; where care proceedings had been started subsequently, files were traced, including following transfer, and data was collected about these proceedings. There were 86 cases in the sample relating to 127 children. In each court area, magistrates' legal advisers and magistrates were interviewed

2

THE DEVELOPMENT OF EMERGENCY PROTECTION POWERS

INTRODUCTION

This chapter traces the development of emergency protection powers in England and Wales from their introduction in the middle of the nineteenth century to the present day. In doing so, it shows the extent to which modern laws and practices are rooted in the past. It also reviews the recent development of the comparable Scottish provisions, which were introduced against a similar background of concerns about social worker accountability and family privacy, but have adopted different mechanisms to achieve these ends. Finally, it examines how emergency removal of children from their parents has been viewed through a human rights lens in Europe and Canada, where there have been major legal challenges to emergency protection laws.

These three accounts of the construction, reconstruction and interpretation of the legal frameworks for emergency protection illustrate shifting power balances between families and the state, and between child welfare workers, the police and the courts. Although the power to remove children for their protection has always rested in law, and the courts have been given the responsibility for approving the use of such powers in many states, lawyers have only become involved in the process relatively recently. Powers to remove and detain children have not therefore been subject to close scrutiny; rather they have been a simple tool, legitimising removal of a child from their family or the streets when a person in authority, usually a police officer or welfare worker, thought that this should be done. From the 1980s onwards, the way this tool has been used has been the subject of repeated and increasing concern, and has become a major impetus for reform. The Children Act 1989 refashioned the tool but it is still used to perform the same functions in many of the same ways as before, as will become clear in the following chapters.

Provision for an immediate response to children in crisis was included in the earliest child protection laws, in keeping with their focus on child rescue. Children and their rescuers could not wait, children needed to be removed from danger directly. There were concerns both with children who threatened the good order of society and with children as victims (Dingwall, Eekelaar & Murray, 1984). Then as now, almost all these children came from the poorest and most marginalised sections of society (Ferguson, 1992; Hendrick, 1994). Such concerns have continued; emergency protection powers are used both to control and to assist children (Masson, 2002; see Chapter 4). The police were given powers to remove and detain children; everyone else had to apply to a magistrate for this authority. There is evidence that the police and child protection agencies (the NSPCC and, later, local authorities) acted both independently and collaboratively in responding to children in crisis. The availability of police powers influenced decisions of social workers and the courts (as it does today; see Chapters 4 and 7).

Both initially and in recent times, parents' rights and the privacy of the family have been a strong influence on law. Intervention has had to be justified. Protection powers were drafted restrictively, and over time, restrictions have been increased. Tensions between the ideals of rescuing children and respecting parental rights have continued. One the one hand, powers have been labelled as Draconian and viewed as requiring control; on the other, there has been concern that they should not be so restrictive as to leave children in danger. Children have been objects of concern with little attention being given to anything but their immediate protection. This continues, although child welfare organisations, most notably the NSPCC have been heavily involved in law reform, little attention has been given to ensuring that law and practice took account of children's rights to family relationships or their participation in decision making. Questions about whether emergency powers are too extensive or are being abused and about how powers can be controlled have recurred, but emergency removal or apprehension has remained a mainstay in child protection practice.

RESCUE AND RESTRAINT THE DEVELOPMENT OF EMERGENCY PROTECTION POWERS

The First Provisions

Powers, now exercised as police protection, have their origins in nineteenth-century laws to rescue, protect and control children from the dangers of society, from their parents and from themselves. The Industrial Schools Act 1857 gave magistrates the power to commit children who had not been convicted of any crime to an Industrial School, where they could be looked after and receive training. These institutions were run by philanthropic or evangelical organisations or groups but often the regime was little different from that in Reformatory Schools for child offenders (Cretney, 2003, 632). The powers to commit children were extensive. Amendments allowed children 'apparently under the age of 14 years' found begging, wandering 'without visible means of support' or 'frequenting the company of thieves' to be committed; parents could also request this for children who were beyond their control (Industrial Schools Act 1861, s.9). Anyone could bring children before the magistrates for a determination. The police investigated the facts and notified the child's parents. Whilst enquiries were being undertaken the child could be sent to the local workhouse for up to seven days (s.10). The workhouse was subsequently defined as a 'place of safety' and used to house children removed from home for their protection. For workhouses to protect children, home conditions must have been dire.

By the 1880s, attention had extended to protecting children from parents; child abuse was seen as 'a major social disease' (Hendrick, 1994, 50). Although there were powers to prosecute parents who ill-treated their children (Poor Law Amendment Act 1868, s. 37), the Poor Law guardians often failed to use them. Action was needed to secure laws that enabled children to be removed from neglectful or abusive parents and to implement them. The creation of local Societies for the Protection of Children (which became the NSPCC in 1889) did this. The London Society campaigned for law reform and later, Inspectors, working on behalf of Societies, used the new powers to rescue children and bring cases to court. In the 1890s, many Societies also provided refuges where children could stay while prosecutions were pending, or with the agreement of their parents, or if they sought to protect themselves by running away (Ferguson, 1992).

The Children's Charter

The Prevention of Cruelty to Children Act 1889, the first 'Children's Charter', removed restrictions on prosecuting parents. It gave the court the power to commit boys aged under 14 and girls under 16 years to the care of a 'fit person' or a relative, where the person with custody of them was convicted of cruelty or ill-treatment (s.5). This is the forerunner of the modern care order. The police were given powers to take child victims of abuse to 'a place of safety' (ss.4, 17). Although prosecution of the person with custody was a precondition for committing the child to another's care, allowing the detention of the child from the time of the parent's arrest gave the widest approach to child protection based on the parent's criminal behaviour. Children could be detained until they could be brought before the court after the person with custody's conviction. In this way, children's temporary care was secured following the arrest of the person with custody, and they were available to provide information or give evidence about their ill-treatment. Protective custody allowed both the protection of the child and of the evidence. After further campaigning by the NSPCC, these protective powers were extended in the Prevention of Cruelty to Children Act 1894 to cover 'any child under the age of 16 who seeks refuge in a place of safety'(s.5(2)).

The 1894 Act included a new power for anyone, acting in the interests of a child, to obtain a warrant from the magistrates to search for an abused or neglected child and detain them in a place of safety. The applicant had to show that there was 'reasonable cause to suspect' that a child 'has been or is being assaulted ... in a manner likely to cause the child unnecessary suffering ...' (s.10). It was this power, the forerunner of the place of safety order and the emergency protection order, which was used by NSPCC Inspectors to investigate allegations of child cruelty and, occasionally, to remove children. The powers in the Industrial Schools Acts and the Prevention of Cruelty Acts were consolidated and extended in the Children Act 1908. Magistrates could grant warrants to allow the search for and/or removal of children. Parents could be arrested for offences against their children, and police officers could remove children to a place of safety. Children brought before the court following their parent's conviction, or those who were begging, destitute or 'lacking adequate parental guardianship' could be committed by the juvenile court to an Industrial School or to the care of a fit person (Cretney, 2003, 648).

Much of the day-to-day work of protecting children was undertaken by NSPCC Inspectors who received complaints, investigated allegations, prosecuted parents, rescued children and supervised families to encourage parents to maintain decent standards. NSPCC Inspectors who wished to remove children from the home had three alternatives. They could persuade parents to agree to enter the workhouse with their children, or to agree to children entering a NSPCC shelter or a children's home. In serious cases, where there was clear evidence of an offence, they could call on a police constable to exercise his powers to arrest the parent and remove the child. In these ways a child could be protected immediately by removal from their home without court proceedings or the involvement of a magistrate. Alternatively, the Inspector could apply to a magistrate for a warrant authorising the child's removal. There is evidence that Inspectors used all of these powers (Ferguson, 1990, 137; Ferguson, 2003, 48–9) Ferguson, who has studied NSPCC records in the north-west commented,

> By 1914, in serious cases, a pattern had emerged in which children were systematically removed from their homes on the basis of professional collaborations begun *before* NSPCC workers consulted their legal department ... Although 'emergency cases' were to remain statistically untypical, the social intervention they legitimated became the defining characteristic of child protection work, and was to remain so through to the Cleveland affair of 1987. (Ferguson, 1992, 164)

Ferguson cites another example where, in 1913, an NSPCC Inspector, accompanied by a police officer, visited a mother who had previously been imprisoned for child neglect. The children appeared 'well-nourished but dirty and verminous.' The officer must have been unwilling to use his powers because the Inspector then called a doctor to examine the children. The doctor recommended that they be taken to the workhouse and the Inspector, relying on the doctor's report, then applied to the court for a warrant for the children's removal. This was granted, the children were removed and the case was reported to the NSPCC legal department (Ferguson, 2003, 48–9). Ferguson comments that this case shows child protection was in the hands of NSPCC Inspectors, with the court rubber stamping their applications. However, it also illustrates the use of additional, professional evidence to establish a case. The Inspector clearly felt it necessary to obtain evidence, not just to assert his own belief that the children needed to be removed. In addition, this case provides an example of the use of these powers where children were not in immediate danger. There are clear parallels with current practices (see Chapters 4 and 7).

NSPCC Inspectors resorted to legal powers where parents would not agree to other arrangements for their children's protection. In the above example, the Inspector is recorded as first asking the parent to go to the workhouse or place their child in a home. Cajoling or threatening parents with police or court powers was part of a continuum from offers of help to the use of coercive powers. According to Ferguson, approximately one in six children who became the subject of an NSPCC investigation were removed from their home as a result, but most were quickly returned (Ferguson, 2003, 33). Prosecution was used in a small minority of cases, approximately 10%. Conviction rates were high, 96%, but few children were made subject of 'fit person' orders (Hendrick, 1994, 56). The majority of cases involved allegations of neglect; violence was a declining feature of child protection cases, a state of affairs which Behlmer ascribes to the increasing professionalism of the NSPCC (Behlmer, 1982, 71,181).

1930s–1960s

Powers to remove and detain children were recast and re-enacted in the Children and Young Persons Act 1932 and consolidated in the 1933 Act. The basic provisions remained the same and were tied to the grounds for a 'fit person' order. Magistrates could grant warrants where a child or young persons had been 'assaulted, ill-treated or neglected . . . in a manner likely to cause . . . unnecessary suffering or injury to health' or where specific offences had been committed in respect of the child. A warrant authorised a police officer to search for, remove and detain a child until they could be brought before the court (s.40). Magistrates could also authorise removal to a place of safety and detention there of any child in need of care and protection who was about to be brought before the juvenile court. Police officers retained their powers to intervene without the authority of a magistrate (s.67).

The Curtis Committee, which was established in 1945, was concerned with the care of children deprived of a normal home life. It focused on the provision made for such children by different legal regimes and in the institutions where they lived. At this time, there were over 125,000 children cared for away from home under various legal powers, 13,000 of whom were the subject of a fit person order. These children, and many more who returned home, are likely to have been removed initially using place of safety powers. The Committee was not concerned with the procedures for removing children from their homes, nor with the grounds for committing them to care but with the care they received. Children removed under place of safety orders were taken to workhouses for 'cleansing and emergency care' and might remain there pending their committal to the care of a local authority or whilst a suitable placement was located. The Ministry of Health admitted that there had been difficulties in keeping to the six week limit on care of children in workhouses (Curtis, 1946, paras 23, 138). During its enquiries, the Committee found children quite unsuitably in workhouses having been removed there under place of safety orders. In one institution, three children, aged 8–12 years who had already spent four months in the workhouse were sleeping with toddlers in the nursery. No plans had yet been made for them. The Committee also recorded that children were occasionally returned to neglectful homes because this was thought better for them than remaining in the workhouse (para 140). There was clearly a shortage of suitable institutions and foster carers, and a lack of urgency in providing suitable care for children who had been removed.

The Curtis Committee recommended that all deprived children should be a State responsibility, cared for by local authorities under the direction of a Children's Officer. Local authorities would be required to care for children subject to fit person orders and to provide 'voluntary care' for children whose parents were unable to look after them. These recommendations were enacted in the Children Act 1948 but the basis for compulsory intervention in the family and for rescuing children remained the Children and Young Persons Act 1933. Local authority children's departments became one of the pillars of the welfare state, undertaking child welfare work until the creation of social services departments in 1970.

LIMITATION AND REFORM – INGLEBY AND THE CYPA 1969

In 1956, the Home Office established a committee to investigate the powers and procedures of the juvenile courts, residential facilities for children brought before the courts as offenders or for their protection, and the pre-vention of cruelty and neglect. Much of the focus of the committee was on delinquency but it provided the opportunity to address some issues that re-lated to children compulsorily removed from their families for any reason. Although there were limits on the duration of an interim order made by a court for the child's detention and on keeping children in workhouses, there were no restrictions on how long a child could be detained in other places of safety pending the first court hearing. This gap was drawn to the attention of the Ingelby Committee, which was concerned about the long delays between a child's removal to a place of safety and the court hearing. The Committee, focusing on welfare rather than rights, recommended that the child should be brought before the next sitting of the juvenile court or before a magistrate within seven days. However, where a child was removed from their home for their own protection, the Committee was less concerned about speedy court proceedings. In such cases, the impact of the proceedings on the child was an important consideration and justified some delay before the hearing:

> Children are taken to places of safety in their own interests, frequently after gross neglect or ill-treatment, and the general principle that persons detained should be detained only on judicial authority does not apply so strongly. Many of these children undergo considerable suffering and strain before arriving at a place of safety and it would not always be in their best interests to subject them to the added strain of a court appearance (and the travelling involved) only a day or two after their removal. (Ingelby Report, 1960, para 126)

The Committee also considered whether the police should have a right to enter premises, without a magistrate's warrant, to search for a child. It was concerned not to provide an unregulated right of entry but recommended that a Police Inspector should have a power to issue written authority to a constable to enter and search for a child (para 128). These recommendations were enacted in the Children and Young Persons Act 1963 and subsequently incorporated in the Children and Young Persons Act 1969, ss.28, 40. The police could remove and detain a child for up to eight days; place of safety orders granted by the court following an application by a social worker or any other person could last for up to 28 days. In either case, removal and detention were based on there being 'reasonable cause to believe' that the grounds for a care order were satisfied. The police could not take a truanting child to a place of safety but a magistrate could issue a place of safety order on the grounds of non-attendance at school. Committing a criminal offence was grounds for a care order, the child could be arrested by a police officer and taken to a place of safety but a magistrate could not issue a place of safety order in respect of such a child (s.28). The court's power to issue warrants under the 1933 Act remained.

There was still no specific provision for a parent to challenge a place of safety order, but, in 1975, a father whose daughter had been removed after allegations of sexual abuse applied for an interim care order for this purpose. Refusal of this order would necessarily lead to the first order being discharged. The magistrates refused to consider his application and he applied for Judicial Review. Lord Widgery commented that the statute was not very clear but suggested that parents were not excluded from making such applications. However, he took the view that it was not necessary for parents to go to such lengths because, 'the arm of the court is quite long enough to stop a local authority from using a power intended to deal with emergencies, on a long term or unfair basis' (*R v. Lincoln (Kesteven) County Justices, ex parte M* 1976). Subsequently, the High Court held that interim care orders could not be used to challenge place of safety orders (*Nottingham County Council v. Q* 1982) leaving parents without an effective means of having the local authority's action reviewed.

GROWING USE AND INCREASED CONCERN

Place of safety orders issued on the application of social workers provided a major route into public care during the 1970s and 1980s. The number of orders increased (Norris & Parton, 1986, 1) – a fact attributed to social services' anxiety provoked by the Public Inquiry into the death of Maria Colwell, an 8-year-old girl who had been killed after she was returned from care to her mother and step-father (Stevenson & Hallett, 1980). In 1981–1982, over 6000 place of safety orders were granted by the courts (Social Services Select Committee, 1984, para 122); the number of warrants issued by Police Inspectors was not recorded. In Hilgendorf's study of legal work for local authority social services departments, conducted in the late 1970s, a place of safety order was obtained before the application for a care order or wardship in 44 out of 57 cases (77%) and in only two cases were the care proceedings not pursued (Hilgendorf, 1981, 8, 70). In three cases, the police had used their place of safety powers to protect children who were not known to social services, including a child sleeping rough, and the police were involved in 'initiating the event or the crisis' in 18 of the 30 neglect cases. Police place of safety powers were used in 25 of the 45 child protection cases in which the police were involved. In nine cases, police officers had 'specifically been requested to do the dirty work such as sorting out violent arguments, providing a show of strength or dealing with a potentially dangerous situation' (Hilgendorf, 1981, 77). Where wardship was used instead of care proceedings, social workers appeared to prefer to obtain authority to remove children from home from a magistrate rather than the High Court. A sample of wardship applications made by local authorities between 1976 and 1984 included 30% where children had initially been protected by place of safety orders (Masson & Morton, 1989, 775).

Research into entry into care provided a rather different picture of the use of place of safety powers. The large number of place of safety orders 'came as a shock' to Dr Jean Packman's team who found that these orders had been considered in half of all admissions. '[T]he emergency was anticipated and the action planned to meet it when it arose – which raised the question of whether such an emergency might have been forestalled by arranging some other, less traumatic admission to care' (Packman, Randall & Jacques, 1986, 53). In the two local authorities in Packman's study, place of safety orders had been used in 60% of cases where children were admitted compulsorily; only 11% of care orders had not been preceded by a such an order or by remand to care (Packman et al., 1986, 53). Just over 40% of place of safety orders were initiated by the police. There was considerable variation between the two authorities, especially in relation to the police use of their powers and the circumstances in which place of safety orders were used. Half the police cases related to teenagers and in 'Shiptown' the Clerk to the Magistrates was said to recommend that the police should use their own powers rather than apply to the court. In 'Clayport' the majority of the place of safety orders were sought because of neglect or abuse, and only 20% related to the child's behaviour; the position was reversed in 'Shiptown' (Packman, Randall & Jacques, 1984, 393, 396). Packman et al. commented,

> Whatever the explanation for such widespread and wide ranging use of these powers, what was very clear was that POSOs are no longer primarily an emergency measure, used to rescue (generally young) children from extreme risk. Rather, they are being used extensively to exert control over unsatisfactory parents and over the unruly child. (Packman et al., 1986, 53)

Six months after the order was made over half of the children had returned home; a quarter had remained away from home only a week. Care orders were made in respect of only 39% of the children and young people (Packman et al., 1984, 398). The research team was concerned about the impact on children of hurried and unplanned removals and placement in residential care. Parents rarely accompanied their children to the placement and visits were generally restricted. Packman commented that entry to care in this way was 'distressing and potentially very damaging' (Packman et al., 1984, 398).

Services for children who were abused or neglected were the focus of a Parliamentary Select Committee inquiry established in 1983. The Social Services Select Committee identified place of safety orders as one of the three mechanisms for entry to care that caused it particular concern (Social Services Select Committee, 1983–4, para 120). Evidence from the Magistrates Association suggested that place of safety orders were seen as 'a routine way of commencing care proceedings' and recommended they should only be used for 'genuine emergencies' (Magistrates Association of England and Wales, 1983, para 2.6). The Committee also received a 'cogent memorandum' from Dr Jean Packman, based on her research suggesting that the power was being abused. Although the Committee found insufficient evidence to establish abuse, it considered that the high number of teenagers being subject to orders and the substantial proportion of children returned home on the expiry of the order were 'good grounds for anxiety' (para 124). Not all the evidence the Committee received was critical. The Association of Directors of Social Services pointed out that magistrates, not social workers decided whether an order should be made. In addition, the NSPCC noted that it was better for an order to be sought than for parents to be persuaded to agree to place their child in voluntary care by the threat of one (para 123).

The length of orders was also an issue. Although there was evidence that orders did not always last for 28 days, the Committee was concerned that children could be removed for so long without parents having an opportunity to challenge the order, as they had in Scotland. Proposals for orders lasting only 72 hours were considered 'totally impractical' by local authority organisations who wanted to have time to consider any future action. Early hearings might lead to more delay if the local authority had had insufficient time to prepare the care application. The Committee proposed a compromise; orders should be reconsidered by a court within a week, and if confirmed, should last a further 21 days (para 140). These ideas were subsequently taken forward in an inter-departmental Review to rationalise and redraft child care law, which was one of the main recommendations of the Committee (para 119).

PROGRESSING REFORM

The Review of Child Care Law took the Select Committee Report as a starting point and commissioned further research on place of safety orders from the Dartington Research Unit. This showed a more limited use of place of safety orders and provided some information about police practice. Police place of safety powers were more likely to be used in the evenings or at weekends; where there was a specialist unit for juvenile work staffed by women officers, there appeared to be a high use of the power. Relationships between police and social services and the arrangements for duty magistrates also affected use; in one inner city area, all cases requiring emergency intervention were passed to the police.The researchers noted:

> There was some tension between police and social services over respective practices in taking place of safety orders: social services thought the police over-interventionist, the police thought social services too lax and too slow to decide on care proceedings after taking a place of safety order (Department of Health and Social Security, 1985, Annex 3 para 13).

It was unusual for orders to be refused by a magistrate. Place of safety orders accounted for between one-fifth and one-eighth of all admissions to care, with wide variations between authorities in the circumstances in which they were used. Three-quarters of children were already known to social services and a third had previously been looked after. Orders were not limited to cases of dire emergency; '[c]rises involving unfamiliar children and their families are very rare, particularly those that necessitate quite literally removal to a place of safety' (Dartington Research Unit, 1985, 18). They too identified control as an issue, emphasising the effect on parents:

> The place of safety order is often a prelude to ensure greater control and is not necessarily for the child's immediate safety. It is the first step in what promises to be a complicated application for a care order. Parents have already lost their children and may thus be more amenable to discussion about social workers' plans for their child's future (Dartington Research Unit, 1985, 18).

The Review issued a detailed discussion paper outlining the current law on place of safety orders and interim care orders in the light of the research evidence and the Select Committee's proposals for review of orders. It canvassed views on the grounds for an order, suggesting that orders might be limited to cases of 'imminent danger'; the length of orders and police detention; whether single magistrates should be able to grant orders; and the court's powers over contact and review (*Review of Child Law*, Department of Health and Social Security, 1985, para 81). It specifically drew attention to the name of the order; the term 'emergency protection order' might avoid confusion (para 73). It would highlight that orders were not routine, and that they should be restricted to cases where the child's protection could not wait.

The Review proposed that there should be a 'rationalised, simple procedure to protect children in emergencies' (Department of Health and Social Security, 1985, para 13.4). It recognised that there were risks to children and families of removing children from the home. The grounds for a place of safety order did not address the purpose of removing the child and this could have led to their frequent use as a means of starting care proceedings. It proposed a new Emergency Protection Order to provide for 'the immediate protection of a child in a genuine emergency' but reflected that the grounds would be too narrow if they were restricted to cases of imminent or impending danger (paras 13.1, 13.8). It rejected a proposal that initial orders (granted without notice) should last for only 72 hours and be followed by a full review hearing, on the basis that this would give local authorities insufficient time to decide whether to withdraw (para 13.22). Instead, it recommended a maximum period of eight days as providing a 'realistic compromise' between the local authority's need to consider whether care proceedings were required and the interests of the parents and the child who had 'not had a chance to challenge the order in court' (para 13.23). The Review thus appears to have accepted that orders would be made without notice to the parents or the child who would only receive information when the order was served on them. Nevertheless, the

Review wanted procedures to be tighter and more consistent than for place of safety orders. There would be a hearing, preferably before specialist magistrates, with written statements where practicable, and formal recording of the reasons for the order (para 13.26–7).

The Review had 'no doubt that the police power is essential where they discover that protection is necessary without delay and where it is impracticable to seek a magistrate's order . . . ' However, they considered that eight days was an 'unnecessarily long period' and recommended that 'initial detention' without a court order should only be allowed for up to 72 hours (para. 13.33). They also recommended that there should be duties on the police to inform the local authority and the parents of the detention, and to hand over the child (and the responsibility for seeking an EPO) to the local authority as soon as possible.

The Review's proposals for an Emergency Protection Order were accepted by the Government. The White Paper stated, 'emergency powers to remove a child at serious risk, which necessarily cannot be preceded by a full court hearing, must be of short duration and subject to court review if the parent wishes to challenge the order' (Department of Health and Social Security, 1987, para 6(e)). It noted that, 'it no longer seems appropriate for a single Justice to make a "place of safety order" for as long as 28 days, without the opportunity of a parent or child contesting it in court'(para 10). As a result of comments on the original proposal, provision was included for a seven-day extension in 'exceptional circumstances' to cover cases where the local authority was not ready to bring care proceedings after the initial eight days (para 45–47).

CRISIS IN CLEVELAND

In the spring of 1987, paediatricians in Cleveland began to detect signs of sexual abuse in increasing numbers of children. Cases were referred to social services, place of safety orders were obtained and children were removed from their families to hospital or foster care. During seven months of intense and controversial child protection activity nearly 300 orders were obtained (Butler-Sloss, 1988, paras 9.4.1–12). Relationships between police and social services broke down completely so it became difficult to investigate cases and prepare further action; hospital services, courts and social workers were overwhelmed. Families caught up in this crisis sought support from their MPs and made contact with the media. The issue of sexual abuse and the powers of social workers to remove children were given massive publicity, frequently tainted with allegations of professional incompetence or even collusion. To address widespread public concern, the Secretary of State for Social Services established a Public Inquiry, chaired by a High Court Judge, Dame Elizabeth Butler-Sloss.

The Inquiry focused on inter-agency relationships and good practice in the identification and management of child sexual abuse. It did not seek to establish whether the allegations had been well-founded, leaving decisions in individual cases to the courts. However, reports that large numbers of children had been returned home were interpreted by some as proving that there had been no abuse (Bell, 1988).

The Inquiry reviewed the law relating to place of safety orders; police powers were not in issue, although the police force's duty to co-operate in child protection certainly was. The magistrates involved did not give evidence and the Inquiry did not consider whether the place of safety orders had been granted appropriately. It was satisfied that the Clerk to the Justices had not improperly influenced magistrates' discretion even though he had apparently suggested to magistrates that granting 28-day orders could help relieve pressure on the courts (para 10.13). However, the Inquiry Report did note that the majority of these orders had been granted during court hours by magistrates in their own homes, contrary to clear understandings between the Clerk and the social services department (para 10.09) and that proper records had not been kept of the number of orders granted (para 10.16). Overall, the Inquiry's wider concerns meant that the courts remained largely unstained by the Cleveland scandal even though it was far from clear that they had exercised judicial discretion and not merely rubber stamped applications.

The Cleveland Report noted that where a child was already in a safe place and there was no immediate fear of removal, 'obtaining an order is likely to cause polarisation of attitudes between social workers and the family at an early stage and may jeopardise co-operation ...' (para 16.14). It welcomed the White Paper proposals subject to a few provisos. It thought that requiring exceptional circumstances for an extension to an EPO 'could create difficulties' and considered that applications should only be heard by a single magistrate if the court was not sitting (para 16.15).

CHILDREN ACT 1989 AND THE REFOCUSING DEBATE

The mechanisms for emergency protection remained the most controversial issue during the passage of the Children Bill and were given close attention (Parton, 1991, 176). The Standing Committee on the Bill included two of the three MPs for the Cleveland area as well as former social workers and child care lawyers. The Secretary of State commented that the government had to steer a safe course between Scylla and Charybdis (Standing Committee B, col. 279). As originally drafted, the Bill contained a single ground for an EPO, requiring the applicant to satisfy the court that 'there is reasonable cause to believe that the child is likely to suffer significant harm' if not removed or detained (cl. 37) and a power where the police were so satisfied to take a child into police protection (cl. 38). It was argued that this test could be too difficult to prove if access to the child was refused. The NSPCC proposed an additional, non-emergency order that would allow the court to order an assessment for up to 28 days and could require the child's removal from home. This was strongly opposed by the Association of Directors of Social Services and by the government who were worried that magistrates and social workers would become confused and orders would be sought inappropriately (Cretney & Masson, 1990, 636). After the NSPCC and ADSS had reached agreement, the government introduced an additional, less restrictive ground for an EPO where access to the child by the local authority or NSPCC was being refused. It also included provision for a child assessment order to last for up to seven days. Lord Mackay admitted during the debate, '[W]e did not get the balance quite right in early versions of the Bill ...' (*Hansard* H.L. Vol. 512, col.784). However, this rather glosses over the conflicts which had to be worked out within the government and between the various organisations concerned with child protection and parents' rights (Parton, 191, 179). In practice, there has been very little use of child assessment orders (Dickens, 1993; Lavery, 1996). Assessment in child protection often requires the active co-operation of parents, and seven days is too short a time to carry out a core assessment.

The government rejected amendments to the Bill designed to enable the court to exclude an adult, rather than remove a child. However, following a recommendation from the Law Commission, the Children Act 1989 was amended by the Family Law Act 1996 so as to enable the court to include an exclusion requirement or accept undertakings with EPOs. The Law Commission was concerned that families could 'lose both ways', by having the suspected abuser excluded and the child removed (Law Commission, 1992, para 6.19). These provisions, too, are seen as having only limited use (Pack, 2001).

Other parts of the Act set the context in which state intervention powers would be used. The Act aimed to reduce the use of compulsory measures by developing preventive services. A general duty was imposed on local authorities to provide services, including day care and accommodation for children in need and their families (s.17). The definition of 'child in need' was 'deliberately wide' to give local authorities broad discretion to develop and provide services (Department of Health, 1991b, para 2.4). The Act emphasised partnership between families and the state in the care of children and encouraged making agreements rather than seeking court orders (Cretney & Masson, 1990, 593). It sought to 'discourage unnecessary court intervention in family life by prohibiting the making of any order' unless it would positively benefit the child (Department of Health, 1993, para 1.15). Local authorities were required to consult parents before making decisions about looking after children, working with them to safeguard their children's welfare once children entered public care. Arrangements for looking after children by agreement were equated with staying with relatives; parents could remove their children at any time and would not have to give notice as the previous law required.

The Act also recognised that both parents and children have rights. State intervention in the family always required a court order, and both parents and children had rights to representation in care and emergency protection proceedings.

In 1995, the government published a research overview on child protection (Dartington Research Unit, 1995). By disseminating research findings about child protection activity and its impact on families and children, it aimed to refocus social services activity away from child protection investigations and towards providing services that would have a positive impact on children's well-being. The objective of refocusing services was to support families and thereby reduce the likelihood of a later crisis. Child protection should not be seen as a matter of responding to incidents, rather of reflecting on the impact on the child of the care provided. Although there were cases where compulsory measures were required, too often investigations only served to upset families; even where concerns were identified no services might be offered. Local authorities had not shifted resources into service provision. Indeed section 17 appeared to have failed in many respects. Local authorities took a long time to grasp the idea of family support, provision was patchy and it was often difficult for families to access services (Department of Health, 2001, 141, 144). Research evidence indicated that proceedings could have been avoided if appropriate interventions had been available earlier (Department of Health, 2001, 58). There were also concerns that proceedings were not being brought soon enough, were used inappropriately and were sometimes threatened in order to get parents to accept accommodation. Overall, research on the workings of the Children Act in the 1990s suggested that 'slow progress had been made in achieving the intended balance between voluntariness and compulsion' (Department of Health, 2001, 51–52, 143).

VICTORIA CLIMBIÉ: POLICING POLICE PROTECTION

Another scandal, the murder of eight-year-old Victoria Climbié and a major Public Inquiry, chaired by Lord Laming, drew attention to problems in protecting children and providing services for children in need, including the way the Metropolitan Police Service investigated crimes against children and operated police protection (Laming, 2003; Masson, 2006b). Lord Laming was highly critical of all the agencies who had been involved with Victoria – social services, health, the NSPCC and the police; there had been 'a gross failing of the system' (para 1.18). His report made specific recommendations about emergency child protection and the use of police protection (Laming, 2003, 375, 381–382). It led to the government requiring self-audits in all agencies (Commission for Health Improvement *et al.*, 2003) and new guidance to the police and all child protection agencies (Home Office, 2003; Department for Education and Skills, 2006).

In April 1999, Victoria was brought to London from Ivory Coast via France, by her great aunt, Mrs Kouao, who had offered to provide her with an education in Europe. Mrs Kouao obtained work in London, sought local authority housing and placed Victoria with a childminder. During this period Mrs Kouao was in repeated contact with various agencies, seeking services as a parent but little attention was paid to Victoria. Concerns about Kouao's care of Victoria led the childminder's daughter to take Victoria to hospital in July 1999. The hospital contacted social services who referred the case to the police Child Abuse Investigation Unit in Brent as a case of 'serious non-accidental injuries'. The constable who took the call agreed with the social worker to place Victoria in police protection but did not visit her or undertake any investigation. The following day the social worker telephoned to say that the paediatrician had concluded the injuries were due to scabies. The constable immediately lifted the police protection. Two weeks later another referral was made from a different hospital where Victoria had been admitted with burns and bruises. Again police and social services investigations were very limited. In November, Mrs Kouao contacted social services alleging Victoria had been sexually abused, a strategy meeting was held but the investigation was not followed through. Mrs Kouao later withdrew her complaint. In February 2000, Victoria was brought to hospital in a state of collapse. She had been tortured and starved for a prolonged period. Victoria died. Kouao and her partner were convicted of her murder in January 2001.

The Inquiry heard evidence that police protection was routinely used by the Metropolitan Police because of the difficulties for local authorities in getting legal advice and making court applications, especially out of normal working hours. The police and social services approach to this power appeared casual; it had been used despite there being no threat to remove Victoria from hospital, and the constable taking the action had also acted as 'designated' officer to supervise the case (para 13.67–9). Police officers appeared to rely on the judgements of other professionals about whether children had been harmed, rather than to form an independent view through investigation. Child protection was viewed as completely different from ordinary policing (para14.57); enquiries were not treated as investigations of serious crimes, and few officers who dealt with child protection had received training to equip them to investigate crime (para 15.12). The Inquiry found deep malaise in the Metropolitan Police Child Abuse Investigation Units. Accommodation was poor, and teams lacked resources; the IT was inadequate (15.39) and there were too few vehicles (para 15.30). Officers and supervisors were poorly trained; the child protection manual was so out of date as to be useless. Overall, managerial oversight was missing; those in senior positions had other responsibilities and gave insufficient attention to managing child protection work.

Before the Report was published, the Metropolitan Police had taken various steps to improve the quality of child protection policing through establishing a new department, Child Protection Command Unit SO5, changes to management, a training programme and updating the child protection manual. However, the impact of the Inquiry on practice is less clear. The report of the self-audits noted,

> [T]here may be an over reliance in some areas on the use of police protection powers, which may not always be in the best interests of children. Some police forces have not issued updated guidance on police protection powers to operational staff...there is a high level of unallocated child protection cases in a few social services departments (Commission for Health Improvement *et al.*, 2003, 5).

EMERGENCY CHILD PROTECTION IN NORTHERN IRELAND

Northern Ireland shares with England and Wales a common history of the development of child protection laws and services. The Prevention of Cruelty to Children Act 1889 applied to Ireland as did the subsequent legislation until the formation of the Northern Irish State in 1921. The NSPCC provided services throughout Ireland until the establishment of the Irish Society for the Protection of Children in 1956 (Department of Health, Social Services and Public Safety, 2003, 153). The Children Act 1908, which consolidated and extended the provisions relating to place of safety orders, remained in force in Northern Ireland until 1950. Later legislation, the Children and Young Persons Acts (NI) 1950 and 1968, established a child welfare system in Northern Ireland similar to that established in 1948 in England, enabled the courts to make 'fit person orders' where children were in need of care or protection and introduced the Ingeby reforms. Police constables and anyone authorised by the courts or by a Justice of the Peace could take a child to a place of safety until proceedings for such an order could be brought (s.70).

The political climate and absence of an independent legislature for many decades left Northern Ireland with this outdated child welfare system. The legislative gap between the two parts of the United Kingdom was closed in 1996 with the implementation of the Children (Northern Ireland) Order 1995, which is closely based on the Children Act 1989. There was, however, little attempt to mould the Children Order to fit with the different structures in Northern Ireland, or the culture of social work practice that had developed during the previous 30 years (Donaldson & Harbison, 2005). The divided society and 'the troubles' created a very different climate for policing. Despite the wholesale reforms of policing following the Good Friday Agreement, police community relations on which child protection policing is founded remain problematic in Northern Ireland.

The 1995 Order provides for emergency intervention to protect children in Northern Ireland, repeating almost word for word the provisions of the Children Act 1989. Children can be taken into police protection (article 65) and courts can make EPOs, and exclude alleged perpetrators to protect children at home (arts 63, 63A and 64). The police are involved in child protection in Northern Ireland; 12 per cent of referrals to the child protection register are made by the police (Department of Health, Social Services and Public Safety, 2002, Table 1.3) and 20 per cent of child protection investigations are conducted jointly with the police (Northern Ireland Statistical and Research Agency, 2005, Table 1.1). As in other parts of the United Kingdom, the police use of their powers remains largely invisible, but the Northern Irish Looked After Children database indicates that about one per cent of admissions were of children in police protection. As in England and for the reasons discussed in Chapter 1, this is likely substantially to underestimate the importance of the power for child protection in Northern Ireland. In its public statement of its child protection policy, the Police Service of Northern Ireland makes specific mention of police protection and notes, echoing the rather more forceful guidance form the Home Office in England and Wales, 'such powers should be used only when necessary, the principle is that wherever possible the decision to remove a child from a parent or carer should be made by a court' (Police Service of Northern Ireland, 2005, para 4).

There is substantial use of emergency protection orders. The Reports of the Children Order Advisory Committee indicate that each year between 2000 and 2005 approximately 100 EPO applications were heard by the courts (Children Order Advisory Committee 2005, appendix 2). The number of applications appears to be reducing but the ratio of EPO applications to care applications remains approximately 1:5, comparable to that observed in England (see Table 1.3). Similarly, almost all applications result in orders and those which do not are withdrawn. The reasons for the withdrawal of applications identified in the EPO Study are discussed in Chapter 7.

Similar issues about children's representation in EPO proceedings have arisen in England and Northern Ireland (see Chapter 7). Guardians ad litem, experienced social workers from NIGALA (the Northern Ireland Guardian ad litem Agency), should be appointed in EPO cases but the short timescales and the limited availability of guardians has meant that this does not occur in majority of cases (NIGALA, 2003). Where a guardian is appointed in EPO proceedings, their recommendation almost always supports the application (CAPITA, 2004).

Overall, the limited information available about emergency intervention suggests that there are likely to be many parallels with the use of court orders in England. The more difficult climate for community policing and the history of policing in Northern Ireland by the Royal Ulster Constabulary means that the police in Northern Ireland face additional difficulties in using their powers to protect children.

NORTH OF THE BORDER – ORKNEY AND REFORM OF SCOTS LAW

Scots law also provided two mechanisms for protecting children in emergencies; the powers were updated and included in the Social Work (Scotland) Act 1968, s.37. Police officers could remove children to a place of safety, and any person could apply to any court or any Justice of the Peace for permission to do so. As in England, almost all place of safety orders were sought by social workers (Clyde, 1992, 16.22). The Scots arrangements differed in one major respect from those in England. The reporter, the official charged with bringing children's cases before the sheriff or a children's hearing 'on the first lawful day' after it had been granted had the power not to pursue the case. Reporters provided 'a second line of protection' for the child and the family (Kearney, 1992, 471) but a practice of delaying hearings meant that the protection was more limited than the legislation appeared to provide.

During the early 1990s, there were concerns about the use of emergency powers in Scotland. As in England, a central issue for policy and practice in child protection has been the balance between voluntary and compulsory measures (McGhee & Francis, 2003, 134). The Scottish Office published a review of child care law in 1990 (Scottish Office, 1990). There were also two public Inquiries in Scotland into the operation of child care and child protection procedures, each of which included consideration of the operation of emergency powers. These two reports focused on key problems with child protection powers: When should they be used? Who should make the decision? How should children's and parents' rights be safeguarded?

The Orkney Inquiry examined the use of Scottish place of safety orders to remove children from their families following allegations of ritual abuse (Clyde, 1992; Asquith 1993). The Fife Inquiry examined, amongst other matters, the way the reporters handled cases where place of safety orders had been used to bring children into public care (Kearney, 1992). In half the cases where social workers had obtained place of safety orders, the reporters in Fife decided not to refer cases to a children's hearing either because they considered there were no grounds for doing so or that continuing the order was contrary to the child's interests (Kearney, 1992, 466). Disagreement between the social work department and the reporter in individual cases reflected wider conflict about the use of compulsory measures of care and the respective roles of social workers and reporters. Both reports raised issues about the proper use of place of safety powers, their use only in emergencies, the trauma they caused to children and to parents and the procedures once orders have been granted.

The reform process drew substantially on the experience in England and Wales (Asquith, 1993, 8) and resulted in the Children (Scotland) Act 1995. However, there are important differences between the two sets of provisions in the way emergency powers are limited and supervised. Scots law provides for eight-day child protection orders (CPOs) (Children (Scotland) Act 1995, ss.57–60), similar to EPOs, child assessment orders (s.55), magistrates' emergency powers and police protection (s.61). Child protection orders can only be granted by a sheriff, a professional judge; there is no provision for prior notification of the parents, or for a hearing. The sheriff's decision is automatically subject to review by a reporter who has power to release the child and must set up a hearing within two working days. The parents and the child can apply to the reporter to have the order discharged even before this hearing. However, recall of orders before the end of the eight-day period when further orders can be made is rare (McGhee & Francis, 2003, 138). Removal or detention for a child's protection can only be authorised by a Justice of the Peace (JP) or a police officer for up to 24 hours. In addition to the criteria for a CPO, the JP or officer must be satisfied that it is not practicable to apply to a sheriff for the order (s.61(5)). Guidance specifically draws local authorities' attention to the need to consider alternatives, and to the importance of placing siblings who are removed together (Scottish Office, 1997, paras 41 and 51).

The implementation of child protection orders led to a 20 per cent decline in the use of emergency powers and increased reliance by social workers on lawyers, but in contrast to England and Wales, many social workers in Scotland make applications without legal representation. McGhee and Francis reflected that the new order had brought greater rigour and accountability to emergency intervention but they were unclear whether children were now more effectively safeguarded, or were left in risky circumstances when urgent action would previously have been taken (2003, 141). No information is available about exercise of police or JP's powers.

CONCERNS ELSEWHERE – HUMAN RIGHTS CHALLENGES TO EMERGENCY INTERVENTION LEGISLATION

In the 1990s, concerns about extensive emergency powers to protect children and limited procedural protection for parents lead to constitutional challenges in Canada and in several European countries (Masson, 2004a, 470). In Canada, Manitoba's child protection laws, which allow an investigating social worker 'who believes on reasonable and probable grounds that a child is endangered' to apprehend a child without a court order, were challenged under the Canadian Charter of Rights and Freedoms, sections 7 and 8. These provisions protect 'rights to life, liberty and security', and safeguard individuals from 'unreasonable search or seizure' by imposing due process standards. At the same time in Finland, parents, assisted by a social worker who had long campaigned against Finnish social welfare practices (Hodson, 2005) challenged the Child Welfare Law 1983 under the European Convention on Human Rights, article 8, which guarantees 'respect for private and family life'. These two cases, *KLW v. Winnipeg* and *K and T v. Finland* were remarkably similar.

Both concerned the removal of newborn babies and their older si\
parents who were longstanding clients of the child welfare service\
viewed as unco-operative. In both States, the law allowed children
moved by social workers without the consent of a court and without a
warning to the family. The procedures available to the parents to rev ... the
original removal worked badly, and long periods passed before the original
decisions were subjected to a thorough review. In *KLW*, the baby eventually
returned home; in *K and T*, she remained in foster care with parental contact,
but the parents successfully retained care of their next child.

Despite their different legal frameworks, the Canadian Supreme Court and
the Grand Chamber of the European Court of Human Rights, largely agreed
what the issues were but reached opposite conclusions in these two cases.
These cases provide a thorough review of the dangers and difficulties of reg-
ulating emergency intervention, protecting children, respecting family rights
and supporting social workers. Each court was divided on what grounds and
procedures for intervention were acceptable, and how to protect both children
and parents. The judges' struggles to balance children's need for protection
and thus the State's need to be able to intervene, with the protection of the
family from oppressive action is apparent from the language they use and the
different aspects of law and practice that they highlighted.

The majority in the Canadian Supreme Court, lead by the Chief Justice
Mme L' Heureux-Dubé, stressed the risk to the 'very survival' of the child
if action were not taken (para 94), and the difficulty of restricting interventions without a court order to emergency cases (paras 99–106). In contrast,
the minority focused on the risk to the family of 'traumatic and disruptive'
action, which could lead to an 'indeterminate period' of separation (para 18).
Reviewing other Canadian child protection statutes, they noted that in some
Provinces warrantless apprehension was restricted to cases where there was
'an immediate risk to health' or 'substantial risk of harm', phrases which
sought to limit intervention and thus protect families (paras 31–33). The minority thought that there should always be an application to a judge, at least
by telephone (para 16) because allowing the person who investigated the case
also to decide that the child should be removed seriously undermined their
capacity to act impartially (para 19). However, the majority considered that
court approval would divert agency resources and that it would not provide
effective protection for parents, 'courts will tend to defer to the agency's assessment ... given the highly compelling purpose for state action' (para 113).
They accepted that parents' rights were sufficiently protected by a prompt
review *after* the removal. Although it did not limit apprehensions to emergencies and only required a review after seven days, the majority held that
the Manitoba's law did not conflict with the principles of fundamental justice. This decision has subsequently been attacked for setting child protection
law 'on a path back to the 1960s ... when the state-interventionist school of
thought' was predominant (Blenner-Hassett, 2004, 162).

K and T was heard twice in the European Court of Human Rights. After the Chamber had unanimously found against it, Finland requested that the case be referred to the Grand Chamber of 17 judges. The majority of the Court found once more that the State had breached the parents' article 8 rights by removing the baby because it had failed to show the 'extraordinary compelling reasons' required for such an 'extremely harsh measure', taken without any consultation with the parents (para 168). However, the majority in the Grand Chamber, disagreeing with the Chamber, accepted that the decision to prevent the parents removing the mother's older child from a children's home where he had been placed with her agreement did *not* breach article 8. Whereas the Chamber viewed this action as unnecessary because the child was safe, the Grand Chamber considered that it was necessary to prevent the child's removal by the parents. In addition, since the boy was already separated from the family, the decision to detain him could not have such an impact on the parents' rights to family life (para 169).

The divisions within the court were more complex than in *KLW*. Ten of the 17 judges in *K and T* issued dissents. Five judges were unwilling to accept that there had been a breach in relation to the removal of the baby, but two of these held that the way the child was removed, immediately after the birth, without any consideration of alternatives itself amounted to a breach of article 8. Those who found no breach thought that 'the court . . . should be more sensitive to the real dilemmas facing the authorities' and preferred to set the balance in favour of placing the child 'beyond the reach of harm'. Another five judges considered that there had been a breach in relation to the older child because 'imminent danger' should be established in order to justify any apprehension without notice.

Overall, there is considerable similarity in the attitudes to children's rights, parents' rights, the position of the child protection agency and the role of the court, expressed by the judges in these two cases. In both cases the pro-apprehension judgements emphasised the need to protect the child from harm in the sense of physical abuse at the hands of the parents. The importance, for the child, of care from the mother – the child's right to family life – was not considered, even though there was no evidence that either the Canadian or the Finnish agency had assessed the risk these mothers posed to their babies, or whether this might be minimised in other ways. The failure to consider children's rights other than their right to protection from physical harm reflects the continued dominance of the rescue philosophy and the invisibility of children's issues in proceedings where children are not represented.

In the four subsequent cases concerning apprehension which have reached the European Court of Human Rights since *K and T* (*P, C and S v. UK*; *Venema v. The Netherlands*; *Covezzi and Morselli v. Italy*; and *Haase v. Germany*), the Court has been willing to accept that States might need to remove children from their parents without a full court hearing but has also stressed the need for sufficient reasons and the importance of involving parents in decisions.

> The Court accepts that when action is taken to protect a child in an emergency, it may not be possible because of the urgency of the situation, to [involve] . . . those having custody of the child. Nor may it even be desirable . . . if [they] . . . are the source of an immediate threat to the child, since giving them prior warning would be liable to deprive the measure of its effectiveness. The court, however, must be satisfied that the national authorities were entitled to consider that there existed circumstances justifying the abrupt removal of the child . . . (*Haase v. Germany*, para 95)

In *P, C and S v. UK*, information about the mother's conviction for harming her older child meant the local authority wanted to assess the parents before the birth of the mother's second child. The parents refused to co-operate, and following the birth, (by emergency caesarean) the local authority obtained a without notice EPO. The baby was removed from the parents, placed in foster care and, after a series of proceedings, adopted. The parents challenged the local authority's and the court's actions in the European Court of Human Rights. The court accepted that the local authority had not breached article 8 by obtaining an emergency protection order without notifying the parents; this procedure was established by law and that the facts showed the necessity of using it. However, because the local authority had not considered alternative ways of protecting the child and failed to consult the parents before implementing the EPO, the parents' rights to family life had been breached (paras 131–3). This approach had been suggested in the concurring judgement of Judge Pellonpää in the Chamber decision of *K and T*. The Court also held that there were further breaches of both article 6(1) the right to fair trial and article 8 in relation to the later care and adoption proceedings (Masson, 2006a).

In contrast with their approach to care cases generally, the judges in the European Court of Human Rights have been unwilling to leave decisions about the appropriateness of exercising apprehension powers to the States themselves. However, they found it difficult to agree boundaries between justified protection and unjustified intervention, and thus could not give a clear ruling but only establish a general basis for review. They did not want to impose their own view of what the national authorities should have done, from the safety of the courtroom. Rather, they put forward an approach which required national authorities to convince the court that their action had been justified, and allowed the court to review the action on the basis of the case presented to them. Their judgements reflect the dilemmas which face national authorities in dealing with these cases, where courts may effectively defer to the decision of the child protection authorities although they have the power to refuse an emergency order. The approach of the courts to EPO applications is examined further in Chapter 7.

The European Court of Human Rights' decisions imply that the balance between protecting children and protecting parents' rights is a fine one. The age of child, the type of harm and the current arrangements for the child's care are all relevant to setting the balance. Providing the case is sufficiently serious, removing children from parents will not breach article 8, even where parents are not notified before powers are obtained. But powers must only be used where they are necessary; parents must generally be consulted before children are taken away from them. Immediate removal of a baby is a 'draconian step', which will only be justified where there is no alternative (*P, C and S*). Where concerns relate to neglect rather than abuse, it will be difficult to convince the court that immediate intervention is appropriate (*Haase v. Germany*), but where the ongoing risk comes from sexual abuse, such intervention can be justified (*Covezzi and Morselli v. Italy*). Powers to prevent parents removing their children when they have already agreed to their being placed in foster care are subject to more limited scrutiny, even where there has been no threat of removal, because the State's powers are less intrusive in these circumstances (*K and T*).

The European Court of Human Rights has not found it necessary to assess emergency intervention powers in terms of article 6(1), the right to fair trial. It has taken the view that article 8 is sufficiently demanding to protect parents' rights, requiring as it does the parents' involvement throughout the process that leads to the child being committed to compulsory care and until the child is reunited with the family (*Johansen v. Norway; Olsson v. Sweden*). On another view, article 6 is inoperable once it is accepted that provision has to be made for immediate removal to protect some children. There is simply no time for a process which could be considered to be a trial. The notion of 'fair trial' would become worthless if it were interpreted to allow an initial decision for the child's removal that can be made administratively (*K and T*) or by a court without any notice to the parents (*P, C and S*) (Masson, 2006a).

The protection the court provides in authorising emergency action must be through restraining applications, not by securing an opportunity for the parents to be heard before the order is made. Parents require a fair hearing in decisions about the continued detention of their child, but this can only be provided if they have information about the local authority's evidence and sufficient notice to obtain representation and prepare their case.

CONCLUSION

There are many continuities between the practice of rescuing children from their violent and neglectful parents in nineteenth-century slums or controlling vagrant children and the operation of emergency protection laws at the beginning of the twenty-first century. Despite the fundamental reform of the laws that govern these decisions by the Children Act 1989, they are still structured much as they were more than a century ago. Parental agreement to their child's placement, sometimes in the face of threats to bring civil (now rarely criminal) proceedings continues to allow social workers to arrange protection without reference to any compulsory powers. This is still seen to be 'a better way' even though concerns about oppressive practice and exhortations to work in partnership leave some social workers and lawyers concerned about this practice (see Chapter 6). The police continue to have a major role in removing children from dangerous situations. They still have powers which they can exercise independently; and close collaborations between police and social workers can avoid the need to apply to the court. The work of the NSPCC has changed considerably in recent years. It has a network of around 200 teams and projects undertaking a wide range of activities to safeguard children. Their work no longer focuses on inspections or investigations in individual families but, with the police and social services, they conduct investigations into complex cases or cases of organised abuse. Although the NSPCC retains the power to seek EPOs, it would be most unusual for it to act independently whilst working with these other agencies. The current use of police protection police is explored in Chapters 3 and 4.

Those drafting child protection powers in Britain and elsewhere have continually entrusted the courts with responsibility for assessing whether intervention should be allowed. Warrantless powers have been seen as inherently more dangerous and open to abuse, and throughout the United Kingdom they have been restricted to police officers, even after the creation of Children's Departments and the professionalisation of child protection social work. However, not all those involved in reviewing the use of emergency powers either in court proceedings or in public enquiries have been convinced that the courts are able to provide effective protection for parents against inappropriate intervention. The European Court of Human Rights has applied the same approach to intervention with and without a court order; the majority in the Canadian Supreme Court did not accept that courts provided a safeguard. The limited evidence from public inquiries in England and Scotland suggests that they do not, but requiring applicants to explain why an order is necessary may discourage some inappropriate applications. This issue is considered in Chapter 7 alongside the study evidence about court practices and in Chapter 9.

Protecting children by removing them from home has never been a routine activity, but when children were considered to need protection, the special powers which allowed immediate removal were used routinely, at least until the late twentieth century when this practice became untenable in the wake of criticism from professionals, scandal and public concern about its misuse. The process of restricting the use of immediate removal has relied on three approaches. First, the imposition of procedural controls, requiring hearings or permission from a judge and/or imposing reviews. Second, restrictive tests limiting use to cases of imminent danger; and third, shortening the duration of powers so that their advantages are balanced with disadvantages. In England and Wales, Northern Ireland and Scotland, the first and third approaches have been used. The courts have formally controlled children's compulsory removal by social workers but the police have always been able to act independently. The Children Act 1989 brought greater formality to decision making; magistrates decided these cases in court not in their homes. Lawyers became more involved, advising magistrates, advising and representing social workers and even representing parents or children who had the right to Legal Aid for these proceedings. The current mechanisms of court control differ; Scots law relies on lawyer judges and requires post order review whereas English (and Northern Irish) law restricts without notice applications and provides for hearings, usually by lay magistrates. The impact of lawyers on the process in local authorities and in the courts is considered in Chapters 6 and 7; the effectiveness of the English provisions in securing accountability examined in Chapter 7. The grounds for obtaining immediate protection orders have never been very restrictive, but the Children Act renamed the order to indicate that its use should be limited to emergencies, an approach which was not followed in Scotland. The length that powers and orders should last has been a recurring theme in reforms in the twentieth century both in England and Wales and in Scotland. Limiting the length of an order and allowing swift review have been key ways to protect the rights of parents and children from oppressive intervention.

The introduction of human rights laws has brought further scrutiny to child protection practices but not resulted in a clear basis for balancing the rights of children to physical safety and of parents to respect for family life, interpreted in this context as involvement in all decisions about their children and the limitation of intervention to cases where it is essential. Human rights judges, recognising the vulnerability of children, especially babies, the huge responsibility child protection laws place on social workers and the wide variety of circumstances where protection may be required, have found it difficult to identify either minimum procedural standards or substantive tests which can distinguish legitimate and illegitimate intervention. Consequently, they have only been able to identify bad laws and practices, not to give clear guidance about the contents of good laws for this difficult area. Only a few elements are clear. Parents must be consulted at least if their whereabouts are known, but this can occur after the order has been obtained. It seems therefore that agreements in the face of a court order can be regarded as securing consultation rather than as oppressive practice. The removal of babies requires exceptional justification, but their vulnerability may well provide this where a parent has harmed a child previously. Where parents and children are already separated, it may be easier to justify powers that prevent parents reclaiming their child. How the introduction of the Human Rights Act 1998 has influenced the approach to EPOs is considered in Chapter 7.

3

THE POLICE, CHILD PROTECTION AND POLICE PROTECTION

INTRODUCTION

Police protection, the power of the police to remove children from harm and keep them in 'protective custody' (Her Majesty's Government, 2005), has wide application. It can be used in any situation where a police officer considers that any person under the age of 18 years is likely to suffer significant harm (Children Act 1989, s.46). In many respects, it is similar to the power of arrest; an officer's decision to arrest a person depends on the need for and justification of police control, which is determined by an officer's assessment of the situation. This chapter reviews how officers used their power to protect children. Drawing on the records of the 311 cases where police protection was used in eight forces and on interviews with officers who used the power, it examines the decisions taken and what happened to the children concerned. The main focus is the decision making – how and why officers decided to use the power, the circumstances in which they used the power, the subsequent decisions about where to take the child and how long he or she should remain in police protection. One aspect of decision making is accountability; the final section of the chapter examines the role of 'designated' officers in reviewing the use of police protection.

THE IMPACT OF POLICE PROTECTION

It was not possible to interview either parents or children about their experiences of police protection. Officer's accounts cannot be proxies for what it was really like for parents or children but gave impressions of how use of the power was received. Officers described parents being relieved that the police had responded to their call, reassured that their child was being looked after, or shocked and distressed beyond words at what had happened. Similarly, although some children were reported as being thankful or '*not too put out*', there were others who were clearly scared, angry and upset. One officer recalled '*one of the worst fights*' he had had trying to get a 12-year-old girl who was being removed from home into a police car. Behaviour and feelings reflect the experience of what it was like to be, or to have one's child, taken into police protection. These differ depending on the reasons the action is taken; the same event may be experienced as child rescue or a raid on the heart of the family, and subsequent events may lead to the original experience being re-assessed.

The two accounts below, taken from other studies, both relate to the use of the power to remove children where children were considered to be at risk because of parental behaviour. In each case, police protection was followed by care proceedings and the child never returned to live with their parents.

A mother's account of police protection

Police had telephone calls to say I was leaving Thomas in the house on his own and stuff like that, which were untrue. I've never left him at all. I think it were neighbour next door actually. Next minute I know, police is at the door. So me first reaction were to grab Thomas. And I held him. They bent me down and put handcuffs on me. They took Thomas in one car and me in another. They took me down to the police station to question me. They put me in a police cell. One of the police said, 'Get in there. You're a danger to yourself and a danger to others.' So that upset me. They just took him. I didn't even know he'd gone. I didn't know where he was or anything. (Booth & Booth, 2004, 57)

A young woman's recollection of police protection 10 years earlier

Susan, aged 17, recalled the night she and her brothers and sisters were removed from home 10 years earlier. Her 13-year-old sister had been accommodated by the local authority after disclosing sexual abuse by her father. This sister went to visit her mother and found that all the children had been alone in the house since the previous evening and told a care worker who then contacted the police.

We heard banging on the door and hid behind the sofa. The police forced entry and put us into a van and took us to the police station. I remember the little ones were crying. I cried as well. I held on to [12-year-old sister].

> We were all really scared. We didn't want to go and we didn't know why they were taking us away.
>
> Susan was then placed in foster care with her brother and younger sister. Her three other siblings were placed elsewhere. (From Masson, Harrison & Pavlovic, 1999)

Even where there was no use of force, those who were aware that police protection had been used (and some were not) felt the power of the state to take control over family life. Although it was only a temporary measure, police protection often initiated the separation of parent and child. Consequently, officers' action had a profound and long-term effect.

POLICE PROTECTION AS POLICE WORK

The police, because of their wide powers, their capacity to act decisively and to use force have become the agency that deals with anything that requires an immediate authoritative intervention (Bittner, 1974). Uniform officers in the course of routine duties are regularly involved in a whole range of 'peace-keeping' activities helping individuals, resolving disputes, exercising control and providing care (Waddington, 1999). Protecting children in a wide range of unexpected situations is one of these responsibilities. Although peacekeeping forms a major part of what officers do, it is given little acknowledgement by police organisations. Police obligations remain 'diffuse and unspecified while operational practice is largely hidden from scrutiny and evaluation' (Punch, 1979, 102). Much of this work has little to do with criminal justice and what officers think of as real policing. In police subculture, it is generally viewed as low status 'rubbish' work (Waddington, 1999).

Police forces are large bureaucracies which impose rules, guidelines and procedures, and supervise their officers. However, discretion is a fundamental element of police work; rules are often vague and require interpretation and situations have to be assessed. Policing is intrinsically difficult to control; constables have substantial discretion because much of what they do occurs when they are working alone or with other constables. Police organisation supports some independent action by officers by leaving it relatively free from scrutiny (Reiner, 2000). Officer's freedom of action is greatest where they are dealing with peacekeeping work rather than criminal matters (Waddington, 1999). In these areas of work, there is less police accountability than for matters that enter the criminal justice system. Officers decide the appropriate approach to take to each situation they face, drawing on their knowledge and experience, police culture and the anticipated consequences of their actions. Officers are concerned not only with the present but how their actions would be viewed by supervisors. They seek to avoid 'within-the-job' trouble, and a major strategy for doing this is to control the information provided to supervisors (Chatterton, 1983). Officer's capacity and willingness to make decisions which keep matters away from the criminal justice system has led to them being seen as an informal court of first instance (Waddington, 1999).

At times of personal or family crisis, the public frequently turn to the police rather than to social services. The police are available at any time, are often easier to contact and are regarded as a first port of call by many who are not clear about the role of social services. Police officers perform emergency welfare services, make referrals to social services and direct individuals to other helping agencies (Punch & Naylor, 1973; Shapland & Vagg, 1988). According to Punch, people call the police not just because other services are not available but because they mistrust social workers and want a decisive, authoritative figure to support them in a dispute (Punch, 1979, 107).

Family disputes, incidents of domestic violence and disputes between parents and teenage children frequently lead to calls to the police. When dealing with disputes, police officers engage in a complex negotiation process seeking commonsense resolutions, applying 'community standards' rather than narrower police perspectives (Waddington, 1999). Their decisions are also guided by the officer's notion of moral culpability (Chatterton, 1983). According to Kemp and colleagues who observed the way the police dealt with 60 disputes (very few of which involved children) the result of the negotiation was most commonly to 'negotiate to nothing' so that no formal police action had to be taken (Kemp, Norris & Fielding, 1992).

In all forces in the police protection study, the decision to use the power was a matter for the individual officer's discretion but there were considerable differences between the eight forces in the way use of the power was organised, supervised and recorded, reflecting differences in the priority given to this work and the concerns of senior officers. In two of the eight forces, Forces J and L, the Inspectors in charge of the specialist Child Abuse Investigation Unit had taken a particular interest in police protection and attempted to ensure that officers knew what they should do when exercising the power. However, in the other six forces, police protection was no one's real concern. It was just a power that officers had, and sometimes had to use; senior officers were not interested in examining how it was being used, or even counting how often this was done.

> We keep statistics, we don't publish them, but we keep them for when people like you ring up and ask for them, 'cause the only people who ever seem interested are the people doing research projects. (Detective Inspector, Child Protection Unit, Force G)

THE ORGANISATION OF CHILD PROTECTION POLICING

Specialist police units to deal with child abuse were introduced in the late 1980s and early 1990s as a result of serious concerns regarding the investigation of child abuse cases, in particular the interviewing of child victims (Hughes, Parker & Gallagher, 1996; Lloyd & Burman 1996). These Child Abuse Investigation Units (CAIUs) gradually developed their own identity with officers building close relationships with social services departments. All forces now have such units, staffed by specially trained officers (Her Majesty's Inspectorate of Constabulary, 2005, 40). They have a wide range of responsibilities, usually including investigating crimes against children in the family or in care homes, supervising sex offenders and supporting child witnesses. However, child protection is 'a whole force responsibility' (Her Majesty's Inspectorate of Constabulary, 1999, 5), 'all police personnel have a responsibility for identifying and taking action in cases of child abuse' (Her Majesty's Inspectorate of Constabulary, 2005, 21) and any officer, not just specialists, can take a child into police protection.

Despite their expertise in child protection, most Child Abuse Investigation Units were not routinely involved in taking police protection. Officers viewed police protection as a power used by uniform officers. The gulf between the work of Child Abuse Investigation Units and day-to-day child protection policing is illustrated by the response of the Head of a CAIU to a question about his force's policies on the use of police protection.

> What do you mean by police protection? . . . It's not something that we deal with under the child protection unit, we investigate offences. The duty to decide whether or not a child should be subject to a PPO is made by the on duty uniform inspector. (Detective Chief Inspector)

There were 42 cases (13.5% of the sample) where police protection was used by CAIU officers, and almost half of these came from the two forces with the lowest use of police protection, Force M and Force I. This would seem to reflect a different approach to police protection in these forces. Their CAIUs were using police protection to a greater extent than elsewhere, and uniformed officers were not responding to crises involving children by using police protection as frequently as in other forces. In Force I, the CAIU operated extended hours and could be contacted via the control room during the evening when many incidents arise. However, a similar pattern was not observed in other forces where the CAIU operated extended hours.

There were also variations between and within forces in the extent to which specialist officers became involved in decisions by uniform officers about the use of police protection. In one force, it appeared from the forms that the duty CAIU officer always went to incidents requiring police protection when she was on duty, but this was not the model in the other divisions there. In all forces, the police protection forms were passed to the CAIU but in some, unless there were allegations of criminal offences which demanded further investigation, forms were only filed. In others, any follow-up with social services was arranged through the CAIU. In Force L, all the designated officers (the officers who have responsibility for overseeing every use of police protection) worked in the Child Abuse Investigation Unit.

In most forces, the vast majority of decisions about using police protection were made by uniform officers, not specialist officers with experience in a range of child protection work. The power was usually exercised by constables or sergeants attending an incident in response to a call to the police from social services, another organisation with responsibilities for safeguarding children such as a hospital or school, or from the child, their family or a member of the public. In some cases officers exercised independent judgement that police protection needed to be used, but where calls came from social services or a hospital, the duty Inspector might instruct officers to use the power.

All officers receive instruction in the power as part of their basic training, but most had no opportunity to build on this during their period as a probationer. Inspectors are also trained about the responsibilities of the 'designated officer' (Her Majesty's Inspectorate of Constabulary, 1999, 3.64–66). For most officers, taking a child into police protection was a rare occurrence – just one of the very many powers officers have by law. Limited familiarity with the power was a factor in officers' confidence and judgement in using it, and in their completion of the forms. It also affected the way designated officers carried out their responsibilities. In the view of Her Majesty's Inspector of Constabulary, lack of training made it difficult for police officers to challenge social workers who wanted police powers to be used so that they could avoid the need to apply for an emergency protection order (Her Majesty's Inspectorate of Constabulary, 2005, 4.12).

EXERCISING POLICE PROTECTION

Police officers are expected to record their use of police protection on forms provided by each force. As might be expected, form filling was not a popular activity and many officers made comments about their force's 'awful' or 'ridiculous' form. All forms have space for recording the reason the power was used and specific actions in relation to the child, including discharge of the power. The way the form is completed reflects officers' understanding of the power and how he or she thinks its use should be explained. The police protection study collected data from these forms to establish why and how the power was used, and to identify officers who were interviewed about their use of the power. Focusing on the form raises questions about dissonance between decision making and recording, the extent to which the form *explains* or *justifies* the action and about whether police officers might take action to protect children without ever completing the form. These issues were explored in the interviews.

Deciding to protect a child and exercising the power of police protection did not always coincide. There were three circumstances where this might occur. First, where the officer recognised that he or she was exercising a police power but was unaware of the procedures and consequently failed to complete the form. Officers' willingness to do this attested to their belief that they had power to remove children when this was necessary, reflecting Bittner's description of the all encompassing nature of the responsibilities placed on the police (Bittner, 1966).

> I actually just removed the child and informed social services, cut out the middle management as it were, the sergeant and the inspector, and obviously [I] wasn't aware of this [police protection] form. It was procedurally incorrect, so my action was corrected. (Police Constable, Force D)

This was not an isolated example, a few other officers recalled bringing children to the police station, knowing that 'they must have a power' but not being sure what it was, and being told to complete a police protection form by the duty inspector or the custody sergeant. Given that officers might only have to use the power occasionally, it was not surprising that some were unsure about 'the paper work'.

Secondly, there were different views about what an officer could do informally. Police are known to act informally where they do not have clear powers (Kemp *et al.*, 1992) and discouragement of informal action is one reason for giving police powers to deal with problems they commonly face (Reiner, 2000). Some officers acknowledged that they had acted informally, avoiding the power because they thought it was not necessary. An officer who found a young child without a carer, or with a parent who was not in a fit state to care for them, might contact a relative or neighbour and arrange temporary care for the child. Such action could have been taken by anyone with the agreement of the parent and needed no police power. But if a parent is too drunk to care for their child it is questionable whether they can consent to care by someone else. Some officers, like this Inspector from Force D considered that where officers assisted in such arrangements they should record it as a use of their powers, 'if we've been involved in that process we should really do it via police protection.' Similarly, a child who had run away might be returned home or asked to go voluntarily to the police station and wait for their parents. Concerns that the police should establish why a child had run away did not mean that police protection had to be used. But if the child refused to go, the power gave the officer authority to take them. An Inspector from Force A saw using police protection as a precaution where children agreed to go to the police station, 'in case they change their mind.' However, there were differences both between and within forces about whether children who had been located after going missing should be taken into police protection.

> Between the inspectors there's a slightly different viewpoint and attitude towards taking police protection. There's times where the children are taken but the forms not completed.... Juveniles who have been reported missing who we find on the street, who are unwilling to come with us... the only power we have is to use police protection... but the paperwork is not completed. (Inspector, Force J)

Thirdly, there were cases of virtual use of the power. Experienced officers recognised that the power could be used but avoided having to do so (and completing the form) through preparation or threats. For example, the risk of abduction from a hospital was sometimes handled by the police making the necessary preparations to take the child into police protection – ensuring that the duty inspector was aware of the situation and that the hospital staff could obtain an immediate response if this became necessary – but not formally using the power. Parents were warned what would happen if they tried to remove the child. Social workers similarly threatened parents to get compliance rather than resorting to court action (see Chapter 6).

> What we say is there is a PPO, and that if there is any attempt to remove the child, it will be live. I would then let [the local station] know ... that if any attempt is made to remove the child a PPO is authorised ... (Inspector, Force I)

Such a halfway approach was not universally accepted:

> We either start police protection or we don't. There's no in between, as far as I'm concerned anyway, and I think my colleagues work the same way. We always explore other possibilities, we look at the individual. (Inspector, Force J)

Exploring other possibilities included checking with social services, or even with a parent to establish whether a voluntary arrangement to protect the child would be agreed. In this way officers avoided the need to use formal powers (Kemp et al., 1992). Local authority lawyers and magistrates' legal advisers also took this approach when considering EPO applications (see Chapter 7). An inspector from Force D recalled a colleague threatening to invoke police protection to put pressure on social services to take responsibility for a 14-year-old who had turned up at the police station after being forced by his parents to leave home.

> [The Inspector] spoke to social services. Social services said, 'Well, he's at the police station now, he's your problem.' So it got to the stage where [the Inspector] said, 'Listen, you've got ten minutes to sort something out and get back to me, otherwise I'm going to invoke the police protection order.' And then they got mobilised, so the police protection order wasn't needed to be filled out, just the threat of it ... It's a very useful bargaining tool. (Inspector, Force D)

The extent of such informal action is unknown. However, a review of all incidents involving children recorded during a month on one force's command and control system revealed no children being taken from their home by officers without the use of police protection with the exception of one child taken together with his mother to a refuge.

THE USE OF POLICE PROTECTION

There are wide variations between forces in the use of police protection. In 1998, use in the 13 forces for which the researchers had data varied between 28 cases in a Force L, which covers a large rural area and a substantial city, and 314 cases in Force N, which covers a suburban and rural area outside London and includes four large towns. There was almost a 10-fold difference in the rate of use between Force J and Force L (see Table 3.1) with Force L making much less use of the power despite covering more than twice the area and having twice as many police officers. Some reasons for these differences are discussed below. They include policies about the use of police protection in particular circumstances, for example in relation to runaways; the extent to

Table 3.1 Number of police protections by Police Force (1998)

Force	Number taken	PP per 1000 under 18s[1]
A	DK[2]	—
B	62	0.38
C	58	0.51
D	293	0.47
E	229	0.64
F	48	0.20
G	90	0.34
H	DK	—
I	30[3]	0.09
J	130	0.79
K	41[4]	—
L	28	0.08
M	78	0.32
N	314	0.7
O	DK	—
P	177	0.35
Total	1578	

[1] Using mid-year estimates for 1998 (Department of Health, 1998b, table A1).
[2] Force did not know and could not establish its use of police protection.
[3] Extrapolated from 3 months data.
[4] Incomplete, four out of five divisions.

which informal action was used and accepted by supervisors; the degree of control specialist officers had over the use of the power; and the reliance on police powers by the social services department.

CIRCUMSTANCES WHERE POLICE PROTECTION IS USED

Case Examples

The following examples, from records and interviews in the two studies illustrate common circumstances that lead to the use of the power. Some details have been changed to maintain anonymity.

Child at risk: Leanne aged 3 months

At around 9 pm on a Sunday evening, the police received a call from a publican about an altercation at a pub close to the police station. Two officers attended and calmed the situation. The parents had been drinking all day with friends, celebrating the birth of their baby. The mother who was drunk was arrested for assaulting the father. The police called an ambulance for the father but he refused to go to hospital. He was very drunk and wanted to take his child. The father was known to the police and one of the officers recalled attending 'domestics' at the parents' home. The officers considered that the father was not in a fit state to care for baby Leanne. The publican offered to keep the child at the pub but the officers were concerned that the father might return and cause trouble. The baby was taken into police protection and, by ambulance, to the police station. After approximately one hour local authority foster carers came and collected Leanne. Force L

Child at risk: Ian aged 2¹/₂ years

At 10 am social services contacted the Inspector at the Child Abuse Investigation Unit with concerns about a mother who was believed to be living with a man convicted of a serious assault on a 2-year-old child. The social worker had been refused access to the home; the man was aggressive and the woman denied that she was the children's mother. The police obtained a photograph from the Criminal Records Office so that they could check the man's identity and an officer went with the social worker to the home twice during the afternoon but there was no one there. A neighbour contacted the grandmother when the family returned and the Inspector, two officers and a social worker from the Emergency Duty Team went to the home The man's identity was confirmed. Ian and his young cousin who was staying with him were taken to their grandmother's home under police protection. The local authority applied for an EPO in respect of Ian the following day. Force I

Children at risk: Adam, aged 8, Alice aged 6 and Annie aged 3

Adam, Alice and Annie were having weekend contact with their divorced father. The father became very drunk and assaulted Adam and 'wrecked the house'. The children were frightened, they barricaded themselves into the flat, leaving their father outside, and called the police. An officer went to the father's flat, he was not convinced that the children could be left there safely and took them into police protection. The mother had gone away for the weekend but the children said there was an aunt who lived locally. The children were taken directly to the aunt's home. Social services were informed. The mother was contacted and later she took the children home. Force A

Abduction: Eve

The mother's first child nearly died because of neglect and was the subject of a care order; the mother and the maternal grandmother both have learning difficulties. At a pre-birth child protection conference a decision was made to register the baby on the child protection register and recommend that the baby be looked after following birth, with only supervised contact with the mother. Arrangements were made for liaison between social services and the maternity services so that the local authority would be informed of the baby's birth. Prior to the birth, the local authority was preparing for care proceedings with a probable plan of adoption. The mother presented herself at a hospital 100 miles away but told nurses that she had come there because E local authority were going to take her baby away. The hospital contacted their local social services emergency duty team who contacted the police. Shortly after she was born, Eve was placed in police protection and E local authority was informed. Before the police protection expired, an EPO was obtained and Eve was removed from hospital and taken to foster carers. Force E

Missing from home: Tony, aged 12

The CAIU were investigating allegations of sexual abuse in respect of two sisters who named their 12-year-old brother, Tony, as the perpetrator. Tony went missing but called his mother using his mobile phone and threatened suicide. The mother contacted the police. Calls to Tony's phone helped to locate him and seven hours later he was picked up by the police. There was insufficient evidence to arrest him and his mother refused to allow him to return home so he was taken into police protection. Social services arranged a foster placement and Tony was taken there from the police station. Force A

Child's behaviour: Dan aged 14 years

Dan's father was in prison and his mother was finding it hard to cope with Dan's behaviour. A month before he was taken into police protection his mother brought him to the police station after they had had an argument and Dan had threatened to kill himself. She found a noose in his bedroom. The Inspector spoke to both of them, they appeared reconciled and went home. The following week there was another incident where Dan tried to hang himself at school and social services were involved but Dan remained at home. Following a third incident on a Sunday morning when Dan assaulted his mother and sister, the mother called the police. The officers who went to Dan's home were aware of the previous incidents and took him into police protection. Social services were contacted. Dan spent 5 hours in the police station front office until a foster placement was found for him. Force D

The Children

Cases where the officer had previous involvement with the child or family were rare. In most cases, the police had little information about the children who they were taking into police protection. Officers responded to the child's situation and were required to record only limited information about the child themselves. Even where social services requested action in respect of a specific child, officers might find other children at the address and consider it necessary to remove them too, as in the case of Ian, above. Name, age and gender were usually but not always available. Younger children might not be able to give their name, and older ones sometimes refused to do so.

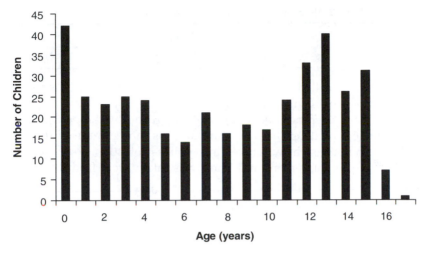

Figure 3.1 The age of children taken into police protection

Any person below the age of 18 years can be taken into police protection, but the power was only used on eight occasions in relation to young people who were over the age of 16 years, see Figure 3.1. Just over a third of the children in the sample were under the age of five years, the largest group, 10 per cent of the total sample were under the age of one year. A quarter of the children were between the ages of five and 11 years and the remaining 40 per cent were aged 11 years or older. Slightly more boys were taken into police protection than girls, but the power was used more frequently in relation to girls over the age of 13 than for teenage boys. These girls were missing from home, 'at risk' or causing concern because of their behaviour. Overall, police protection was used in relation to older children far more frequently than emergency protection orders; only 10 out of 127 applications for EPOs were made in relation to children over the age of 10 years.

The 311 cases involved a total of 420 children. Three-quarters of the incidents in the study concerned only one child, and another sixth two children. Most cases involving more than one child related to children at home, who were at risk or left without a carer.

Use of Police Protection in the Eight Forces

Table 3.2 breaks down the case sample from the police protection study, showing the circumstances in which the power was used in each of the eight forces. It also illustrates the differences between forces in the way the power was used.

Table 3.2 Reason for use of police protection by Police Force

Reason	Force								Total
	A	D	E	F	I	J	L	M	
Missing from home	15	10	14	4	1	8	4	2	58
Domestic violence	0	2	2	1	3	1	3	0	12
On street	4	4	4	3	0	2	2	1	20
At risk	10	25	19	7	21	11	14	16	123
Parent's arrest	3	3	0	0	1	1	0	0	8
Behaviour	9	6	13	2	2	6	0	2	40
Home alone	5	3	5	2	2	2	4	0	23
Abduction	3	3	3	1	3	1	2	1	17
Disputes	0	0	3	2	0	1	1	1	8
Total	49	56	63	22	33	33	30	23	309[1]

[1] Missing data in two cases

'At risk' cases were the most common, accounting for almost 40 per cent of use overall but over 60 per cent of cases in Forces I and M. The next largest category, children missing from home, were almost 20 per cent of the sample but the power was only used in such circumstances once in Force I and twice in Force M. Indeed only Force J routinely took missing children into police protection although others did so where there were additional concerns as there were with Tony (above). Concerns about children's behaviour led to the use of police protection in 13 per cent of the sample cases but none from Force L. These cases, which might involve the police looking after young people in the police station for a considerable time until a placement was found, were often a source of conflict with social services. They are discussed in Chapter 4.

In most cases the police protection form gave more details about the incident. A third of 'at risk' cases involved parents who were incapable of caring because they were under the influence of drink or drugs; 12 per cent had a parent whose mental health was thought to be a risk to their children; and a quarter involved children who were thought to have non-accidental injuries. There were cases where the form only stated that the child was 'at risk' and others where the only information given was *'scabies'* or *'severe dental decay'* – child protection concerns that would not on their own be seen as justifying an immediate response, especially not from the police. This suggests that the supervision of the power, or at least of form filling, did not seek to challenge officers' initial decisions to use it, a view corroborated by the interviews with officers.

In many cases, the need for immediate protection was clear and there were some highly charged incidents. However, there were a few cases where the use of emergency removal was more questionable, particularly in the light of the *Working Together* guidance about balancing risks to the child of removal, of harm if they are not removed, and the need to secure evidence for prosecutions (Home Office *et al.,* 1991, para 3.8). For example, in one case where specialist officers were interviewing a child who alleged sexual abuse they instructed uniform colleagues to collect the child's three siblings from school, under police protection. These children were released to their parents three hours later. Nothing further was recorded on the police protection form.

Of the 58 incidents where police protection was used in relation to children missing from home, 15 concerned children who were missing from local authority care. Running away is a major issue; it has been estimated that there are over 100,000 incidents in England and Scotland, and that over 40,000 children and young people go missing each year (Abrahams & Mungall, 1992; Children's Society, 1999, 38).

Children in state care are known to run away more frequently than those living with their families; Abrahams and Mungall found that 30 per cent of young runaways were missing from substitute care, the majority from residential care (Wade, Biehal, Clayden & Stein, 1998, 5). Following up absences from substitute care puts considerable strain on police resources (Local Government Association and Association of Chief Police Officers, 1997). Concerns have also been expressed that sometimes such young people are not taken sufficiently seriously, and that running away may be a cry for help where a young person is being abused (Kirkwood, 1993; Waterhouse, 1999). Officers expressed exasperation at dealing with children who ran away repeatedly; some commented that insufficient control was exerted to keep children in care homes.

> If they're not there at a particular time, the staff tell us. We're then obliged to record them as a missing person, and they basically are manipulating the system. When they've had enough, they will go home, eat, bath, change their clothes and go again. And every time we have to do the missing persons report, because of the age you cannot discount that ... what we're getting [is] 6 o'clock in the morning is phone calls from them saying, 'We're cold, we want to go home, come and collect us.' (Inspector, Force E)

> You deal with so many, so many times a day, same names over and over again ... and it's a real half hearted ... you really have to try and prevent that ... say yeah, I know its so and so, I know this is the fiftieth time this week he has gone missing, but we do have to try and find him. And we find him, he'll be missing again within the hour. (Sergeant, Force L)

There were 23 incidents, when police protection was used where children had been left at home alone. Twenty of the 47 children involved were aged less than six years. Officers were generally unaware of how long the parent had been (and would be) absent. Some of the children showed signs of obvious neglect, and some homes had no food available. In one incident, three children under the age of five years were found locked in a bedroom after a call by the landlord. They were taken to hospital because of their condition. Others were found in homes with obvious dangers, for example unguarded fires or open front doors. Removing children under police protection was not the only police response to such cases, officers sometimes found neighbours or relatives who would act as babysitters and at least one sent a colleague to find the mother at a local leisure centre. Such informal action could obviate the need to use police protection to take the child to the police station and to complete the form; parent and child could be re-united and the parent advised to take more care in future.

Children were picked up in public places and taken into police protection on 20 occasions. In five cases, children were taken from a parent who was incapable of caring for them, generally because of intoxication. One child was also picked up drunk. Seven children had been lost, including one who was found unconscious and another who had been found alone in a park by an over-cautious member of the public who called the police. Two children were hitch-hiking on the motorway, one appeared to be soliciting and no details were given for the remaining four.

The abduction or threatened abduction of a child led to the use of police protection in 17 cases. There were three distinct circumstances where the power was used, to prevent parents removing children from hospital, either newborn babies or children thought to have been abused; to stop parents taking children who were being looked after by the local authority; and where a parent without residence removed a child from (or failed to return their child to) the parent with care. Where children were in hospital or being looked after, police protection was frequently followed by the local authority seeking an EPO. These were examples of urgent, often precautionary action, but in a few, such as the case of Eve, above, parents were trying to evade the attentions of social services.

Incidents of domestic violence resulted in the use of police protection if neither parent was in a fit state to look after the children. This might happen, as in the case of Leanne (above), where one parent was arrested and the other was incapable of caring because of injury or intoxication. Although police are commonly called to deal with violent incidents in the home, use of police protection was rare, accounting for only 12 incidents in the sample, despite the current emphasis given to 'taking positive action' by arresting the perpetrator in such cases. In most cases, alternatives were open to the police; the victim was able either to continue caring for the children or to make arrangements with relatives or neighbours to do so. One child, aged eight years, came into police protection because, unlike his brothers and sisters, he refused to stay with relatives after such an incident. Parental arrest also led to children being taken into police protection in eight other cases. These included cases where parents were arrested at an incident or in their own home under a warrant.

The main factor which led to the use of police protection in these cases was the parents' failure to make or to agree other arrangements for their children's care. Police officers removing the carer could not leave children home alone and therefore had no alternative but to use their powers to ensure the children were looked after.

The Time Police Protection was Used

In the majority of cases, police protection was used out of normal office hours. In over half the cases, action was taken between 4.30 pm and midnight, and in another sixth between midnight and 6 am. Distribution over the week was fairly even, with slightly fewer cases on Saturdays and Sundays. Contrary to what most police officers believed, more applications were made on Mondays, not Fridays. There were only 58 cases (20 per cent) where the power was used on a weekday between 9 am and 4.30 pm. Given the emphasis on seeking court orders (above, Chapter 1), police protection should only be used at such times if immediate action is required, making proceedings impracticable. Also, for part of the year at least, most children would be at school during at these times. Just under half of these daytime applications related to children 'at risk' and a quarter concerned children's behaviour. There were slight differences between forces in the proportions of cases where police protection was used during office hours, with Force D doing this least and Force L (where much of the work was channelled though the CAIU) most. It does not appear that police protection was frequently used at a time and in circumstances in which an application to protect the child should have been made to a court.

THE DECISION TO TAKE A CHILD INTO POLICE PROTECTION

There are many parallels between police protection and the emergency apprehension of mentally ill people researched by Bittner in the 1960s. Bittner noted that this work was the proper business of the police with legal rules specifying police action and comparable to arrest. However, officers disliked it because it was not well regarded by superiors or colleagues, because of the time it took and the difficulties of dealing with psychiatric hospitals. They did not feel competent to make decisions that apprehension was required, and viewed compulsory hospital admission as punitive and stigmatising. Nevertheless, they took action where the person concerned presented a serious problem for the police (for example by being a danger to themselves or others) and no alternative course of action was available. Officers also recognised that a slight change in their approach could lead to much more of this difficult work with many more people being apprehended (Bittner, 1966). This point was also reflected in comments about police protection, for example by the inspector from Force A, quoted below.

The decision to take a child into police protection is subject to very little control. This is apparent from officers' willingness to write reasons that do not appear to satisfy the test in the Act. Officers recognised that assessing whether the power should be used was a matter for their professional judgement, and not something which was likely to be questioned.

> It's your call at the time, nobody ever disputes it…nobody else was there, so they can't criticise, because you're the only one there…(Police Constable, Force E)

The only criticisms from senior officers recalled in the interviews related to decisions *not* to exercise the power. None of the officers interviewed was aware of any case where use of the power had been questioned in the courts. During the study the researchers heard of one such case (not in any of the forces in the sample) where this had occurred. A young woman aged 21, picked up in a red light area and taken into police protection, obtained compensation for unlawful imprisonment because she was too old to be subjected to the power. More recently, a successful action has been taken against the Chief Constable of Merseyside where a police officer used police protection to remove a child on behalf of social services. A social worker had already obtained an EPO but not a warrant for the child's removal by the police (*Langley v Liverpool City Council and the Chief Constable of Merseyside Police* 2005). Nevertheless, some officers viewed the decision presented by use of the power as a difficult one. This was because, like Bittner's officers, they lacked confidence in dealing with the key issue, the assessment of 'significant harm' to a child and felt the power was 'draconian'. A few officers, like this Inspector, referred specifically to the impact on the child of being removed:

> The exercise of that power is quite crucial, because if you misuse it, to remove children from home unnecessarily would be quite devastating, so it has to be exercised properly, and people should be trained to do that. (Inspector, Force A)

But more officers appeared concerned about harm occurring to a child where they had failed to use their power. Comments about the circumstances where they had acted revealed concern about the plight of the children, especially younger ones. The notion that one should 'err on the side of caution' was frequently repeated, as was the need for officers to 'cover their backs'. These comments are all the more powerful because they were made before the death of Victoria Climbié, and the substantial attention in the Inquiry and the media to failure by police officers to take effective action. Even though there was little supervision of this work, concern for children's well-being and the desire to avoid criticism appeared as powerful influences on the decision to use the power.

Where officers were unsure about what to do they relied on colleagues, especially those who had experience working in a CAIU, or they contacted their sergeant or the duty Inspector. Sometimes, they were able to do this from the incident, but in other cases they brought the child to the police station (necessarily under police protection) in order to clarify the further steps they should take.

The 'significant harm' test is open to different interpretations. Police officers acknowledged that they could not just apply their own standards but found it difficult to decide what was bad enough to justify using the power. Cases where children were in their own home with a parent, and those where parents complained about their daughter's sexual activity were the most difficult.

> But I think all our standards have dropped somewhat. The truth is, you wouldn't keep a dog in some of the circumstances, the houses that we actually go to, but the kid's brought up in that environment . . . We're not the moral judges here, we've just got to ensure the safety of children . . . There are so many young people that you could actually take that power with, but you don't, and that's a moral issue. (Inspector, Force A)

> We sometimes put our own standards on things, you go into some houses and say, 'Oh this is terrible!' But compared to what we are used to, that child might be perfectly happy in that environment. All right [it is] a bit dirty but they're with their parents, they're happy. That's always the difficulty in saying, 'I believe this child could suffer significant harm if they stay at the address.' (Inspector, Force F)

Officers in other forces made similar comments about the police being more (or less) willing than the public to identify risk. Significant harm is situational; the scene presented to the officer attending it may convince him or her that a risk exists or that it does not. Officers were particularly concerned about the vulnerability of young children; perceptions about those approaching adulthood could be quite different.

> Sixteen-year-old lad reported missing from home, and I find him at 2 a.m. with his girlfriend who's having his baby. He must have been six foot three and like a brick outhouse . . . he could have fought half [the town] and won. And yet the next day there's some confusion, 'Well you should have brought him in.' No significant harm would have come to this lad. (Police Constable, Force D)

The breadth of the concept of significant harm and the lack of any external check when the power is exercised places responsibility on the officers exercising it to ensure that it is used appropriately. The very nature of the power means that the officer attending the scene largely determines whether or not the power is used. Even where the officer is unsure and consults a sergeant or inspector, the officer's account of the scene is crucial in deciding what advice to give. Also, the demeanour and personal skills of the officer may calm a situation so that it appears safe for the child to remain, or help to persuade a parent that they should agree to let someone else take care of their child. The Children Act 1989 provides a safeguard by requiring that the use of the power is investigated by a designated officer. Rather than ensuring that the initial decision is appropriate and holding the officer to account, the Act protects the child and family by providing for an automatic review by a senior officer and release of the child at that point where it is safe to do so.

CARING FOR CHILDREN IN POLICE PROTECTION

First Destination

Once an officer has decided to take a child into police protection he or she also has to decide *where* to take them unless either the power has been used to prevent the child's removal from where they were currently staying or a social worker is able to take the child directly to a placement. The Children Act 1989 requires the officer to remove the child to 'suitable accommodation', this is not defined but the 1991 Home Office Circular stated this 'will clearly not be police premises except for a short period in exceptional circumstances' (Home Office, 1991, para 15). The revised Circular expands on this,

> The term 'suitable accommodation' would normally mean local authority accommodation, a registered children's home or foster care. If the designated officer and social services consider it appropriate, the child may also be placed with relatives or other appropriate carers ... (para 25) ... A child under police protection should not therefore be brought to the police station except in exceptional circumstances, such as the lack of immediately available local authority accommodation, and then only for a short period. (Home Office, 2003, para 28)

None of the forces had direct access to social services accommodation; obtaining local authority accommodation for a child required contact with the social services department. In practice, social services accommodation was only exceptionally available immediately, unless use of the power had been at the request of social services. In just over 20 per cent of cases, children who were removed under police protection were taken direct to a placement; another four per cent, mostly very young children, were taken to hospital. Even where social services instigated the police action, a placement had not always been arranged before the child was removed. Twenty per cent of children taken into police protection on behalf of social services were taken to the police station initially because a placement was not immediately available for them. Out of office hours, arrangements had to be made via the emergency duty team. The limited numbers of staff in emergency duty teams and shortages of accommodation together meant that there could be a delay of some hours before a placement could be identified and the child taken there.

Going to the Police Station

Inevitably many children were brought to the police station to wait for somewhere to stay. Although many officers regarded the police station as a place of last resort, they felt that they had no option but to take children there. In three-quarters of the cases where children were removed under police protection and this information was recorded, they were taken to a police station. Almost 200 children were known to have been taken to the police station, half of them, aged 12 years or older.

> Ninety-nine times it's not ideal to bring children back to the police station, but at the end of the day, it was late on Friday night, you have to make the most of it, and I don't think she was too put by it... She thoroughly enjoyed it. (Police Constable, Force L)

Being taken to the police station could mean a substantial journey because only a few are open 24 hours a day. Officers were concerned about transporting young children because police cars did not have child restraints. There was general agreement amongst all the Inspectors interviewed that children taken into police protection should never enter the police station via the custody area. However, this route was used occasionally if an officer thought he had arrested the child and it was the custody sergeant or designated officer who identified police protection as the appropriate power, or if the officer thought that the child should wait to be collected by social services in the juvenile detention room.

Care in Police Stations

The legal position of children taken to police stations under police protection is unclear. Children are not free to leave but are not treated as if they are formally detained. Although Police and Criminal Evidence Act, Code C, applies to people 'in custody at police stations, whether or not they have been arrested for an offence and those removed to a police station... under s.135

and 136 of the Mental Health Act 1983', it makes no reference to children in police protection. Nor is there any mention of the Code in the Home Office Circular. Officers in the study did not consider PACE to be applicable to children brought into police protection although in one force the custody officer included such children in the register of 'volunteers'. There appeared to be no formal rules governing how children should be cared for, nor were they under the protective oversight of the custody officer. Children were not supposed to be at police stations, and officers who brought them there had to do what they could to accommodate them temporarily.

Finding somewhere suitable in the police station where children could be kept safe was a problem for all forces. None of the police stations had a dedicated family room; officers had to find the least unsuitable place, a canteen, recreation room or interview room. Wherever children were put they had to be accompanied, or at least supervised. Officers were concerned to prevent children becoming too upset, and about their behaviour, particularly that they might run away. Occasionally, the only way to control 'streetwise' young people was to place them in cells, juvenile detention rooms or the holding area of the custody suite. But most officers regarded the use of detention facilities as 'not an option' at least until they found themselves responsible for a young person who could not be contained in any other way. Young people placed in cells included a boy of 15, thought to be a suicide risk, who was waiting to be examined by the police surgeon; a severely autistic boy, aged 11, whose behaviour presented a danger to himself and others; and four siblings who had run away and ran round the police station and out into the road.

Children needed to be looked after, given something to eat and drink, and reassured about what would happen to them. They were kept occupied with television, or even a tour of the police station with opportunities to try on helmets! Makeshift beds were created on chairs and benches for children who wanted to sleep. Although some officers were unsure about relating to children, they spoke about doing what they could to help them. Where food was not available at the police station, officers stopped at petrol stations to buy crisps and sweets, shared their lunch boxes, or even went out to get fish and chips. Officers from all eight forces recounted tales of looking after children they or colleagues had brought in. Where children did not misbehave 'babysitting' (as it was generally termed) might not be onerous, but Inspectors were concerned about the impact on staffing, especially where there were few officers on duty. They volunteered that junior officers might be chosen for this task because their inexperience meant that they could not be given the full range of policing work.

> It's not the youngest because, 'You're the youngest you're doing it.' It's the youngest because you're a foot walker, if you were a driver we'd have you out in a car. Also it's good experience for them. (Inspector, Force D)

There were only two forces, Force D and Force I, where the length of time children spent in the police station was generally recorded accurately. It appeared that in these forces at least, the time children spent there was quite short. In Force I, where the power was largely used at the request of social services, fewer than 10 per cent of children spent more than two hours in the police station. In Force D, where over a third of children were taken into police protection because of their behaviour, being missing from home or they were found on the street, just over 50 per cent spent as long there. In a few cases, older children who had run away from home or local authority care spent prolonged periods in a police station, in one case 17 hours.

Subsequent Placement

In just over a quarter of the cases where children were initially taken to the police station, they left there to return to their parents. Return to parents was most common where children were missing from home or found on the street, occurring in almost half of cases. Only 10 per cent of cases where children were 'at risk' ended with children going home from police protection. In nearly 60 per cent of cases, children were taken to local authority placements – residential homes or foster carers. Most of these cases involved children 'at risk' or those taken into police protection because of their behaviour. In the remaining cases, children went to stay with relatives or friends. The nature of arrangements with relatives or friends was unclear from the police records; it was uncertain whether this was a protective arrangement with the children remaining in police protection, and whether the placement was approved by social services. In the majority of cases children placed with relatives had been considered 'at risk' but the police documentation did not indicate whether this risk had passed.

INDEPENDENT OVERSIGHT – THE ROLE OF THE DESIGNATED OFFICER

Once at the police station, the necessary telephone calls could be made to relatives and to social services so that a placement could be located and parents who were not present when the child was taken could be informed. These inquiries and completing the police protection form might be undertaken by the officer who took the child into police protection or by the designated officer. The Home Office Circular 2003 makes it clear that the designated officer provides 'independent oversight' of use of the power (para 8) and also has responsibility for completing the form (para 10). However, at the time of the research, guidance described this role as being 'responsible for enquiries' and made no reference to recording the actions taken (Home Office, 1991, para 19).

In seven of the eight forces, uniform officers, usually Inspectors but sometimes sergeants, took the role of designated officer. In Force L, all officers from the Child Abuse Investigation Unit, of whatever rank, acted as designated officers. This had a considerable impact on the exercise of the role because these officers were only available during office hours. If police protection was taken outside this time, the officer who had used the power had no supervision but could get support by telephone. Nevertheless, officers in Force L thought that this was a good arrangement; the CAIU staff were all experienced in child protection and had a close relationship with social services staff. They saw themselves as more capable of dealing with issues relating to police protection than duty Inspectors whose experience in these matters was likely to be very limited.

> My previous experience of having an Inspector do them is, you would find an inspector, and nine times out of ten, it would be the first one they've done, or they wouldn't know what to do, or there would be a little bit of panic. (Sergeant, Force L)

When this was discussed at the two police focus groups, conducted by the researchers at the end of the study, officers from all other forces were critical of the practice in Force L. Their main criticism related to the availability of specialist staff, but there were also questions of rank. One constable summed up these points:

> I think it is better having it with the inspector there, he's on hand, he can see what is happening, he's got an overall view of it... it takes the onus off us, so I would prefer to have the inspector there to make any decisions.(Police Constable, Force A)

In Force L, use of police protection was low, a third of cases were referred by social services and in a quarter the action was taken by a CAIU officer. Occasions where a uniform officer took a child into police protection when the CAIU was closed were few, so the problems that other officers saw with the arrangement in Force L rarely occurred.

Approaches to Acting as Designated Officer

Except in Force L, there was general acceptance that the designated officer must be informed of police protection as soon as possible and that it was their responsibility to authorise or sanction the continued use of the power. Two patterns of working, 'hands-on' and 'hands-off' emerged from the interviews with the designated officers in the other seven forces. These were not the result of hard and fast policies in forces, rather they operated within forces according to the preferred style of individual officers, or sometimes according to the case.

Where designated officers were 'hands on' they were involved in completing many of the tasks required by the legislation, and checking what the officer had done. They visited the child, talked to them, liaised with social services, and took an active part in the process from the time when the officer taking police protection first alerted them to the situation. In some cases the designated officer was also involved in the initial decision to take police protection.

> You've got this role, it's just a question of making sure that the officer comes to you, that all that has been done that should have been done, and all the relevant people have been informed, that the paperwork has been completed ... It's my role to make sure, what the full background of the case was, which is what I did do, and to inform her what was happening, what a police protection order meant, why we couldn't let her stay at the house she wanted to stay at. We got from her why she didn't want to go back [home]. (Inspector, Force F)

Many inspectors expected to get personally involved in every police protection incident. This followed the pre-Children Act approach where the police power was an Inspector's warrant and from the fact that inspectors saw the power to remove a child as a major responsibility, which had to be taken seriously. One inspector commented that some officers thought of police protection as 'just getting the designated officer to sign the form', whereas he saw the power as a serious issue, with himself carrying the responsibility. Inspectors who acted in this way sometimes identified informal action by an officer as use of the power.

Where designated officers were 'hands-off' they acted more as a supervisor, leaving the officer to carry out the bulk of the work, but checking the form. There could be practical reasons for this; the inspector could be based at another station or be dealing with a major incident. In other cases, this approach occurred because there was nothing left to do or the Inspector thought there was no need for greater involvement.

> Of all the ones I've ever dealt with, this was actually dealt with by the time I'd got there ... Obviously the reason why the inspector gets involved is because the form demands an inspector's signature as the designated officer, but the inquiries are in the main done by the sergeant, and my experience mainly of them has been as a sergeant, doing the actual investigations. It's getting the inspector's signature and then completing it [themselves]. (Inspector, Force D)

The 'hands-off' approach might mean that the designated officer did little more than sign the form, sometimes it seems from the quote above, before it had been completed, and going along with decisions made by the officer. In such cases there was no effective control over the use of the power, forms were not completed fully or accurately, and forces lacked the information necessary to check what actions had been taken. This was in marked contrast to the approach taken by custody officers where people (adults or children) are detained under the Police and Criminal Evidence Act 1984, where thorough records must be (and are) kept.

ENDING POLICE PROTECTION

It is the designated officer's responsibility to determine whether there is no longer a risk of significant harm and the child should be released from police protection. In any event the power can last no longer than 72 hours. However, many officers of all ranks were confused about when police protection ended. It was a common misconception that police protection ended when the child left the police station. Conversely, in one force it was the view that police protection always lasted for 72 hours. Linking police protection with presence at the police station suggests confusion with arrest; the notion that the power always lasts 72 hours suggests that the designated officers were not mindful of their responsibilities. As a consequence of these errors, the length of time the child remained in police protection could only be established reliably in three of the eight forces, J, E and A. One of these forces included specific guidance about the duration of police protection on its forms, and in the other two, the designated officers generally ensured that this part of the form was completed correctly. Even so it only possible to determine how long the power had been in place in 103 out of 146 cases from these three forces.

In 70 per cent of these cases, police protection lasted no longer than six hours. As might be expected, there was considerable variation in the length of police protection depending on the circumstances in which it was used; police protection was more likely to end within six hours where children had been reported missing from home (81 per cent of these cases) than where they were believed to be 'at risk' (55 per cent). Similarly, police protection was more likely to end quickly where children returned home than if they entered local authority accommodation. Only 15 per cent of the children who returned home spent longer than six hours in police protection.

Where children ceased to be in police protection but remained in a local authority placement, the social services department made other legal arrangements. Ending police protection might therefore make little difference to the child or the parents. The local authority could reach an agreement with the parents for the child to be accommodated (or to stay with relatives or friends). If parents would not agree, the local authority could apply for an EPO and start care proceedings. In these cases, the length of police protection depended on the time taken to obtain an EPO. This is considered in Chapter 7.

UNDERSTANDING THE POLICE POWER

> But police protection, like all child protection matters, is not well understood by most officers, and I think, as a result of that, it's probably a misused power, in the main. (Inspector, Force A)

This officer was the only one who claimed that police protection was frequently misused. Lack of understanding was linked by other officers to a failure to use the power, or to recognise that the action they had taken was a use of the power. More specifically, many officers were unclear about the powers they had in relation to children in police protection, thinking that they had parental responsibility or that they were powerless if children refused to co-operate. There was much confusion about the responsibility the police had after children had been placed by social services; as noted above, it was a common misconception that children left police protection when they left the police station. The place was suffused with the power so the power was not recognised as existing independently.

CONCLUSION

Child protection was not a national policing priority and therefore did not receive the resources (money or management) committed to other areas of policing (Masson, 2006b). Although many officers noted that the police were 'a 24/7 service' with wide powers to safeguard children, their focus remained crime control, including the investigation and prevention of offences. Like other aspects of peacekeeping it had low status. The power was just another tool that any officer might have to use to solve a problem with the care or control of children which could not be sorted out in any other way. Small, specialist CAIUs, which were available for only part of the day, could not respond to all cases where police protection was required

For the most part, officers interviewed in the study took their responsibilities in relation to police protection seriously and were keen to improve practice but they also viewed this work negatively. They remained uncertain how practice could be improved, and where their responsibilities fitted in to the bigger picture of child protection. Exercising the power was seen as the last resort in a crisis relating to a child, not as a way of securing a safety net for children. In part this reflected the nature of the power which could be used in a wide variety of circumstances, most of which allowed for no preparation or planning, and impacted on any individual officer only rarely. It also related to institutional uncertainty about the role of the police in child protection and the limited attention which has been given to this area by central government and, consequently, by forces.

Police responsibilities for child protection are unlikely to be taken away. Someone has to have the power to do something where immediate action has to be taken (Bittner, 1974). Police protection is a formal power but its wide drafting leaves officers with a broad scope for action. The power is available for all eventualities where children need protection and this cannot be arranged in another way. The wide construction and limited force oversight means that officers effectively set their own thresholds for intervention and that their standards are rarely challenged. Review by the designated officer ensures that misjudgements can be rectified quickly but little attention is given to the power by senior officers. Although police protection is similar to arrest in many ways, like other areas of police work unrelated to criminal justice, decisions about its use are subject to more limited control. Children do not have the protection that others detained at the police station have under the Police and Criminal Evidence Act 1984.

New emphasis on safeguarding and promoting children's welfare developed through *Every Child Matters* (Her Majesty's Treasury, 2003) and the Children Act 2004 seems unlikely to make a substantial difference to child protection policing. The focus of guidance on this Act remains the welfare of children within the criminal justice system because children are perpetrators, witnesses or victims; little attention is given to police officers' civil powers to protect children. Moreover, concerns about social services' avoidance of the courts through reliance on police powers, reflected in both the Home Office Circular (Home Office, 2003) and *Working Together* (Department for Education and Skills, 2006) may mean that even less attention is given to the power because of an underlying message that it should not be used. The issue of police and social services collaboration in emergency intervention is discussed in the following chapter.

4

WORKING TOGETHER? THE POLICE, SOCIAL SERVICES AND POLICE PROTECTION

Basically the PPOs, they're divided into two. One where we act for social services because it's out of hours and they can't initiate it themselves. Then the other ones are the types where we sort of stumble upon something. (Inspector, Force J)

INTRODUCTION

Drawing on the police protection and EPO studies, this chapter examines how the police and social services departments worked together and independently in providing a response to child protection emergencies. It identifies the different concerns of the two agencies and considers the issues that arise in such cases from the perspectives of police officers, social workers and social services managers.

Whereas both police officers and social workers have responsibilities to children at risk of significant harm, they operate in very different contexts. For social services, child protection is the 'heavy end' of extensive duties to safeguard and promote the welfare of children in need in the community. For the police, it can arise across a diverse range of unrelated policing activities (Her Majesty's Inspectorate of Constabulary, 1999, 61) and, outside specialist Child Abuse Investigation Units, it is generally peripheral in mainstream policing (Punch, 1979; Waddington, 1999; see also Chapter 3). Consequently, the police and social workers view thresholds for action differently and disagree about what is the appropriate response to a specific crisis. At the most basic level, these are conflicts about power and resources.

The local authority social services department is the agency with the main responsibility for protecting children but only the police have powers which they can use directly to protect children by removing or detaining them. Social workers can only act with parental agreement, or after obtaining a court order. There are occasions when social workers want the police to use their power but officers are unwilling to do so, and others where the police take action and social workers consider that they should not have done so. Local authority social service departments have duties to provide accommodation and to make enquiries when children are taken into police protection (Children Act 1989, ss.21, 47). Whenever the police use their power, they make demands on social services resources. Although there are circumstances where the police identify children whom social services recognise need to be protected, police action can disrupt social services plans and lead to demands for resources which would otherwise be resisted.

Even where there is agreement that action is required, the speed or otherwise with which each agency is able to respond impacts on the other. The police failure to respond sufficiently quickly to prevent a parent disappearing may result in the need to apply for an EPO with a warrant or a recovery order (ss.48, 50). Similarly, a slow response providing a placement for a child can result in police time being spent looking after the child at the police station and locating a relative or friend to provide care. Where both agencies consider themselves under-resourced, the ability of each to create work for, and shift responsibilities onto, the other provides a context for uneasy relationships. Officers recognised this, 'I don't think they [social services] enjoy us taking people into police protection because we are forcing their arm by legislation. They are like anybody else, they have limited resources' (Inspector Force M). And social services managers considered that there was not enough discussion before action was taken, 'Increasingly it is our experience that we are informed by the police that they have or are on the point of doing, or taking police protection . . . so it very much tends to be their initiative' (Social Services Manager, Area L).

RELATIONSHIPS BETWEEN POLICE AND SOCIAL SERVICES

In the past, police social services relations have been problematic, most publicly during the Cleveland crisis when there was a complete breakdown in co-operation between the agencies in the investigation of allegations of child sexual abuse (Butler-Sloss, 1988; Campbell, 1988). Hallett and Stevenson noted that conflicts of values, different priorities and ambiguities of agency function meant attempts at co-operative working between police and social services were fraught with difficulty (Hallett & Stevenson, 1992, 133). Since the enactment of the Children Act 1989 and the publication of *Working Together* (Home Office *et al.*, 1991) and the *Memorandum of Good Practice* (Home Office *et al.*, 1992) joint police social services investigations have become an essential component of child protection work. Close working relationships have been established between police CAIUs and child protection teams. Co-operation has been facilitated by local Area Child Protection Committees, interagency forums with responsibilities to develop and agree local policies and procedures and to encourage effective working relationships between different services and professional groups (Home Office *et al.*, 1991; Department of Health *et al.*, 2003, 33). Local Safeguarding Children Boards, statutory bodies set up under the Children Act 2004, have now been given this responsibility.

As discussed in Chapter 3, the use of police protection provides a very different context for police/social services relations than planned investigations into sexual or physical abuse by specialist officers. In most forces, uniform officers, not specialist officers from the CAIU, make decisions about the use of the power. Cases where children require immediate protection under police powers most commonly occur outside the normal working day; in only 20 per cent of cases where police protection was used was this action taken during the normal working day. Consequently, calls from the police to social services, for example requests to provide information or emergency accommodation for a child in police protection, are handled by the Emergency Duty Team (EDT) not by locally based, specialist child protection or family placement workers. Liaison over the use of police protection is generally between uniform inspectors acting as designated officers and social workers from EDT. Although some EDT staff retained their posts for a remarkably long time, relationships did not appear to be established between them and uniform officers as they are between child protection specialists. As one social services manager commented:

> Traditionally we have a good relationship with [force] police, mainly out of co-terminosity with the child abuse investigation unit being in [town]. I thought latterly that our good relationship with CAIU officers has been at some expense with maintaining the same sort of relationship we would have with local policing units. We tend to speak to CAIU officers and have lots of accord with them, when we speak to non-CAIU personnel it does seem different. (Social Services Manager, Area M)

Social services managers found the police organisation rather 'difficult to infiltrate' but good liaison with the CAIU could help build relationships with designated officers. In Area E, social work managers had arranged meetings with senior police officers to help develop co-operative working, and in Area J, the Inspector from the CAIU had arranged meetings with social services and briefings for designated officers for this purpose.

THE NATURE OF THE EDT SERVICE

In 1998, in its plan for modernising social services, the government stressed the need for local authorities 'to provide reliable and sufficient emergency out-of-hours services ... for urgent family situations where there are risks to children ...'(Department of Health, 1998a, para 2.58). However, the Social Services Inspectorate found that there was a narrow approach to 'emergency services' which accepted that 'intervention is only warranted if a service users' situation would not hold until daytime or mainstream services are available' (Social Services Inspectorate, 1999, para 1.18). Throughout the duration of research, the local authorities in the study provided only this limited level of service for emergencies.

The arrangements local authorities make for social services out of normal working hours vary; some run their own teams but others, particularly smaller authorities may commission such services from neighbouring authorities. Emergency duty teams have a generic remit handling calls about care for the elderly, people with severe mental health difficulties, families (including foster carers) in crisis and child protection. In the SSI study, children and families were the main service users, accounting for 48 per cent of users with 'looked after child (absconding)' accounting for 10 per cent of calls and 'requests for accommodation', 'general family support' and 'looked after child (other)' each accounting for about 5 per cent of calls (Social Services Inspectorate, 1999, 27). Three-quarters of those using the service were already known to the social services department (para 7.6). Not all calls require the same amount of work. Mental health assessments (5 per cent of calls) are particularly time consuming and necessitate a visit to the person concerned, with half lasting more than three hours. But many other calls can be handled by telephone. Overall, EDT social workers dealt with 45 per cent of cases in less than half an hour and made a call-out visit in just under 15 per cent of cases (Social Services Inspectorate, 1999, para 6.21). Forty-five per cent of calls were found by the EDT to necessitate no action or only advice, but 23 per cent required a service from them and over 10 per cent from another social services department provider. Where services were required, locating it could be time consuming; the shortage of emergency foster placements, particularly for older children, which was noted by the SSI (para 7.9), continues in most areas.

Most of the EDT services in the SSI study were based in social services department offices or residential premises. In one, staff operated from their own homes and in another staff could choose whether to do so or to use a central office base. Working from home reflects practices before the establishment of emergency duty teams when some mainstream social workers were on-call at night and weekends. Wherever staff are based, they need good access to social services information such as databases on users, services (for example foster home vacancies) and the child protection register. The SSI found that none of the services could access current social services files, service user data bases were frequently incomplete or out of date and that EDT staff experienced problems in using IT. Child protection registers and placement vacancies were generally up to date on the computer and copies were also faxed regularly (Social Services Inspectorate, 1999, paras 7.9–11).

The small number of workers (many services had only one worker on duty at any time), the concentration of calls in the evening and the nature of the work mean that callers may experience delays in speaking to an EDT social worker. The SSI noted the importance of a prompt response and advised social services departments to monitor response times and staffing levels. Generally it considered that there was a need for improvement in out-of-hours services and that local authorities needed to reconsider whether services should be limited to an emergency response, the extent to which more services should be open all hours, and co-operation with other agencies and services to provide out-of-hours services (Social Services Inspectorate, 1999, 1.31–2). The Climbié Report also stressed the need to improve out-of-hours services. It recommended that specialist services should be available to respond to children and family problems at any time (Laming, 2003, para 6.181) and that local authorities should also have access to legal advice in relation to emergency action to protect children 24 hours a day (para 5.128).

EDT SERVICES IN THE POLICE PROTECTION STUDY

The six EDT services included in the police protection study generally reflected the range of services seen by the SSI. It appeared that not all of these services had moved with the times but there were some attempts to improve them.

> Out of hours will be just the kind [of service] not really bothered about, and obviously part of what I am trying to do is to make sure that [it is] much more part of, an integrated part of, the directorate's work . . . (Social Services Manager, Area E)

Some were located in social services premises, including one close to a main police station, whereas others operated from social worker's homes. These workers generally had poorer access to social services department data and little equipment, for example, one had no fax machine. This impacted on the work they could do and the time it took.

I have had many an occasion when the social worker cannot actually get into the office, or get hold of the files on nights. They don't appear to have full records available, which doesn't make it easier on you if you're dealing with somebody you know full well social services may have more details of, relatives on their files, but they can't access those files. (Inspector, Force D)

Areas covered by a single EDT were extensive, especially where the EDT was provided by a county council; in one authority social workers had to travel for up to 90 minutes to make some visits. The police knew that there were very few EDT social workers and were critical of the service provided and poor response times.

And the input of staff into these issues is really minimal. You get a duty social worker in the night, who is pulled in all directions. (Inspector, Force E)

I've had so many cases with social services where either they won't physically come out or they try to negotiate a lot on the telephone . . . ' (Inspector, Force J)

Despite the pressure it placed on the police, some officers recognised the efforts that EDT workers made and remained sympathetic and appreciative.

Well it just takes too long. Trying to get social services out is absolutely horren-dous. I'm not saying it is their fault, they're busy, but that's what upsets us the most. (Police Constable, Force E)

Officers (in all forces) also avoided the need to rely on social services by trying to identify potential carers for children in police protection themselves, a practice which has now been recognised in the Home Office Circular (Home Office, 2003, paras 25, 30).

Albeit social services have a responsibility to place the child, we often will do the digging in terms of other relatives because it saves time as well if we are getting the details of the relatives, and we're checking as to whether they'd be prepared to house the child initially. (Inspector, Force D)

However, taking on such responsibilities masked the deficiencies of social services. In effect, the police had accepted that local authorities were not able to fulfil their statutory obligations within the timescale the police wanted so they tried to reduce their dependency on social services. Officers' expectations of social services were low but responsive action was praised. When EDT provided a speedy response 'they were brilliant' and they could be 'very very helpful when trying to find some suitable accommodation'. But the excuse that social services had inadequate resources met with an angry retort that 'the whole world is under-resourced' from another Inspector.

SOCIAL SERVICES REQUESTS FOR POLICE ASSISTANCE

Social workers sought police support in relation to child protection where the risk of violence or refusal of entry necessitated the use of police presence and powers, or where action was needed in an emergency and it was not possible to obtain a court order for a child's removal immediately. For example, in **case 22**, the social worker arranged for police attendance when she served the EPO application so that the child could be taken into police protection if the parent did not agree to the child being accommodated until the hearing later that day. Other examples where police provided support involved cases appearing to be more serious and involving threats to social workers or reports that there were guns in the house. In **case 83**, the social worker requested police assistance to take a three-year-old girl into police protection after her mother, who was suspected of burning out her home, had refused to agree to her going into foster care. However, the police failed to attend immediately and the mother disappeared with the child. The local authority applied for an EPO with a warrant the following day and the child was located and placed in foster care.

Social services were recorded by police as the source of the child protection referral in almost 20 per cent of cases where police protection was used; referral rates were even higher where the CAIU had substantial input in decisions about the use of police protection. In 29 cases (a third of the EPO study sample) the children had initially been protected with police powers exercised at the request of social services. These included four cases where parents refused to agree to their children being accommodated and two where having agreed they removed their children from foster care or failed to return them after contact. As shown in Figure 4.1, there were also four cases where children were left without carers and seven where parents refused access to social workers or children disappeared and there were child protection concerns.

Social workers, managers and local authority lawyers regarded the police as generally supportive in dealing with child protection emergencies. The comment from a social worker in Area E was typical, 'We have good relations with our child protection police so they will arrange PPO if we ask.' The police officers interviewed accepted their role in providing assistance to social services. This was all part of working together. Police officers generally responded positively to requests for police protection, so long as they were satisfied that there were grounds but there were occasions were the police refused to use their power. However, Her Majesty's Inspectorate of Constabulary seems to expect a more rigorous approach by the police to social services' requests. They have suggested that non-specialist officers' limited training in child protection made it difficult for them to challenge social services' requests for police protection (Her Majesty's Inspectorate of Constabulary, 2005, 4.12). Overall,

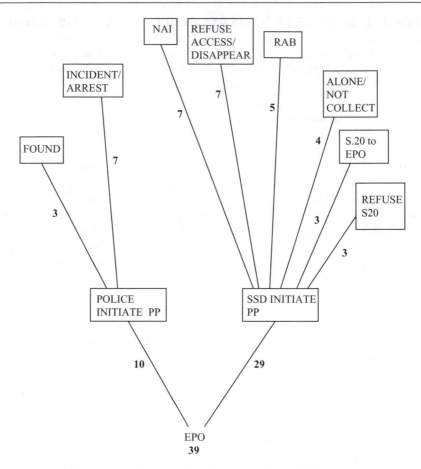

Figure 4.1   The use of police protection in EPO cases

agreeing to social services requests is both a matter of being co-operative and of lacking the knowledge and understanding to make an assessment which could justify refusal.

SOCIAL SERVICES AND POLICE PROTECTION

Guidance (see p. 14) stresses that court proceedings should be used to secure emergency protection wherever possible, and that police protection should only be used where immediate action is required. This was accepted by most of the local authority lawyers interviewed. Lawyers from each of the six authorities in the EPO study spontaneously commented that they thought it inappropriate to turn to the police where it was practicable to make an EPO application. Relying on the police was illegitimate, and would undermine relationships with them, making it harder to get co-operation in other cases.

> We'd always try and go for emergency protection rather than using police protection because to keep going for police protection is an abuse of their powers. And they don't like doing it either. They will limit the ... times they're prepared to do it. And also it's not an answer to rely on somebody else, if we can get it into court, we should be doing it ourselves. (Local Authority Lawyer, Area J)

A social work manager in the same authority agreed that 'doing things properly', required making arrangements to use the courts for applications during office hours. Only one local authority lawyer specifically made the case for using police protection more routinely, because it was a more limited power, allowed the social worker time to make a proper application to the court and ensured that the police were present when the child was removed:

> [My advice is to use police protection] wherever possible, I think for a number of reasons. Firstly, it goes by the least possible order. Secondly, it gives the social worker time to prepare a proper application. And thirdly, it gives you the all important thing that you're unlikely to have with an EPO ... you have an independent body attending the property and removing the child with you. (Local Authority lawyer, Area E)

A social work manager from the same authority commented negatively about the high use of police protection there, and indicated that attempts were being made to move away from reliance on the police.

> I was horrified with the high number of police protection compared to [the authority where interviewee worked previously]. There are some structural difficulties we have got between the police, social services and the judiciary here ... The majority of cases taken in the day time are in conjunction with social services ... [the police] come along to assist and expedite the process ... There is a broad intention within our directorate to make more use of EPOs but basically we are facing long fights in the courts, particularly the family court. We also have the system here, where we have to go through our legal services to get agreement, whereas I believe that a decision whether or not to seek an EPO should be a social work decision ... (Social Services Manager, Area E)

REASONS FOR RELYING ON POLICE PROTECTION

There were two main reasons why social services resorted to police protection, to avoid the need to make an application for an EPO outside the normal working day or where children needed immediate protection. The survey of magistrates' courts established that there were mechanisms for dealing with family proceedings out of hours in 36 out of 39 magistrates' courts areas. However, arranging to make an EPO application when the court office was closed was not easy. In most areas, a list of telephone numbers for magistrates' legal advisers was available; any person wanting to make an application had to work through the list to find which legal adviser could make the arrangements. Also, in 11 areas, the list was not directly available to the local authority, and contact with legal advisers out of hours was arranged by the police. Only four court areas operated a formal rota of advisers to deal with family cases when the court office was closed. Even though there were arrangements for out-of-hours applications, little use was made of them. Over a quarter of the magistrates' legal advisers interviewed could either not recall the last time there had been such an application for an EPO, or said that there had only been one or two in the last five or 10 years. In nearly a quarter of areas, magistrates' legal advisers said that they understood that out-of-hours cases were dealt with by the police. One noted that although provision was made for such applications, 'the culture is that police protection is the best way.' Only four clerks commented that the police took a negative approach to requests for children to be placed in police protection.

The courts in Areas E, J and M did not have formal systems for dealing with EPO applications out of normal court hours but provided phone numbers so magistrates' legal advisers could be contacted. The small number of cases meant that a formal rota was not considered a justifiable expense. In all three areas, magistrates' legal advisers gave examples of hearing EPO applications in the evening or on a Saturday, but each of these cases related to an application which had been warned or made when the court office was open. Five of the six local authorities made arrangements for legal advice at evenings and weekends, usually by providing the EDT with a contact number for a local authority lawyer. In the other authority such arrangements were only made for Bank Holidays. In all three areas, such calls were very rare; both social workers and local authority lawyers expected that children would be protected by the police at such times. One experienced lawyer said, 'I haven't actually applied for an EPO out of hours. Because you do have this thing . . . called police protection' (Local Authority lawyer, Area J). A social worker in the same area referred to the use of police protection being 'custom and practice', not policy. Relying on police protection out of hours was routine in other areas too, the only problem mentioned with this approach was that over Bank Holidays 72 hours might not be long enough.

Where immediate action was required, local authority lawyers in Areas E and J acknowledged that police protection had to be used.

> But if you decide you need an order; then how quickly do you need an order? If it's very, very quick, then that's when you look at the issue of police protection, because there's no way if you get a phone call at 3.30 today you are going to get an EPO today. It just doesn't happen in [this area] I know it does in some places but it doesn't here. So if it's that bad then that's where you advise the social worker to hang up the phone and stop wasting time talking to me and go and talk to the police because that is where they are going to get more assistance at this point in the day . . . (Local Authority lawyer, Area E)

The courts in these areas took a restrictive approach to hearing without notice applications, and in Area E would not even consider setting up a court until it had received an application in writing. Consequently, obtaining an EPO could take a number of hours. This was not mentioned by any of the three local authority lawyers interviewed in Area M, where the courts were much more willing to allow EPO applications to be made without notice, and to hear oral evidence without any written statement. During normal court hours, whether the social worker made a request to the police was determined by how quickly an EPO could be obtained.

Out-of-hours applications and immediate crises were not the only cases where local authorities sought to rely on police powers. There were some suggestions that the police could be less demanding in terms of evidence, but no clear examples were given of this occurring. One Inspector recalled being asked, and refusing, to use the power when a court application could not be made because the local authority 'haven't got sufficient evidence' and there were a few examples of children being taken into police protection after courts had refused to hear an EPO application without notice. Conversely, a legal adviser recalled the court granting an order after the police had refused to use their power. However, it was clear to social workers, local authority lawyers and the police that it was *simpler* to approach the police than to make an application to the court. This resulted in requests to the police where children needed protecting, but problems had not suddenly arisen and, with planning, protection could have been obtained through the courts.

> The impression I got...the [CAIU] said, social services on this occasion opted for police protection as an easy way out...I mean the child did very much need to be taken, but it was an easy way out and they were avoiding taking the EPO...It's perhaps one of the areas of friction between police and social services. (Sergeant, Force L)

Some officers recalled refusing such requests, making clear that this was a police power, and the officer exercising it had to be satisfied that the child's current circumstances justified its use.

> Why most PPOs are instigated is because social services haven't got time to go for EPO, which is in court. They'll often come to me for a PP, and if for me nothing's changed, then I won't give a PPO. It has to be something that says that if we don't do something now there could be a danger. (Inspector, Force I)

THE POLICE POWER

The Inquiry into the death of Victoria Climbié heard an account of how the decision was made to take Victoria into police protection. When she was first seen in hospital with suspected non-accidental injuries, a child protection referral was made to the local social services department by the doctor who examined her. The social worker then contacted the hospital and established that Victoria had been admitted to hospital. She telephoned Brent CAIU and spoke to a police constable. 'Together [the social worker and the officer] agreed to take Victoria into police protection' (Laming, 2003, para 5.124). Neither the social worker nor the police officer had seen Victoria, nor did they apparently consider whether there was a risk that she would be removed from hospital. The decision to protect Victoria was based on the fact that her injuries were non-accidental and justified her admission to hospital. Lord Laming was highly critical of the social services and police action. It was not clear that police protection was required, and it was not appropriate to use it without an officer first seeing Victoria. In effect both social service and police had used the power 'as a holding measure' justifying delaying any further investigation until the next day (Laming, 2003, paras 5.125, 13.69–70).

How might other forces have responded to the social worker's call about a child who had been admitted to hospital with suspected non-accidental injuries? The forces in the study certainly regarded police protection as a routine or administrative means of preventing children's removal from hospital pending an application for an EPO but an officer usually attended the hospital when police protection was exercised. Where parents were considered to be unfit, arrangements for police protection might be made in preparation for a baby's birth. Also, where a child was brought to the hospital with serious injuries caused by abuse, he or she might be detained in hospital under police protection. There were nine cases in the EPO study where social services requested children who were in hospital be taken into police protection, five were newborn babies, three were children who were thought to have been abused and one was admitted with her sick mother who later refused to cooperate with arrangements for the baby's discharge. Although an officer from the CAIU in Force L said, '[Y]ou can't decide to take police protection unless you're there.' This approach was not always applied where action was taken to prevent children's removal from hospital.

In the other 20 cases in the EPO study of police protection at social services request, use of the power involved specific action, removing the child from the parent (16 cases) or providing care where children had been left alone (four cases). In seven of these cases, police assistance was needed either to find children or to gain access to the home (see Figure 4.1). In all of these cases the police accepted that the power should be used. However, police protection was not available in every case. The police had to be persuaded it was appropriate for them to use their powers. Officers were very clear that it was their decision whether or not 'to give the power'; they had to assess the child's situation. Social workers (or more usually their managers) were left to persuade the police that action was required:

> We can influence, they might take advice as well but the power rests with them, and we can influence and goad but ultimately they can take it. And I have had it both ways, and in the day time we have wanted them to do police protection and they would not take it; and we have been suggesting that there is no need for police protection and they have overridden us and said, 'This is an emergency' and have taken it. (Social Services Manager, Area E)

In Area E, the difficulties the local authority experienced with the court's approach to without notice EPO applications meant that they regularly requested police assistance. Indeed, the magistrates' legal advisers were reported by the local authority lawyers as suggesting that requests should be made to the police rather than to the courts. Caught between the powers of both police and magistrates' legal advisers to refuse an emergency response, the local authority had sought to negotiate with both. An understanding had been reached with the courts that courts would be made available for EPO applications made during working hours and an arrangement was put in place for higher level consideration of applications for without notice hearings. A meeting between social work managers and the Assistant Chief Constable took place and was thought by a social services manager to have raised social services' credibility with the police and improved understanding of the pressures on social services in dealing with child protection crises.

REFERRALS TO THE POLICE FROM MOTHERS AND OTHERS

Although the police occasionally did stumble upon a child who needed to be protected in the course of ordinary policing, police protection was more likely to be used in response to a referral about a child. A source of referral was identified in just over 60 per cent of the cases in the police protection study. Family members, most commonly mothers, were the main referrers, accounting for a third of all referrals, and children referred themselves in another 15 per cent of cases. Mothers, including foster mothers, contacted the police when their children were missing from home and also where they were having severe problems with the child's behaviour. These problems included self-harm and violence or threats of violence to a parent, a carer or a sibling. For example, a boy with severe learning difficulties attacked his mother, and a nine-year-old girl threatened her foster mother with a pair of scissors. The police also received calls from members of the public (and from relatives) who were concerned about children being abused or left at home alone.

There were 40 incidents in the police protection study where the child's behaviour precipitated the use of the power. Most of these incidents arose out of disputes with parents, step-parents or carers to which the police were called, but two involved children who had set fire to their homes. Calling the police reflected the desperation carers felt, and also the expectation that a response would be forthcoming (Punch, 1979). In some instances there had been a previous request to social services to remove the child but this had been refused. Even where social services would have offered services from a specialist team, they were generally unable to provide an immediate response which the police could offer and the parents wanted (Biehal, Clayden & Byford, 2000, 34).

Both police officers and social work managers agreed that families frequently turned to the police because the response from social services was insufficient. Families had to wait too long for social services to provide a service, and what was offered was not what parents felt was needed. The comments from the social services manager in Area L and the police officer in Force J reflected experience generally:

> Because often families are at the end of their tether, they have been asking for relief or a resource and we have not been able to provide it in the kind of timescale that the family [expect]. It is often very minor incidents that cause the family to crack and involve the police, and I think they see it as an immediate way of resolving their difficulties. And I think quite often the police have got real concerns about putting a vulnerable child back into what they see as a very fragile situation . . . I don't think this is an appropriate use of pp. (Social Services Manager, Area L)

> I think a lot of the time, social services don't take enough notice of parents that call us and say, 'I can't cope anymore . . . I want you to get social services to come out and take him into care.' And it's not as easy as that. It's difficult to get parents to realise that they can't just offload their children . . . But when you speak to social services, [they] perhaps say, 'We can't do anything tonight, I'm not coming out . . .' And we're in a bit of a stalemate, and we're stuck in the middle. And I think it would be nice if social services actually get a bit more involved with older ones at that sort of stage. (Police Constable, Force J)

The police wanted social services to be more involved; they felt caught in the middle, dumped on by parents and left to deal with situations which were not the proper concern of the police, and which were better dealt with by social services.

> . . . we're just getting dumped on here. This is not a police matter, if they don't want to make a complaint [against the child], this is not a police matter, it's social services should be sorting that out. And you have to say, 'Is there not a better place that the child could be taken rather than here [police station]?' He should go straight to social services. (Inspector, Force A)

As the above quotes suggest, for some police it was easier to deal with young people's behaviour if parents were prepared to make a complaint that could be handled as a criminal matter, but others accepted that parents were trying to do what was best in a situation where they felt unable to cope. There were advantages to the police and to families in responding to violent behaviour by children towards parents as a child protection matter. If it was not possible to sort out the family problem and calm the situation, officers had to rely on their powers (Kemp *et al.*, 1992). The police could defuse the situation by removing the child under police protection without the necessity to engage with the criminal law and allied procedures, including referral to the Crown Prosecution Service and the involvement of the Youth Offending Team. Avoiding this work is all the more desirable where there is an expectation that there will be no prosecution because any complaint against the child will be withdrawn. For the child, the use of police protection avoids coming into contact with the criminal justice system. However, by-passing the Youth Offending Team may mean that the family does not receive support with the child's behaviour. This could be made available through a social services department referral on the basis that the child is in need but there was little evidence of such follow-up work after the use of police protection.

SOCIAL SERVICES RESPONSE TO POLICE ACTION

There were no cases in the EPO study where a court order had been sought because of disputes between parents and teenage children, indeed EPO applications in relation to teenage children were very rare (see Chapter 5, Figure 5.1). The parents who called the police because of their children's behaviour generally wanted their children to be taken away (at least temporarily) and would have agreed to local authority accommodation if a social worker had offered it. The police use of their power in these cases was very far removed from the social work understanding of emergency child protection powers, which were sought by social workers only where parents would not agree to arrangements voluntarily.

Although social workers were willing to rely on the police when they wanted a child to be protected, they were critical of the way the police use their power independently, particularly where this necessitated finding accommodation for a child. Police protection is effectively the only way in which a child can become looked after without an assessment by a local authority social worker that accommodation is required. Decisions to admit to accommodation are not usually matters for individual social workers but require managers or resource panels to agree to this (Packman & Hall, 1998, 30). Social workers do accept emergency admissions to accommodation but these often follow weeks during which social workers have resisted parental pressure for such a service. Packman and Hall found high rates of emergency admissions to accommodation for adolescents with 60 per cent of admissions occurring without a planning meeting and within 24 hours of the referral. Some of these resulted from the use of police protection (Packman & Hall, 1998, 79).

Where accommodation was offered to provide 'time out' for an adolescent in dispute with parents, time limits and conditions were imposed so that the family worked with social workers on solving the underlying problems (Packman & Hall, 1998, 83).

Police action which could by-pass social services admissions processes was considered inappropriate by social workers and managers. Even where a social worker had recently refused to accommodate a child, the parents could contact the police who might exercise their power. Such a decision overrode the social services assessment and made a demand on social services scarce resources. For example, following a fight between parents and a teenage girl over her relationship with her boyfriend, which resulted in her being taken to hospital, a social worker persuaded the parents to take their daughter home. When they reached home there was another incident, the police were called and the girl was taken into police protection. The social worker was very critical of the police action, which she saw as upsetting the agreement that she had brokered earlier in the evening.

The social services managers interviewed were all concerned about the way the police used their power, particularly their willingness to remove children where parents had contacted the police in a crisis. They thought that the police tended to be *'over reactive'*, responding to *'police anxieties'* rather than risks to children, and that parents exaggerated problems to get the police to respond. These managers considered that the police lacked the skills and experience to deal with such cases, and that taking the child into police protection was not an appropriate response.

> I do think that it is probably the one occasion we have never been able to resolve and police officers who have not had appropriate training will take a young person from their home at the request of a parent and bring them to the police station. For me that is the scenario that has never been resolved, and there has always been a lack of understanding from a social work perspective believing that you cannot take a PPO if the parents are asking for an accommodation. (Social Services Manager, Area D)

These cases, most of which involved teenagers, were not emergency situations as far as social services managers were concerned but reflected difficult relationships and needed a response which took account of that, not the exercise of police power to control children. In the managers' view, the police had insufficient training or experience to assess whether removing the child was an appropriate course of action. Rather than resolving problems, this disrupted existing plans and made it more difficult for social services to work with the parents and child to maintain the child at home.

> ... and the police get really irritated in a way, making us respond regardless of what our plans may be. That can have repercussions. (Social Services Manager, Area E)

Getting a child back home after he or she had been removed could be even more difficult with children refusing to go and parents refusing to have them back alternately. One teenage girl spent 17 hours in the police station while police attempted to get social services to make arrangements for her and then the social worker tried to arrange her return home. Finally, she went with the social worker to the social services office for further attempts at negotiation with her parents.

Social services managers found it hard to accept that individual police officers, without specific training, had the power to decide to take a child into police protection. One manager from Area L suggested that the power should be restricted to Inspectors. Instead of independent police action, social work managers wanted there to be consultation with EDT social workers about these cases, before the police removed a child.

> Rather than remove the child, I would much prefer the police to ring social services ... and quite often we can intervene over the phone and reassure the family that the local authority will have a planned intervention the following morning. (Social Services Manager, Area D)

Although it might not be possible for a social worker to visit the family, issues should be discussed:

> We may not be able to go out and visit them, but we would certainly like to look at the issues around why they are taking out a police protection order because sometimes they are not appropriate. Sometimes it has more to do with police anxieties than actually with the law or with the risks for the children. (Social Worker, Area L)

Most police officers would have welcomed support from social services but they considered it impracticable to have to wait for social services before taking action, and they rejected the notion that their power was subject to social services' agreement.

POLICE ACTION TO PUT PRESSURE ON SOCIAL SERVICES

Just as social workers occasionally wanted the police to exercise their power to take a child into police protection although there was no immediate crisis, some police officers considered using the power with the intention of levering a social services response. A few officers, who were familiar with the power and the requirement for the local authority to provide accommodation, recognised that police protection had the potential to engage social services and might thus provide a way forward in dealing with an otherwise intractable problem. A community officer in Force A hoped that taking an unruly teenager into police protection rather than dealing with his behaviour as a criminal matter would lead social services to establish why his parents were not controlling him.

> I knew that there was no means of [14-year-old boy] being controlled by anybody, so come the second or third time of him getting into trouble, I actually took police protection out, to try and force the hand of social services ... (Police Constable, Force A)

In the event this was unsuccessful because the social services department did not recognise the boy to be in need of protection. Rather than showing the power of police authority, the action reinforced the powerlessness of adults in dealing with teenagers who are unruly. The officer's coercive action had come to nothing and shown the boy that he could act with impunity. Another officer having attempted to get action by referring the case of a teenage girl who was continually going missing also said she had tried to force social services to act by using police protection:

> School and social services, I had made them aware of all this on a number of occasions ... to be honest I was sick of banging my head against a brick wall. I had spoken to the parents and they were at their wits end ... we had a meeting set up with social services ... and when I broached the school on the subject, I was getting a negative response ... I just felt that things weren't happening and I just felt that a stigma was being attached to the fact she was a problem child but no one was saying 'Well, why is she a problem child? Why is she causing problems? Why is it no one will help her?' (Police Constable, Force M)

Cases where police officers admitted trying to manipulate social services by using police protection in relation to troubled and troublesome children were rare. Few officers were sufficiently aware of the power and the workings of social services. Their powers under the criminal law, and now the use of anti-social behaviour orders (ASBOs), provided considerable scope for handling such cases in other ways.

COUNTER MOVES: SOCIAL SERVICES RESPONSE TO POLICE ACTION

Although social services could not refuse to take responsibility for a child in police protection, their duty was to safeguard and promote the welfare of the child, not to comply with police expectations. Difficulties in finding place-ments, and the advantages of working with parents to improve parenting whilst children were at home both operated to encourage social workers to return children to parents. Twenty per cent of children went home to their parents from police protection without any intermediate placement, others returned there after a night in foster care. Just as police officers were critical of social services lack of action where relationships between parents and children had broken down, they thought that social workers were too eager to return children to conditions the police considered to be unsatisfactory:

> [I] spoke to social services and the kids were with us for four or five hours, and at the end of that, because of the time that had elapsed, they were then happy to put the kids back with mum, and in my view [she] weren't fit to have the kids . . . (Inspector, Force A)

However, the police had no means of getting their concerns heard by social services. Not one of the areas studied had a protocol relating to the use of police protection, and systems had not been established to review decisions across the two services. This reflected the low status of this work in the police, with managements having little or no interest in it, leaving it for officers to sort out, and social services managers' uncertainty about working with police outside CAIUs.

STUMBLING UPON CASES – POLICE PROTECTION DURING ORDINARY POLICING

There were 40 incidents in the police protection study (12 per cent of the sample) where police officers found children in need of protection whilst on the beat, responding to calls about other matters or executing warrants. In 20 of these cases, children were taken into police protection because they were lost, or found in the care of a person who was clearly incapable of caring for them, most commonly someone who was intoxicated. There were 12 incidents where police were called to a home because of a violent dispute between the adults, and children were removed into police protection. Only if neither parent could look after the child was the power used. These cases generally involved the arrest of one parent, with the other too drunk to make arrangements for, or to look after the children, as in the case of baby Leanne, in Chapter 3. Occasionally police protection was used following the arrest of a person who had a child in their care, for example a parent who was shoplifting with a baby or following a drugs raid where there were children on the premises. If parents were arrested at their home, they had usually been given time to make arrangements for their children, only where they refused to do so did the police resort to taking children into police protection. There were eight cases where children were taken into police protection because they were left without a carer when their parents were arrested.

In the EPO study, there were 10 cases (12 per cent of the sample), all involving young children, where the police used police protection in similar circumstances, and the local authority followed this with an application for an EPO (see Figure 4.1). It appeared that the police never used their power to apply for an EPO on behalf of social services. Unplanned, independent use by the police of police protection leading to an EPO application was regarded as unusual by social services managers. In most cases where police used their powers independently, the power 'lapsed', situations resolved and children returned home, sometimes after a period of accommodation. Cases where police use of their power was followed by an EPO application included three cases where children were found in vehicles, either alone or with adults who were unconscious, and six cases where a lone parent was arrested. Further investigations in these cases, and sometimes further incidents, convinced social services that care proceedings were necessary to secure the long-term protection of these children. Emergency protection orders were therefore obtained to continue the children's protection pending the hearing of an application for an interim care order. The other case involved serious incidents of domestic violence and the EPO application was withdrawn when the mother agreed to move to a refuge with the child (**case 59**). There may have been other cases where police protection was followed by an application for a care or supervision order with the child either returning home or being accommodated by agreement pending the care proceedings. Such further action could not be identified from police records which, in most forces, did not routinely or reliably record cases where the local authority had applied for an EPO.

THE DIFFERENT PERSPECTIVES OF POLICE AND SOCIAL SERVICES STAFF

At the heart of the relationship between police and social services was a conflict of roles and expectations. Although 'working together' had evolved (or been imposed) between child protection workers and CAIU staff, there was not the same sense of common purpose between EDT staff and uniform officers. Rather each wanted to change the way the other agency approached their work, especially in cases involving conflict between parents and their adolescent children. Only in the area covered by Force I, where police protection was rarely used except at the request of social services (see Table 3.2), did it appear that both social services and the police were generally happy about the way the other approached police protection.

The difference between social services' and police perspectives on the use of police protection is partly accounted for by the potential duration of each agency's involvement after the power was used, and the consequent demands the power placed on their resources. Generally the police focused on the current situation; the cases where they used the power to 'kick start' social services' involvement with children believed to have long-term problems were exceptional. The police saw their action as providing the required emergency response to a crisis; officers took children into police protection because of the situation that confronted them (and concern that they would be criticised if they took no action and the child suffered further harm). Although where they could take a child was an issue, officers were not concerned about how the child would be cared for beyond the time it took to locate somewhere safe for the child to go. Police protection was viewed as a very short-term, temporary measure. Indeed, it was a common misconception among officers of all ranks and in five of the eight forces that police protection ended when the social worker collected the child from the police station.

In contrast for social services, the police decision triggered duties which could have long-term implications both in terms of the social work (and legal department) resources required and the impact on the child and family. The duty to accommodate potentially lasts until the child reaches the age of 18 years, and it is generally recognised to be far more difficult to return a child who has been removed than to maintain him or her within their family (Bullock, Little & Millham, 1993). The duty to consider further enquiries in respect of a child in police protection may lead to the child protection juggernaut trundling through the family with numerous meetings, assessments and even court hearings. The social services department's responsibility means that social workers cannot disregard the impact of the process on the child. The consequences of entry to public care are known to be hazardous for children (Utting, 1992; Farmer & Owen, 1995). Social workers are expected to weigh up the consequences of different types of interventions, and to work with families wherever possible. All these elements require social workers to take a longer-term perspective on intervention. From such a standpoint, an apparent crisis may look less severe, and the implications of removing a child or not returning them demand more consideration. This is particularly true where the family is already known to social services, is not rejecting services and the decision to remove was made without social work involvement.

Although each agency was critical of the other's approach, it was clear that staff had a common experience of police protection. Police officers recognised, but did not agree, that social workers thought they removed children too readily. They accepted that social workers' greater experience in child protection, their longer term involvement with families and the wider range of cases they saw could give them a different perspective, but felt that when police officers removed a child they were responding to the emergency before them in the only tenable way. As an Inspector from Force D commented, 'There are different agendas for police and social services. Social services case files may say, "not as bad as appears" but we, police, don't have that. We have to react to emergency situations.' Social workers understood that the police were frustrated about the time it took for them to provide accommodation but saw the solution as fewer requests not increased provision. They suggested that if the police involved them earlier they could prevent the need for police protection (and for accommodating the child). In effect, the different perspectives produced different thresholds for intervention, with social workers viewing that operated by the police as too low. Different expectations of how cases should be dealt with also meant that occasionally staff from each agency tried to force the hand of the other, a fact that both 'sides' acknowledged.

DEVELOPING MORE CO-OPERATIVE WORKING

Overall, there is a need to improve co-operation between police and social services, particularly between uniform officers and Emergency Duty Teams, in responding to child protection emergencies. The current practices meant that individual cases could become sites of conflict and misunderstanding because officers and social workers saw each other as creating difficulties. Co-operation was regarded as successful where there was a quick response by one agency doing what the other wanted. This could happen where resources, workers and placements, were readily available, and where views about what was appropriate naturally coincided, for example cases concerning young children who were severely neglected or without any carer. It also occurred where cases could be handled with few resources, for example use of the power to prevent a child's removal from hospital. However, only in Areas E and J had there been any attempt by managers in the two agencies to reach a common approach, and even in these areas this appeared to be limited to addressing specific problems.

The SSI recommended that formal protocols should be agreed for the provision of services out of hours between local authorities and other agencies such as the police and the health service (Social Services Inspectorate, 1999, para 5.37). These should set out agencies' commitments and provide mechanisms for resolving problems. None of the eight police forces had formal arrangements with EDT services, although all the social services departments mentioned close working relationships with police Child Abuse Investigation Units, and some of these were backed by written agreements. There was some recognition in both agencies that protocols which covered co-operation over police protection would be a good idea.

> There should be an agreement by all the parties involved about the issues and the taking of police protection, otherwise everyone has different standards. (Inspector, Force D)

> I think the implications are vital, we need an understanding of each other's roles, and an understanding of the law is paramount. (Social Services Manager, Area L)

Social services were unsure whether it would be possible to achieve co-operative working with uniform officers because these officers were thought to lack sufficient knowledge about child protection and using police protection was always portrayed as a matter for the discretion of the individual officer. In the view of a social services manager in Area E, a joint protocol might just mean that 'ultimately the responsibility [for taking police protection] lies with the police officer.' For most police forces there was a different problem. They wanted any protocol to cover their whole force area. For many forces, this would mean getting agreement with a number of local authorities, (and even more if police reorganisation reduces the number of forces). Despite the strong common lead provided by central government guidance on child protection, the different resources, priorities and policies in local authorities would make negotiating agreed approaches and response times very difficult.

Better co-operation over cases relating to difficult adolescents requires better social services provision, especially out of ordinary working hours, so that parents and children do not have to resort to calling the police when a crisis occurs. If such a service existed, police officers could be expected to call on it to mediate instead of trying themselves, and using police protection to remove the child if the situation could not be calmed. In addition to providing advice and counselling, such a service should also have refuge or crash pad facilities for temporary respite care. Protocols between police and social services for accessing such provision would need to be agreed, and should not be by-passed by using police protection. Where parents are effectively asking for their children to be accommodated, social workers not police officers should decide what services are provided, even though the decision is made in the evening or during a weekend. Further, if the decision is not to provide accommodation, the police should not be able to override it through police protection as if allowing an appeal.

In cases of immediate risk, preventing children's removal from hospital or foster care, or removing them from abusive or grossly neglectful homes, co-operation was generally good. However, the existence of the police power provided social services with the possibility of avoiding the checks and balances operated by the courts (see Chapter 7). The limited experience in child protection of police officers, particularly those working outside CAIUs, means they do not have the background knowledge to assess requests from social services departments. This made them reluctant to refuse to use police powers unless the grounds for doing so were obviously weak. In practice, they generally acceded to requests. If police protection is to be reserved for exceptional cases in line with official guidance (Home Office, 2003; Department for Education and Skills, 2006), a different approach will be required for considering the use of police powers at the request of social services. Requiring a senior social services manager to take responsibility for requests could ensure that police protection is not used to avoid legal department or court controls. It would also ensure that managers, not just front line workers, were aware of the pressures emergency child protection placed on services. However, close scrutiny of action within the local authority could also create the basis for social workers having their own powers to protect children in emergencies, a matter which is discussed in detail in Chapter 9.

POWER AND POLICE PROTECTION

The exercise of police protection is an exercise of power, but that power is not simply exercised by police officers over children. It impacts on families, on social workers and on the officers themselves. Nor does the power flow in one direction. Children are ultimately protected or controlled by the power, but this may allow them to be rescued from oppressive power in the family or to escape the stigmatising effects of the criminal justice system. In a few cases, young people, recognising that police officers had power, sought to help themselves by calling the police. Other young people may experience police protection as an overwhelming exercise of power, a sudden intervention without forewarning or explanations about where they would stay or for how long. For those who went into residential care this powerlessness was overlaid with anxiety, even when they were glad to be away from home (Packman & Hall, 1998, 254).

Social workers viewed many cases involving 'difficult adolescents' as ones where the police used their power inappropriately to make social services provide accommodation in circumstances where children were better remaining at home. Packman and Hall's interviews with parents suggested that some parents contrived to have their children accommodated where social services had repeatedly refused to provide this (Packman & Hall, 1998, 213), a view reflected by social services managers in the police protection study. Parents resented social workers' efforts to offer preventive services instead of accommodation; they saw the police as 'more sympathetic' and able to use their powers to support parents against both difficult children and unhelpful social workers. In effect, turning to the police was a way parents could exercise power in such circumstances. Other researchers have noted that parents feel a loss of control once social services become involved with their families (Farmer & Owen, 1995). Decisions about children's return seemed to be in the hands of social workers or the young people themselves so children might return when parents wanted a longer break or remain away from home when parents preferred them to return (Packman & Hall, 1998, 228). The need for help from outside the family and children's experiences away from home, both served to undermine parental authority, potentially leaving relationships more problematic than when the child was initially removed (Bullock et al., 1993; Farmer & Owen, 1995; Packman & Hall, 1998).

Police officers' initial feelings of power when resolving a problem with police protection could quickly disappear when they were left to look after young people whilst the social worker tried to make arrangements for placements. Police officers felt that both parents and social services passed their responsibilities to the police. In relation to the protection of younger children, police protection appeared to police officers to be more like a responsibility than a power. They were concerned that children might be harmed if they failed to act and that they would be blamed. Similarly, when officers were requested by social services to use police protection, they generally felt they should take action unless they were clear that action was outside the power.

Social services managers and local authority lawyers recognised that the police power had advantages although they expressed concerns about relying on the police too much. For lawyers, police action avoided the need to submit to the power of the magistrates' legal adviser and convince him or her that that the case justified an immediate hearing. It also reduced somewhat the time pressures of preparing an EPO application for the court. For social work managers, it meant that a social worker did not have to be burdened with the unpleasant and fraught task of removing the child; the police took this responsibility even though a social worker might attend with them. Getting the police to use their power allowed the manager to protect children and social work staff.

Overall the exercise of police protection had a substantial impact on agencies, professionals and individual families who became involved with it. Professionals were generally able to turn it to their advantage, and occasionally parents and children did so too.

5

CHILDREN, FAMILIES AND APPLICATIONS FOR EMERGENCY PROTECTION ORDERS

INTRODUCTION

This chapter provides a description of the children, who were subject to emergency protection order applications, and their families, and outlines the circumstances in which emergency protection orders (EPOs) were sought. It aims to explore the use of EPOs and to make comparisons with other research in child protection where coercive interventions were not used. Its primary sources are the application for the EPO (forms C1 and C13) and the social worker's written statement to the court, which may have been available to the court for the EPO hearing, or have been filed only after the order was made. It also draws on other documents from the court file (such as the children's guardian's report in subsequent proceedings), interviews with social workers and lawyers and the social services department's records. The totality of this material gives a somewhat fuller and clearer picture of the child and families' circumstances than is likely to have been available when the court considered the EPO application. This additional information provides details that allows comparisons to be made with children and families in other studies.

Although the researchers have drawn on information about the children and their families provided to the courts, they do not claim that this is an objective account of the families' circumstances. Both written records and interview data are necessarily selective and instrumental. Social work records are completed for a purpose. They record social work activity and social workers' observations and assessments of parents, children and family circumstances. In the area of child protection, contemporaneous records are frequently relied on to build a case for intervention, providing the basis for the social worker's statement in proceedings or the chronology required by the court. Alternatively, they can justify case closure. This selectivity can be reinforced in research interviews, for example when the interviewee seeks to explain how a decision came to be made:

> Obviously I am only concentrating on the negatives as I am picking things out as to why we had to have a [child protection] conference. This is a mother in many ways who is absolutely excellent with the children, so I am only picking out why we had to have a conference. (Social worker, Area J)

A study of emergency protection, based on court records, is bound to focus on the negative aspects of children's care. The main source of information is that provided to the court by the applicant local authority and was selected by them to explain the need for the order. Only rarely is this balanced by any information from the parents. At this stage of proceedings, parents' evidence is necessarily oral and unprepared rather than written and drawn from existing records. Moreover, it was less obvious in the court file, appearing in the notes of evidence and (possibly) the magistrates' reasons, rather than as a written statement.

THE APPLICATION FOR AN EPO

The application provides the headlines to the court, the basic information about the child and the reasons for seeking an order. Although much of its contents are objective they are also selective. The forms are designed to provide the court with key information about the application so that the magistrates' legal adviser can make the necessary arrangements for the hearing and prepare the magistrates for the decisions they will have to make. The application is completed by the local authority social worker with a view to obtaining an EPO, and consequently there is a focus on the child's immediate need for protection rather than their general well-being. This selectivity is compounded by the limited information that the local authority may have when seeking an EPO, or more frequently, by the limited time available for completing the form and any statements.

As well as details about the child, the child's carers and parents, the applicant must give information about their own involvement with the child, including whether the child is on the child protection register and their plans for the child. In some cases, the local authority may lack key information about the child, for example if the child is living with a lone mother they might not know the name of the father, or where young children have been found home alone, the identities of either parent. Newborn babies might not have been named, and where a pregnant woman has left home with the intention of avoiding social services' attentions, the local authority might not even be certain that the child has been born. Where there has been no prior involvement with the family by the their social services department, the local authority making the application may be unaware of other children in the family, previous proceedings or the involvement of another social services department. However, so long as the court is satisfied that the child exists, the lack of descriptive or identifying information is not a barrier to obtaining an order. Court orders cannot be granted in respect of unborn children (*Re F*, 1988).

APPLICATIONS IN THE EPO STUDY

The sample consisted of all the cases in the three court areas where EPOs were sought during a 12-month period between 2000 and 2002, and all children in these cases in respect of whom an EPO applicant was made. There were 86 cases and 127 children. Nearly three-quarters of the cases concerned only one child, another 14% related to two children and a similar proportion concerned three or more children. In almost three-quarters of cases, EPO applications were made in respect of all the eligible children in the family. In another seven families (8 per cent of the sample), siblings were subsequently included in court proceedings when applications were made for interim care orders (ICO). Bobby, **case 110**, is an example; he became subject to care proceedings only after an EPO had been obtained in respect of his new baby brother.

Protection by agreement and the use of EPOs

In **case 110**, an ICO application was made in respect of Bobby shortly after his baby brother had been protected at birth using an EPO. Their mother had been a repeated victim of domestic violence and Bobby aged 5 years was exhibiting extreme temper tantrums and was beyond his mother's control. A core assessment had identified Bobby as a child in need; various services had been provided but Ms Jones missed some appointments and failed to accept that her partner posed a risk to Bobby. Both brothers were placed on the child protection register before the baby was born. There were clearly sufficient grounds to bring care proceedings in relation to Bobby before his brother was born. However, he was protected by his mother agreeing that he should be placed with her mother. In this way Ms Jones was spared the further stress of care proceedings at the end of her pregnancy.

There were only 15 families where siblings did not become the subject of proceedings when or after an EPO had been sought. In three of these cases, the initial EPO application was not followed by care proceedings and only limited information was available about the family. In the remaining 12 cases, the siblings who remained outside the care proceedings were usually living in a different household and consequently were not subject to the same risks as the children involved in the proceedings.

In twenty-six families (30 per cent of the sample) the child for whom the EPO application was made was a first/only child. Many children shared their home with half-siblings, some had full or half-siblings living elsewhere, most commonly in foster care. In 14 families, almost a quarter of the sample of families with other children, the siblings were recorded as already being subject to care orders. These families were, like those in Hunt and colleagues' study of care proceedings, 'complex and dislocated' (Hunt *et al.*,1999, 20).

THE CHILDREN

There were 70 boys and 57 girls in the sample of 127 children, with more boys than girls at all ages, with the exception of children over the age of 10 years. This contrasts with studies of children on child protection registers where girls out number boys (Devaney, 2004). The larger number of girls relates to registrations of adolescent girls under the category of sexual abuse, an issue which only exceptionally led to an EPO application However, police protection was used to control young women engaging in sexual activity. There was only one such case in the EPO study:

In **case 35**, an EPO was sought in relation to Corinne, a 14-year-old girl who was missing from residential care and believed to be involved with sex and drugs. The application for an EPO and a recovery order were the precursor to an application for a secure accommodation order, the third in two years. No care order had been sought in relation to Corinne and she remained accommodated with her mother's agreement. If there had been a care order, no EPO would have been required and the local authority would have been able to apply for a recovery order directly.

In one other case (**case 5**, discussed below) another 14-year-old girl's risky behaviour, her mentally ill mother's encouragement of it and the mother's inability to exert any control were major factors in the decision to care bring proceedings but the EPO was precipitated by other matters.

The minority ethnic populations were low in each of the areas. The application form does not require information about the child's ethnicity and this information was not available for 14 children from the sample of 127. Over 80 per cent of the children were white British, there were six children of dual heritage and four black African children in the sample.

Age

Most of the children who were subject to EPO applications were very young; a far higher proportion of these applications than police protection cases related to children under the age of one year, and there were correspondingly fewer applications for children over the age of 10 years. Forty-two children (a third of the sample) were aged between one and five years; six out of 10 children were under the age of five years when the EPO application was made. Thirty-seven children (29 per cent of the sample) were aged between five and 10 years and only 10 children (eight per cent of the sample) were older than 10 years. All but two of these older children were protected with younger siblings when they had both been left alone, with unsuitable carers, or when there was a family crisis precipitated by a violent incident or deterioration in their carer's mental health (see Figure 5.1).

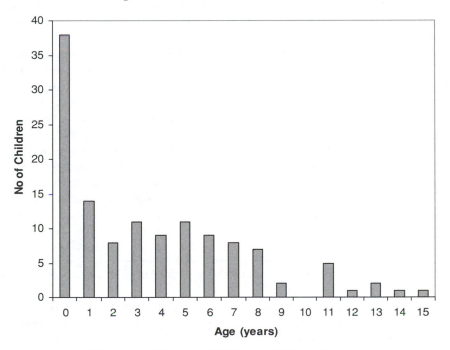

Figure 5.1   The age of children at EPO application

There were 38 EPO applications (30 per cent of the sample) that had been made in respect of children under the age of one year and 16 of these (12.6 per cent) concerned children under a month old who were removed at or shortly after birth. A similar rate of proceedings was observed in Booth and Booth's study of care proceedings; 11 per cent of those care applications related to children aged less than one month and a third of the cases relating to parents with learning difficulties involved proceedings taken in respect of new born babies (Booth and Booth, 2004, 19, 24). If these figures were replicated across the country over 400 new babies would be removed each year.

Removal at birth occurred in three distinct situations: where previous children have been harmed and parents were considered to be unable to care for a new baby; where children were born suffering from the effects of drug or alcohol abuse; and where the parent's behaviour shortly after the birth placed the child in danger. Most of the first group of cases are 'planned emergencies' where EPOs and/or police protection are used to provide an immediate response once it is known that the child has been born, or if the mother wants to take her baby from hospital. Planning may start as soon as the mother's pregnancy is known but the need to assess the parents' parenting capacity may mean that the decision to arrange for the baby's removal may only occur shortly before the birth. In such cases, women have no opportunity to consider whether they will continue with the pregnancy even though it is very unlikely that they will be able to keep the baby (Care Services Improvement Partnership, 2006).

Of the 16 families where babies were removed at, or shortly after birth, only three were the mother's first children, and two of these had been subject to child protection plans during pregnancy. Indeed, social services' earlier involvement due to the inadequate care of previous children was a major factor in the decision to remove children like baby Bates, **case 1**, below. In eight of the 16 families, siblings had been removed in earlier proceedings, and in another three (including **case 54**, below) a child had died in circumstances which were thought to amount to homicide. Two first-time mothers placed their new babies at risk, one by threatening to remove her from the special care baby unit (**case 43**, below) and the other by returning to a violent partner (**case 73**, below). Three children were suffering from conditions relating to substance abuse.

Case 1: Planned removal of a new baby at risk of neglect and abuse

A referral was made by the social services department for the area where Mr and Mrs Bates had previously been living. Mrs Bates was known to be pregnant and was chronically depressed; Mr Bates had moderate learning difficulties. The referral reported persistent concerns about poor home conditions, including poor hygiene, lack of food and bed clothes relating to the Bates' previous children, and about them being left with unsuitable carers. The older children had disclosed sexual abuse. Social workers' attempts to work with the parents to secure satisfactory care for their children had been unsuccessful. Mr and Mrs Bates had been convicted of child cruelty and their four children had been removed and made subject to care orders. The younger children had been adopted. The couple were believed to have moved in order to avoid the attentions of social workers. They were living in a caravan and therefore considered to be likely to move again.

A legal strategy meeting was held immediately following the referral. Because of concerns that the parents would disappear and that the mother would not seek medical help at the birth of the baby, arrangements were discussed for the child's protection without any prior notification to the parents. A case conference was arranged, attended by the police, the community midwife, the clinical nurse manager, a social worker from the family's previous home area, and social workers and managers from the family's current home area. The parents were not invited. The baby's name was placed on the child protection register and plans agreed for the child's protection from birth. The baby was taken into police protection shortly after birth and placed with foster carers. The local authority immediately filed its application for an EPO to be heard on full notice; the parents and CAFCASS were notified. The hearing was attended by the social worker, her managers and a local authority lawyer, the parents, their solicitor and the solicitor for the child. At the hearing, which lasted three hours, the social worker gave evidence of the previous proceedings. The EPO application was not contested, and an order was made for five days; contact was left to the discretion of the local authority. The local authority immediately applied for an ICO but a hearing could not be arranged before the expiry of the EPO, the following day they applied for the EPO to be extended until the date of the ICO hearing. This renewal hearing was attended by the parents' solicitor but the parents did not attend. The renewal application was not contested.

The Bates' next child also became the subject of care proceedings but in her case the initial separation was achieved with the parents' agreement.

Case 73: Planned protection of baby expected by woman in a violent relationship

A referral was made from the local hospital. Ms Thomas, aged 17 years, and 6 months pregnant, had been admitted after an assault and was saying that she did not want the baby. There were also concerns that she was taking drugs. She left hospital without providing further information. A second referral was received three weeks later after Ms Thomas was again admitted to hospital following an overdose. The next day social workers from the mental health and children's teams made a joint visit to Ms Thomas to plan the baby's protection. Although Ms Thomas initially spoke of concerns that she would harm the baby and wanting to have it adopted she changed her mind. There were a series of further incidents of domestic violence. Although Ms Thomas did not wish to press charges, the police took evidence and obtained photographs of her injuries. Ms Thomas left her partner and returned to live with her mother. Arrangements were agreed for a core assessment, Ms Thomas was told that if she returned to her violent partner (who was not the baby's father) the local authority would take legal advice and she was put in touch with Women's Aid. Ms Thomas gave birth to Tammy and was discharged home to her mother's house the same day, with arrangements for daily visits from the community midwife.

Later the same week the health visitor contacted social services to say that Ms Thomas had returned to her boyfriend's home with Tammy. Arrangements were made with the police to visit Ms Thomas at her boyfriend's house in order to persuade her to return with Tammy to her mother's home. If she would not agree, Tammy was to be removed by the police under police protection. There was no response at the address, or to repeated visits made by the police. The same day, local authority applied without notice for an EPO and a recovery order. The orders were passed to the police and the EDT was informed. The following day, Ms Thomas and Tammy were found and taken to the police station. Ms Thomas returned to her mother's home and Tammy was placed in foster care. An ICO application was made to be heard before the eight-day EPO expired.

In comparison with other studies of child protection, which have focused on children on the child protection register (Farmer & Owen, 1995, table 5) or identified as suffering or at risk of significant harm (Brandon *et al.*, 1999), the children for whom EPO applications were made were younger. One reason for this is the frequent use of EPOs to remove new born babies. Also, younger children are particularly vulnerable where standards of care are very low, and thus immediate intervention to protect them may be thought necessary.

THE FAMILIES

Family Composition

The EPO applications provided very little information about the child's parents and carers. Fathers without parental responsibility (most unmarried fathers at the time of the research) are not respondents to the proceedings and no details have to be included on the application if they are not living with the child. In 23 families (just over a quarter of the sample), the children's parents were living together. It was more common for the parents to be separated (49 families, 81 children) and in 12 families (15 children) the father was either deceased or his identity was not known to social services. Only just over a third of children had fathers with parental responsibility, and in most cases this was because the parents were married.

At the point when the emergency intervention was initiated, 60 families (70 per cent of the sample) had their children currently living with them. In the remaining 26 families, the children were in hospital, were accommodated by social services or were living with relatives. The substantial use of police protection meant that few families had their children living with them by the time the EPO application was made (see Chapter 6, especially Figure 6.1). Where children were living with a parent, this was most likely to be their mother. Thirty families in the EPO study (35 per cent of the sample) were headed by a lone mother, and six by a lone father. This is a slightly lower proportion than found by Hunt and colleagues where 52% of families were headed by a lone parent (Hunt *et al.*, 1999) and in other studies of children involved in the child protection process (Brandon *et al.*, 1999; Devaney, 2004). In only 15 families (17 per cent of the sample) was the child was living with both parents when protective action was taken, in another nine families (10 per cent of the sample) the child was living with the mother and her partner. Overall, a quarter of children were living in a household with two adults, at least one of whom was a parent. Also, the EPO precipitated immediate separation of the adults in a number of families where exclusion of the male perpetrator was crucial for the child's protection, for example, **case 4**, below, which involved sexual abuse of a toddler by the mother's partner, and **case 59** where the mother was a victim of repeated and severe violence from her partner and agreed to go to a refuge. On this basis the EPO application was withdrawn.

Parents' problems

Being brought up in state care, domestic violence, substance abuse, mental health difficulties or learning difficulties are known to impact on parents' parenting capacity although many people parent successfully despite these adversities (Cleaver & Freeman, 1999). Some information was available about the parents' difficulties in the statement provided by the social worker to the court, or where this was given orally, in the reasons given by the magistrates for making the order. Although the researchers were able to supplement this with information they obtained through interviews and record reading, the material collected is still likely to underestimate these problems in the study families. Problems such as domestic violence and substance misuse are not always identified by or disclosed to social workers (Thoburn, Lewis & Shemmings, 1995; Cleaver & Freeman, 1999). In Booth and Booth's (2004) study of care proceedings, parents' learning difficulties were often documented in psychologist's reports on the parents which were unlikely to be available for the EPO hearing. Indeed higher rates of substance abuse, mental illness and domestic violence have been identified in other studies of care proceedings (Cleaver & Freeman, 1999, table 3; Brophy, 2006, 15).

Out of 86 families there appeared to be just 20 (23% of the sample) where neither parent experienced at least one of the major problems, listed above, which are known to impact on parenting capacity. In 41 families (48 % of the sample) at least one of these problems was noted and in the remainder two or more. This compares with such problems in the families of a third of *children* in Booth and Booth's study, which included sensory disability but not domestic violence or a care background. In their study, five per cent of parents involved in care proceedings had a sensory disability (Booth & Booth, 2004, table 7).

Problems with drug or alcohol misuse were the most prevalent, both on their own and in combination with other problems, occurring in over 40% of families. The high proportion of such cases may relate to the fact that substance misuse led to repeated incidents where children were placed at risk and the police became involved; drink and drugs cases were common in the police protection study (see Chapter 3). Neglect associated with drug misuse was a major feature of cases, particularly in one of the three areas. Peter and his sisters (**cases 60–63**, below) are typical.

Cases 60–63: Long-term neglect, children left home alone

The family had been involved with social services since the oldest child, Peter (now aged 11) was 3 years old. There had been repeated neglect of Peter and his two younger half-sisters, including the children being left alone over night. The children were reported as having poor school attendance and being unkempt and hungry. Their names were entered on the child protection register and although there had been little if any improvement in the children's care they were deregistered a year before the EPO was sought. The mother was a heroin user who financed her habit through shoplifting. Both fathers were in prison.

Peter told his teacher that he and his sisters were alone the previous night and had had nothing to eat. The school contacted social services; this was the third referral by the school in a week. The earlier referrals concerned the mother's failure to collect the girls from school and Peter's disclosure to his teacher that his mother took drugs. The local authority applied without notice for an EPO; an order was granted for six days and Peter and his sisters were placed with relatives. The social worker established that the mother had been arrested and had not told the police that her children would be alone. The local authority applied for an ICO to be heard before the EPO expired.

Similarly, in **case 42**, both parents were drug users and the mother was involved in prostitution to finance this. An EPO was obtained after the parents disappeared leaving the child with an unrelated teenage carer. In **case 47**, the police took the child into police protection when the mother was arrested at a drugs raid and the local authority followed this with an EPO, and in **case 102**, the mother was too drunk to agree to her child being accommodated when she was arrested; her child was taken into police protection. In **case 38**, a new baby was removed from her mother because she was born with opiate dependency and in **case 108**, the child's removal at birth related to birth with foetal alcohol syndrome and his parents' 'chaotic and self-destructive lifestyle', which mirrored their behaviour with their previous child who had been adopted.

Severe domestic violence was also common, being mentioned in 22 families, a quarter of the sample. Indeed in seven families, intervention was precipitated by incidents of domestic violence, including for the protection of baby Tammy (**case 73**) outlined above. In 17 families, there were concerns about the parents' mental health and, in three of these the parent's breakdown of mental health precipitated the application. In **case 34**, a lone father who was mentally ill made threats to kill people including himself and his child. He was sectioned under the Mental Health Act and an EPO was obtained in respect of the child. In **case 93**, the mother who was receiving treatment in the community for her psychiatric problems punched one of her children in the street, requested that she be accommodated and disclosed thoughts of harming her; both children were made subject to EPOs. In **case 20**, the mother's outburst and collapse at the case conference led to her admission to a psychiatric unit and the decision that a court order rather than a voluntary agreement should be used to protect her daughter who was living temporarily with her grandmother. This mother had previously been diagnosed with a mental illness.

INVOLVEMENT WITH SOCIAL SERVICES AND THE COURTS

Long involvement with social services was a major feature of most of the families in the EPO study. Only five families were not known to social services immediately prior to the intervention. All these cases concerned children who had been identified by medical staff as having non-accidental injuries; Katie, **case 92** below, is an example. In four of these families, the injured child was initially taken into police protection at the request of the local authority, the other case concerned allegations of salt poisoning, which led to the arrest of both parents whilst the child remained in hospital.

Case 92: Non-accidental injury in a family previously unknown to social services

Katie, aged 9 months, was brought by her parents to the casualty department in a state of collapse. They said that she had had a prolonged fit. She was admitted to hospital and various tests were undertaken. A CT scan indicated a brain haemorrhage and eye examination showed bilateral retinal haemorrhage. These injuries were considered to be a strong indication of non-accidental injury through shaking. Late in the afternoon four days later, Katie was well enough to be discharged from hospital and her parents were waiting to take her home. The consultant made a child protection referral to social services who immediately contacted the police. There had been no prior warning to the parents that they were under suspicion, or that Katie would not be discharged to them. Katie's parents were unwilling to leave her in hospital so police protection was taken. The following morning the social worker contacted the legal department. It was agreed that an application would be made for an EPO before the police protection expired. The court agreed to abridge notice for an EPO hearing the following morning. The parents were served with the court papers at the social services office and advised to obtain a solicitor for the proceedings. The local authority obtained a medical report from Katie's consultant; the social worker prepared a statement about the events leading to the use of police protection. Counsel was briefed to represent the local authority and CAFCASS were notified.

At the EPO hearing, attended by counsel for the local authority, the social worker, Katie's solicitor, her parents and their solicitor, the parents agreed to allow the disclosure of relevant medical records and not to contest the EPO. An EPO was granted for five days to fit in with the court's timetable. The local authority undertook to file an application for an ICO to be heard before the EPO expired. Katie was placed with local authority foster parents and arrangements were made for supervised contact between Katie and her parents three times week.

In addition, there were 15 children who were not known to social services before the incident that provoked the EPO, although their 10 families were involved with social services or had been in the recent past. In **case 111**, the father thrashed his son causing a fracture for failing to do a chore. The boy's older sister had been accommodated by the local authority after a breakdown of her relationships with her parents. The other cases either concerned very young children who had not apparently come to the attention of social services even though there had been previous social services involvement with their parents or siblings, or parents with mental health difficulties whose dealings with the mental health team had not involved any referral in relation to their children. For example, a referral was only made to social services about baby Tom (**case 43**) when relationships between his young mother and the paediatric team broke down and she threatened to remove him from the special care baby unit. Tom's mother was known to social services because of difficulties between her and her parents shortly before and during her pregnancy. In **cases 106** and **107**, considerable concern had been expressed about a three-year-old boy who had repeatedly been seen in the Accident and Emergency Department of the local hospital and whose mother had been observed to treat him roughly and shout at him at nursery. Emergency protection orders were sought for this boy and his three-month-old sister after a nurse at the children's hospital where the baby had been admitted with feeding difficulties saw the mother punch him.

Eight other families had been known to the social services department in the study for less than three months, although at least three of these had been involved with social services elsewhere, including a family where the lone father had mental health difficulties and there was a long history of child protection concerns and refusing services (**case 34**). Two of these cases concerned first children removed at birth, and three others involved sudden crises (two families where children were found home alone and one where they were removed during domestic violence). Only one of the cases of short-term involvement by social services appeared to have involved intensive support for the family, **case 12**. This was also a rare case where the EPO was not precipitated by an incident but occurred in the context of increasing concerns.

Case 12: EPO for neglect without any specific incident

Christine's mother had only moved into the area shortly before baby Christine was born; her partner was not her baby's father. The mother was a troubled young woman, estranged from her family after an abusive childhood and was thought to be depressed. The couple were living in a shabby flat and dependent on social security. Christine had been born prematurely and they were having difficulty caring adequately for her. When she was six weeks old, Christine's name was placed on the child protection register because of neglect. The concerns related to poor hygiene and erratic feeding and poor budgeting; the couple never seemed to have money for heating which was metered. A written agreement was made with the couple to allow regular visits from the social work team and to co-operate with them. The social worker was so anxious about Christine's care that she continued to visit whilst she was on leave. Despite daily visits and support from a family aide and the social worker, the couple did not appear motivated to care for Christine. The flat was filthy with sacks of rubbish and dirty bottles; they repeatedly had no milk for Christine and continued to miss her feeds. Christine began to lose weight.

An EPO was sought after the social worker concluded that visits and cajoling were not going to bring about adequate care. This was one of the few cases where there appeared to be no specific incident precipitating the application. Indeed, despite the high level of concern this case was viewed as problematic for emergency intervention because there had been no specific incident of harm. Both the social worker and the local authority lawyer were unsure that an EPO would be granted 'just for neglect'. The social worker was adamant that action needed to be taken and that it was not possible leave Christine in the care of 'these people who can't be bothered to get up and feed her.' The lawyer and manager accepted the social worker's assessment of the seriousness of the situation and agreed that an EPO application could be made. Difficulties in preparing the papers and finding a court where the application could be heard led to the application being heard in the evening and the local authority being represented by a solicitor from private practice. The parents were given a short period of notice and taken to the hearing by the social worker. Concern that it might be difficult to convince the magistrates that an EPO should be granted meant that particular attention was given to marshalling evidence about the child's care. Both the social worker and social work assistant gave evidence and the social worker also provided the court with a letter from the community paediatrician about weight loss in young babies. The parents objected to the order and denied that they had failed to feed the baby but their evidence was not accepted. After a hearing lasting over three hours (one of the longest in the sample) the order was granted, Christine was placed in foster care and an application was made for an ICO.

Sixty two families (60 per cent of the sample where this information was available) had been known to the social services department for over two years and half of these for more than five years. In general, these were families with multiple problems, and their long involvement with social services had included periods when their children were looked after and previous child protection proceedings.

Child Protection Registration

There were a number of cases in the sample where it appeared surprising to the researchers that the catalogue of injuries and incidents recorded had not resulted in the arrangement of a child protection case conference. Indeed, had the information, which was collated for the care proceedings, been drawn together earlier, an application for a care order might have been made without resorting to emergency intervention in response to the latest crisis. Similar failures to take an overview have repeatedly been noted in child death inquiry reports (Reder, Duncan & Gray, 1993; Sinclair & Bullock 2002).

In 42 families, the children who were the subject of the EPO proceedings were on the child protection register and, in another seven families, the child had previously been on the register. These figures are similar to those found in an earlier study of care proceedings under the Children Act 1989 (Hunt et al., 1999), but lower than the 73 per cent found by Brophy and colleagues (Brophy et al., 2003). Overall, 59 children in the sample were known currently to be registered and at least another 10 had previously been registered. Registration indicates that there is a current child protection plan and thus indicates that social services have serious concerns. Children on the register are more likely to be subject to legal proceedings than other children with a child protection referral (Gibbons, Conroy & Bell, 1995). Part of the protection plan may include seeking an EPO or bringing care proceedings if there are further incidents; breach of the parent's agreement with social services was a precipitating factor for many EPO applications. However, lack of registration does not necessarily indicate that the child does not need protection. Cases involving neglect are less likely to be registered than those with specific allegations of abuse (Gordon & Gibbons, 1998) and registration practices are known to vary between local authorities (Gibbons & Bell, 1994; Pugh, 2006). As one social worker replied to the question, 'Was the child on the register?', 'No, but he should have been.'

Previous Court Proceedings

The serious nature of social services previous concerns about the families in the study is clear from the information about previous court proceedings. Only 24 families (40 per cent of the sample with other children) had not already been involved in any court proceedings. There were 26 families (43 per cent of this sample) who had previously been involved in care proceedings and 11 families had been involved in private law proceedings, disputes over residence, contact or parental responsibility and domestic violence injunctions. Hunt and colleagues found a similar rate of previous involvement in child protection proceedings in their sample of care cases, begun shortly after the implementation of the Children Act (Hunt *et al.*,1999). These figures are high given the relatively low use of court proceedings generally; only about 10 per cent of separating parents use the courts (Blackwell & Dawe, 2003), although many of those who do have major parenting difficulties which may bring them in contact with social services (Trinder, Connolly, Kellett & Notley, 2005). Care proceedings are even rarer (Department for Education and Skills, 2004). It appears that a substantial proportion of families involved in care proceedings have either been there before or will come again, usually with another child. Little attention has been given to this, yet their previous experiences are likely to influence parents' actions and reactions to legal proceedings, those of their social workers and court decisions.

Seven children from four families who were currently the subject of emergency intervention had been involved in previous care proceedings. Applications in relation to three of these children had been withdrawn and care orders had been granted and later discharged for four others. This should serve as a reminder that, despite the resources expended in care proceedings, the assessments made in them are not guaranteed to be right. Problems may resurface and improvements made may not be sustained. Also, that court control over the withdrawal of applications does not ensure that children will continue to be safe without an order. In at least 11 families there had been a previous EPO, in five cases for the child in the study and in six cases in respect of siblings. The sample included one child who was the subject of two, separate EPOs in 12 months and another child where a second EPO was known to have been obtained after the fieldwork period. Given that 16 children were subject to EPOs at birth and could not have been involved in proceedings earlier and 26 children had no siblings there was a substantial re-use of both emergency intervention and care proceedings in the study families. **Case 4** is an example:

Case 4: a two-year chronology of child protection interventions

Month 0:   Pre-birth case conference child's name placed on CPR. Birth; EPO
Month 1:   Placement of mother and baby at residential assessment unit
Month 6:   Care proceedings withdrawn at final hearing
             Name removed from CPR.
Month13:   Housing crisis
Month 16:   Further housing crisis; temporary accommodation requested
Month 19:   Mother witnessed indecent assault on child by partner, Police called
Month 20:   Child admitted to hospital; mother discharged child

---

Month 21:	Child admitted to hospital
	EDT contacted injuries include bite marks
	Sexual abuse diagnosed
	Police protection
	EPO application
	EPO withdrawn – agreement
Month 22:	Placement at mother and baby home and care proceedings

The repeated use of EPOs may indicate a particularly confrontational relationship between the social services department and the parents where the stakes are rapidly raised and swift, coercive action is thought necessary by the local authority to obtain protective control. Interviews with social workers, their managers and local authority lawyers indicated a general wish to limit the use of EPOs. Indeed, one social worker, commenting on the removal of a subsequent child from a family in the study noted:

> There is another baby, they are going through it again except they did not have an EPO, they [the local authority] did it the right way this time and they did it with [accommodation]. (Social worker, Area J)

Once an EPO has been considered necessary, there may be less restraint on using one again, or such complete lack of trust between the social workers and parents that negotiated arrangements seem impossible. To the extent that the study shows long-term and repeated, compulsory child protection action, it reflects both a failure of parenting and the limits of social work intervention. Despite social services involvement, some parents were not able to change sufficiently to care adequately for their children or make their subsequent children safe. Within this context, both social workers and families trust in each other was likely to be weak, making parents less willing to make and keep protective arrangements and social workers more willing to resort to compulsory intervention, a theme that is explored in the next chapter.

THE USE OF EPOs

As the examples given above indicate, emergency protection orders were sought by local authorities in a wide range of circumstances where children were considered to be at risk. These were not necessarily matters of life and death but situations where the risks of harm to children was considered to be too high to be managed without an order or the child's current care was so inadequate that it could not be to be allowed to continue, even for the few days it would take to obtain an interim care order. Some social workers recounted being acutely anxious about the safety of children before the order was obtained. This anxiety made them press their managers and the local authority lawyer to agree to legal proceedings. Additional concerns, about the parents' reaction and possible disappearance with the children if they were notified of the local authority's intention to seek an ICO, also encouraged both swifter action and bringing proceedings without informing parents, in order to prevent them harming their children further.

EPOs were sought in response to incidents. It is an inherent aspect of child protection work to concentrate on incidents; specific referrals are more likely to result in investigation than more general concerns (Platt, 2006b). In part, the focus on incidents reflected the need to present a case which would satisfy the court that an EPO was required, and the matter could not be left to the ordinary course of care proceedings. Very serious incidents such as life-threatening injuries to children and homicide of a sibling were generally seen by lawyers and social workers as justifying an application for an EPO but there were those who accepted that adequate protection could be arranged through agreements with parents even in these cases. The quotation below is from a local authority lawyer but was echoed by social workers and managers.

> You can almost tell from how an EPO comes in what office it's coming from ... our [name] office, they rang me yesterday on duty with a case where they are actively trying to pursue a voluntary accommodation of the child who has suffered non-accidental injury. The police are investigating it. They feel quite rightly in this case, that this child can stay with the paternal grandmother, so they have no intention at all at this point in time of seeking an order from the court and if they do so, it would be an ICO because they think that their placement that they have with the paternal grandmother is enough to satisfy the [child's needs]. If you were to take that to most of our other offices, they would be straight on the phone asking for an EPO now... (Local Authority Lawyer, Area E)

Although most of the families were known to be experiencing prolonged and severe difficulties in providing adequate care for their children, the EPO application was almost always driven by a specific incident where a child had been seriously harmed or placed at risk of significant harm. These incidents were not necessarily any more serious than previous occasions where children's care had been unsatisfactory but they provoked a concerted response from the local authority because they were viewed as indicating that it was no longer possible to protect the child by relying on the parents. A common feature in most cases was the parents' refusal to co-operate with social services, or the belief, that they could not be trusted to co-operate. This might be based on the local authority and other professions having limited knowledge about the family, knowing them only because of the specific incident, as in the case of Katie (**case 92**). More commonly it was the result of previous dealings with the family where the parents had shown themselves to be unreliable or unwilling to work with social services. This appeared to be the case in relation to Mr and Mrs Bates (**case 1**), Ms Thomas (**case 73**), Peter's mother (**cases 60–63**), Christine's parents (**case 12**) and Ms Martin (**cases 5–6**) and the parents of Rachel and Sarah (**cases 53–54**) below.

Cases 5 and 6: Breach of agreement for children's protection

The social services department had been working with Ms Martin and her children for many years. Ms Martin had bi-polar disorder and there were times when she became acutely unwell, obsessed with sex, destructive and unable to care for or control her children. In the past, she had had relationships with paedophiles and was thought to have encouraged her daughter to meet with them. Ms Martin stopped taking her medication and her behaviour deteriorated. Her daughter, Linda aged 15 years, was out of control, stealing from her mother, taking drugs and staying out at night. Ms Martin's children had been on the child protection register previously and were re-registered a few weeks before the EPOs were obtained, Linda under 'sexual abuse' and Joe, aged 10, under 'physical abuse'. Shortly afterwards, Linda went away with an older man known to be involved in prostitution and drugs, and was missing for over a week. Tensions in the home were high with Ms Martin hitting Joe and being verbally abusive. Ms Martin also told the social worker that she had thoughts of killing the children and committing suicide. The social worker was so anxious about the family that she or the mental health social worker visited daily. The social worker persuaded the mother to agree to Joe going to stay with his aunt but the mother would not agree to Linda going into foster care. The social worker contacted the legal department with a view to applying for EPOs but was told that she should seek a further agreement with the mother. A child protection conference was arranged and before it took place the mother agreed to Linda being fostered.

Having received further worrying information about the mother's care, the local authority decided to bring care proceedings. The mother was informed and advised to consult a solicitor. She became very angry and assaulted the social worker. A few days later she took Linda from her foster home, attempted to take Joe from his aunt, and drove off. She did not return to her home; neither Ms Martin nor Linda could be found. On the morning of the first directions hearing in the care proceedings, the local authority applied for EPOs for both children. At this hearing, which was attended by the mother's solicitor, a local authority solicitor, the children's guardian and solicitor and the social

---

worker's manager, EPOs were granted for eight days and directions were made for an ICO hearing the following week. On the same day, the mother reappeared and was persuaded by the social worker to let Linda return to foster care.

Cases 53 and 54: Removal of children following the death of a sibling due to NAI

The family first came to the notice of social services a few months after their first child, Terry, was born. An anonymous referral reported neglect and domestic violence. There was an investigation and a child protection case conference but Terry's name was not place on the child protection register. Two years later following the birth of Rachel, a similar referral was made, which also alleged drug misuse by the father; the children were taken into police protection and placed with their mother in a refuge. The children were included on the child protection register under the category of neglect. The following month, the father was convicted of burglary and imprisoned. Shortly afterwards, the mother began a new relationship and became pregnant. A comprehensive assessment was undertaken and a child protection plan drawn up; nursery placements were arranged for the children and the family were given support to obtain re-housing. At a review conference six months later concerns were raised about the mother's co-operation and the new partner's history; he had convictions for assaulting a child and was violent to his former wife. The mother did not accept this information; her relationship with the social worker deteriorated. Shortly afterwards, the family was re-housed in a different district in the authority; new arrangements needed to be made for social work support and nursery care. A visit to the family's new home raised no concerns.

Two weeks later, the mother and her partner called an ambulance saying Terry was unwell. Terry was found to be dead on admission to the children's hospital. The explanation given of Terry's condition did not fit the post-mortem results. Terry had suffered a massive blow and had a fractured skull and other older injuries. The mother and stepfather were arrested and Rachel went to stay with a relative. The following day a strategy meeting was held and a decision was made to obtain an EPO in respect of Rachel with an order for no contact with her mother, father and her mother's partner. Later that day at a without notice hearing, an EPO was granted for seven days. The mother and her partner were released from custody pending further investigations. The local authority applied for and obtained an ICO.

A child protection case conference was then held in respect of the mother's unborn child and this child was included on the child protection register. The mother's partner was arrested, charged with murder and re-manded in custody. A month later, Sarah was born. The following day, the local authority applied for an EPO; the court agreed that this should be heard with short notice to the mother. After discussions between the mother, her solicitor and the local authority, the mother agreed to Sarah being accommodated and to supervised contact. The local authority with-drew its application for an EPO and applied for an ICO to be consolidated with the care proceedings relating to Rachel.

CONCLUSION

In many respects the children and families who were subject to applications for emergency protection orders were similar to children and families in-volved in care proceedings without emergency intervention. Indeed, local authorities occasionally sought an EPO for one child in the family and ap-plied, on notice, for an interim care order in respect of their siblings. A high proportion of parents with care had major problems such as mental health dif-ficulties or substance abuse, which undermined their parenting capacity. Most families were already known to social services before the incident that pre-cipitated emergency intervention and more than a third had been through the process before, at least in the form of care proceedings. Similarities between EPOs and care cases might be expected given the high proportion of EPOs that were followed by care proceedings and the very variable rates in which differ-ent local authorities resorted to EPOs (see Table 1.3 and Figure 7.1). The issue to be explained is therefore not that child protection proceedings were brought but why emergency proceedings were thought to be necessary in these cases.

Children who became subject to EPO applications were very young; 30 per cent were under the age of one year. Their age and dependency made them particularly vulnerable, increasing the risks of delay in bringing proceedings and providing one reason for bringing emergency proceedings.

EPOs appeared to be incident driven, but the process of obtaining an EPO encouraged social workers to focus on an incident that could be said to justify swift protective action. In this sense, the cases were emergencies, but few con-formed to the narrower notion of a sudden and unexpected event and only a handful involved families who were not known to social services. Rather they were cases where there were already serious concerns about parenting, where a further incident was seen to justify moving immediately from working on a voluntary or partnership basis to court proceedings. The factors that led the social workers to seek emergency powers in these cases, the legal advice they obtained before applying and whether cases might have been handled differently are discussed in the next chapter.

6

LOCAL AUTHORITY DECISIONS TO SEEK EMERGENCY PROTECTION

INTRODUCTION

Child protection social work is incident driven (Cleaver, Walker & Meadows, 2004; Platt, 2006a), but social workers' response to referrals raising concerns is influenced by its context not only the incident itself. Where social workers are already monitoring or supporting families where there are child protection concerns, visits and discussions are incidents in themselves, providing further opportunities to assess the need for intervention and reassuring workers that children are safe or raising the level of concern. In order to make decisions about what action is required, social workers consider the source of referrals, their number and specificity and the seriousness of the concerns raised alongside their previous knowledge about the family (Buckley, 2003). Personal, professional and agency issues are part of the context, which shapes the action taken (Reder & Duncan, 1999; Horwath, 2006).

In the cases in the EPO study, the response to the most recent incident was to remove or detain the child, either by initiating police protection, which was followed by and EPO, or directly by seeking an EPO. Thus, the social workers had in these cases taken the less common approach to ensuring the child's protection of using compulsory powers rather than continuing to try to work in partnership and rely on parental co-operation (Brandon *et al.*, 1999). This necessitated engaging with the law, working with the local authority's legal department and satisfying the courts that such action was justified. This chapter discusses the factors that appeared to influence the use of emergency powers and examines the agency context for this decision making. It explores the processes in local authorities through which such decisions were taken, particularly the balance of power in decision making between the social worker with responsibility for the case, her manager and the local authority lawyer.

THE AGENCY CONTEXT

In common with many local authority social services departments, all six of the local authorities in the study were subject to work-force pressures, which meant that they had unfilled posts and high proportions of staff with limited experience. In Area M, the staff had the most experience; between 60 and 70 per cent of social workers in these authorities had worked there for three years or more, but only 15 per cent had worked as long in the shire country that formed the bulk of Area E. This authority had responded to its severe staffing problems by recruiting social workers overseas. These workers were generally highly qualified but had little knowledge of, and training for, the legal context in which they were now operating. Area J had reorganised its workforce to create a courts team in order to secure social workers for all cases currently subject to proceedings. This had impacted on other teams by removing staff, and also meant that the social worker involved in the care proceedings was unlikely to have worked on the case previously. The need for liaison with staff who had previously worked with the family was a further drain on caseworkers' time. Worker stress was an issue in all authorities and led to further staff shortages as over-stressed staff took periods of sick leave. In all three areas, there were unallocated or 'team allocated' child protection cases, and in addition there were cases awaiting assessments, some of which would probably have identified child protection issues.

The three shire counties had all recently been involved in inquiries into the handling of child protection cases where children had been killed or seriously injured despite social services involvement. These cases added to social worker anxiety, particularly in the authority where the inquiry and the parents' prosecution were the subject of national media coverage. Such attention has been identified as contributing to a climate that encourages intervention rather than seeking to manage risk though working with parents (Ayre, 2001; Scourfield, 2003). During the later stages of the research, the Climbié Inquiry (Laming, 2003) received extensive publicity; some interviewees referred to this as necessitating a re-examination of how cases were dealt with, suggesting an even greater use of intervention.

> The criticisms from the Laming Inquiry have started to affect people's judgement so, for example, the police are a bit twitchy when they are perhaps busy and take the decision to remove under police protection more readily than they used to and that is true for social workers as well. So I think that is starting to be the reaction. (LA Lawyer, Area M)

Reports from the Social Services Inspectorate covering roughly the same period as the research were available for all authorities in the study except
one of the unitary authorities. These provided an external evaluation of the
effectiveness of the councils' services for children and families. The Inspectorate's report on Area J noted deficiencies in practice which required urgent
action. Standards were inconsistent, case recording was poor, including for
child protection cases, and case conference administration was inadequate.
Staff compliance with local authority procedures was also low. Although
there was less criticism of the authorities which made up Area M, the Inspectorate also commented on inconsistency in child protection thresholds,
the variable quality of staff decision making and some failure to follow procedures and implement decisions. The authorities in Area E did not escape
criticism but the main concerns related to the low numbers of staff, their lack
of experience and the variable quality of assessments.

These assessments were reflected in some of the interviews for the research.
Social workers from Areas J and E referred to cases which had been given too
little attention and suggested that, in their authorities, lack of resources could
mean that cases might drift without the proper support and end in a crisis
necessitating an EPO.

> I wish we had more resources to work with families more closely, and to be
> able to express our concerns and to pursue things without having to go to
> the extent of an EPO, in general. Sometimes...we don't in [Area] have any
> funds now for children in need work, and sometimes cases just drift, and
> then a crisis occurs and you end up doing an EPO. And then you can end
> up with the children going home. And the stress of that, you know, is enor-
> mous. Whereas if you could have kept the children at home in the first place,
> but put in more of a service, you might have been able to avoid an EPO.
> (Social worker Area J)

The view that EPOs were required because of the local authority's failure
to provide preventative services was also expressed by solicitors in private
practice in these areas.

> Because of the persistent under funding of the social services in [Area], both
> before and after the reorganisation, there seems to be a lot of moderately routine
> work with children and families that's not getting done because they just don't
> have the bodies to go out and do it. Then an emergency arises...And then they
> find themselves galvanised into taking emergency proceedings. So I would say
> that if social services was doing its job properly, there would be less need for an
> EPO...(Solicitor, Area E)

One social worker in Area E recalled becoming so concerned about the limited action on a case involving neglect by a chronically depressed woman
that she asked for it to be allocated to her. Shortly afterwards she was

able to get the agreement of the local authority to make an application for an EPO.

> I think one needs to look at the wider context of what was happening in the local team. I think that things were pretty chaotic in the team at that point in time; we had a team manager who was struggling to make decisions on cases, I mean we had such a backlog of cases.... There were hundreds and hundreds of unallocated cases. On this particular one there had been recommendations to go to child protection conference, core assessment, but nothing had happened. So when I picked up the case, I was really alarmed...So this case had not received the attention that it should have. (Social worker, Area E)

In this case, the incident that precipitated the EPO was observed on a planned visit to the mother's home. The social worker had difficulty gaining entry because the mother had to be woken. The children were not at school and were seen sitting on a third floor window sill. The home conditions were very poor (**case 115**).

Local Authority Legal Services

Each of the authorities had its own in-house legal department which provided advice on individual cases, initiated proceedings and undertook advocacy in Children Act proceedings, except in long or complex cases and those in the High Court where counsel were usually instructed. In all areas there was some pressure to keep costs down by not instructing counsel, but the use of barristers was important for meeting case demands. Pressure of work and the need to keep costs down meant that in all three areas, local authority lawyers attended fewer cases conferences than they had in the past. Lawyers from Areas M and E noted that attending cases conferences and being involved in early planning could help to avoid the need to bring proceedings. In all areas, barristers were sometimes used to cover EPO hearings if a local authority lawyer was not available, and in Area J, private practice solicitors were occasionally instructed to act as the authority's agent in EPO cases. The use of external lawyers was seen as having some disadvantages, local authority lawyers could 'lose the feel for a case', social workers received less support at court, and the court might make directions or impose timescales that the local authority would not have accepted.

The Social Services Inspectorate made few comments about the provision of legal advice for social services departments but did note that arrangements in Area J needed to be improved and those in parts of Areas M and E were good. In the report on the other authority in Area M, there was no specific reference to legal services but the Inspectorate noted that strategy meetings

rarely took place and telephone calls about strategy decisions v
recorded.

THE PROCESS OF MAKING DECISIONS ABOUT EMERGENCY INTERVENTION

Law and managerialism have become dominant strategies in delivering social work services, transforming welfare values and concepts (Dickens, 2005,
329). Local authorities operate a range of gate-keeping strategies designed to
control access to expensive resources and to ensure that services are provided
fairly and arbitrary decisions are not made (Packman & Hall, 1998). Provision
of accommodation and bringing care proceedings are commonly subject to
such managerial control. In addition, *Working Together* advises that a strategy
discussion involving the social services department, the police and other relevant agencies should take place 'whenever there is reasonable cause to suspect that a child is suffering . . . significant harm' (Department of Health *et al.*,
1999, para 5.28; Department for Education and Skills, 2006, para 5.54). The
most recent guidance states that 'those participating should be senior . . . and
able to make decisions on behalf of their agencies' and specifically refers to
the strategy discussion 'determining if legal action is required' (paras 5.45–5).
The 1999 guidance, which applied during the research and is repeated in the
2006 edition, only stated that:

> Planned emergency action will normally take place following an immediate
> strategy discussion . . . Where a single agency has to act immediately to protect
> a child, a strategy discussion should take place as soon as possible after such
> action to plan next steps. Legal advice should normally be obtained before initi-
> ating legal action, particularly when an Emergency Protection Order is sought.
> (Department of Health *et al.*, 1999, para 5.24)

The practice in the study areas largely accorded with this guidance. Where
emergency action was pre-planned as in the case of decisions taken at pre-
birth case conferences to remove babies, health services staff and the police
were involved. Parents might have access to legal advice at this time but
there was little the parent's lawyer could do except prepare to oppose any
application once the child had been born.

> . . . it was known that the baby was going to be born in about 4 to 5 months. Social
> services called a pre-birth child protection conference which was attended by
> the police and it was minuted at that child protection conference that when
> the baby was born the police would immediately take out police protection for
> which an incident number was allocated . . . And I wrote to the legal department
> at [local authority] and told them what had happened and made it clear that we

would oppose any such action by emergency court proceedings if need be . . . In
that particular case the mother was gently persuaded to agree to the baby being
accommodated voluntarily without her knowing about it. And the child was
subsequently taken into care. (Solicitor, Area E)

There were a few other cases where a contingency plan was made to seek an
EPO if a particular event occurred. For example, in a case where a child had
yo-yoed between home and accommodation a decision was made to seek an
EPO if the parent made another request for the child to be accommodated.
However, it was more usual for decisions about emergency intervention to be
taken in response to an incident and be made following telephone discussions
with managers, local authority lawyers and, if police protection was required,
the police.

Management Input in EPO Decisions

In all six local authorities, the process of deciding to seek an EPO, involved
the case being considered by a social services manager. This was usually at the
level above team manager, although where cases were likely to be sensitive,
for example where a child had gone missing and publicity might be needed to
find him or her, senior management were likely to be informed and consulted.
In contrast with police officers who saw decisions about police protection
being for them alone, none of the social workers interviewed expected to be
able, or to be required, to make the decision to seek an EPO alone. Where
the appropriate manager was not available, they consulted a more senior
manager, a manager in another area of the authority, or failing them, a local
authority lawyer.

> I would never make an arbitrary decision about taking a matter to an EPO, I
> would always have to do it with my consultant, with my team manager, and he
> would then consult up the line. I can't make it myself. And if he wasn't available,
> I would ring the service manager, talk it over with her. (Social worker, Area J)

The same approach with the same level of managerial responsibility was
taken in the three authorities where little use was made of EPOs. In common
with research on provision of accommodation (Dickens, Howell, Thoburn &
Schofield, 2005), limited use of EPOs appeared to relate to the prevailing culture in the department, not tighter control mechanisms. Indeed, one of these
authorities had greater controls on starting care proceedings than on applying
for EPOs but still used EPOs in a very small proportion of its care cases. Nevertheless, social work managers and lawyers who attended the project's focus
groups generally believed that requiring approval at a high level within an authority could ensure that senior management took responsibility for decisions

whether to seek orders or not, and that emergency applications were restricted to cases where they were essential.

The same controls did not appear to apply where police protection was sought. Although in many cases the use of police protection was discussed with (and even proposed by) the legal department (see Chapter 4), it was possible for a social worker, with the support of their team manager, to by-pass agency controls and request police assistance. Duty Inspectors generally asked about the child's circumstances, why police protection was needed and why court action could not be taken. However, they did not seem to be aware that the problem with bringing proceedings could relate to a decision by a social services manager rather than the more common problem of time or the availability of a court. A team manager in Area M gave an example where the agency's controls on emergency intervention had been side-stepped in this way.

> Our thinking was to tell mum and serve the papers [for care proceedings]. Next week the health visitor went to the house and was very concerned about the home. There was either no carer for the child or no appropriate carer...The social worker was concerned about leaving the child there over the weekend. The team manager spoke to the area manager about seeking an EPO. The reply back was, 'No to an EPO.' So [the team manager] consulted with police for police protection. (Social work team manager, Area M)

Such practice did not seem to be widespread but indicates that the agency controls were not as tight as senior managers intended.

Lawyers and Social Workers – Who Decides to Bring Proceedings?

Working relationships between social workers and lawyers acting for the local authority have been seen as involving considerable tensions, particularly in relation to the solicitor's role in taking decisions about how a case is handled (Hilgendorf, 1981; Grace, 1994; Dickens, 2004, 2006). Hilgendorf identified three distinct roles that lawyers acting for a local authority took: *legal consultant*, where the lawyer merely advised on the law and presented the case in a detached way; *social work advocate* where the lawyer played a greater part in securing the outcome by advocating on behalf of the social worker in court; and *legal member of the team* where the lawyer was actively involved in making decisions on the case. Hunt and colleagues noted that the introduction of the Children Act 1989 greatly strengthened the local authority lawyer's role in controlling access to legal proceedings; legal departments expanded and it became inconceivable to bring proceedings without consultation with the legal department (Hunt *et al.*, 1999, 164). More recently, Dickens concluded that rather than distinct roles local authority lawyers took a continuum of approaches. These reflected the way they balanced their responsibilities to the five interests they served – the local authority, the social services department, the social worker, the child and the court. Lawyers were more or less involved in cases depending on the stage of the proceedings, the competence and experience of the social worker, the supervision the social worker was getting, other pressures on the social worker, and their own caseload. Duties to the court, for example to disclose information, took priority (as they should for all solicitors) even if this might be disadvantageous to the department's case (Dickens 2004, 2005).

Different views have been expressed about whether involvement of the legal department tends to raise or lower thresholds for intervention. Whereas the prevailing view of social workers in Hunt and colleagues' study was that lawyers interpreted the grounds for care or EPO proceedings more restrictively than the courts, some lawyers and social workers interviewed by Dickens suggested that lawyers were more willing to bring proceedings than social workers. Social workers in the EPO study commented that lawyers lacked the capacity to deal with the sort of risks that social workers had to live with and therefore operated low thresholds. Lawyers gave a different reason for their approach; they felt it necessary to press for legal action to be taken because managers were reluctant to bring proceedings because of the expense.

Legal Advice about EPOs

The National Survey of Magistrates Courts only identified four court areas where social workers commonly made EPO applications without being represented by a lawyer. Even in these areas, such practice was usually restricted to applications made without notice to the parents, so the social worker only had to present the case to the magistrates and respond to their questions. Whether the social workers in these areas first had to obtain advice from the local authority lawyers was not clear.

In all six local authorities in the court study, the decision to take proceedings necessitated contacting the local authority legal department. Any social worker who contacted the court direct was referred to their local authority lawyer by the magistrates' legal adviser. Before contacting the legal department, individual social workers were generally expected to discuss the case with their team manager. Where the social worker was inexperienced, contact with the lawyer might be made by their manager. If a decision were made to apply for an EPO, the legal department provided the forms, gave advice about completing them, contacted the court to discuss the timing of the hearing and to establish whether notice had to be given to the parents, and arranged representation for the hearing.

The tensions between social workers and lawyers were clear from the discussions about the use of EPOs. Whereas some social workers viewed the decision as a joint one, others considered that they instructed the solicitor to make the application. Even then the solicitor had a role to advise whether or not the criteria for an order were made out.

> I think the decision to go for an EPO is initially the social worker's decision, discussed with the team manager . . . and then we would ring up legal services. They would elicit from us whether they think the criteria have been met . . . If you like, the decision making is both [departments] but we are in a legal sphere so they would be advising us not to [apply] if they thought we didn't have grounds. (Social worker, Area J)

> At the end of the day we still try and treat it like a conventional solicitor – client relationship. We are asking them whether they think threshold criteria are met, whether they think we can evidence risk of significant harm. . . and do they think it is an appropriate application. And those are the questions we want them to answer. (Social work team manager, Area E)

With one exception, the lawyers all saw the decision as being made by the social services department. The lawyer's role was to provide legal advice and this included ensuring that it was necessary and appropriate for an EPO application to be made before contacting the court. The response below was typical in all three areas.

> I will tell them the likelihood of success, and what legal grounds they have. But at the end of the day, they instruct me. They are my clients, and if they say, 'We want to put this before the court, and I hear what you say, but we still want to put it before the court.' Then we will go. Because the final decision isn't mine, it's theirs. (Local Authority Lawyer, Area J)

But just as social workers might seek to avoid adverse decisions by turning to the police, lawyers might seek to have instructions withdrawn. Where a lawyer was concerned about the action social services were proposing, he or she would speak to someone more senior in social services with a view to having the instructions countermanded. This was an element of the lawyer's responsibility to ensure that the local authority did not take proceedings inappropriately.

> It can vary a bit on the lawyers because they have to make a decision based on their experience and what they're hearing and what the social services want as well. And in the end it should be the social services who make the decision, unless we think they are barking mad, in which case we'll go to somebody higher up in social services . . . (Local Authority Lawyer, Area E)

Both lawyers and social work managers expressed some concerns about lawyers being given too much responsibility – being asked what action *should* be taken, rather than whether an EPO *could* be sought. This might happen where the social worker and manager had little experience or there was no manager available to take social work decisions. Lawyers commented that they were sometimes put in the position of the social worker's manager.

> We instruct solicitors ... I'm very clear about it. Some people are less clear about that and so the solicitor would actually give the advice that you should go for an EPO ... That is putting the casework decision and the legal decision on the lawyer's shoulder and we are allowing them to make that decision. There is varying practice but ... I am telling you where I am coming from. (Social work team manager, Area J)

> I would be the first to say that I get quite unhappy at times as to what our role should be in relation to the interplay between ourselves and the social services department. About the decision – who takes the decision for an EPO and where our role begins and ends, and it varies of course to social worker and to team manager, and area, as to what their expectations are. I know one of the issues I have with the Head of Legal is that on occasions it feels like we are used as substitute team managers. (Local Authority Lawyer, Area M)

Closer consideration of the advice given also showed that the lawyers told social workers what they had to do before an EPO could be sought. For example, a social worker might be told to try to get parents' agreement for the child to be placed in foster care. Such direction was presented as legal advice, on the basis that it was 'an expectation the court would make' when considering the application. The use of knowledge of court practice as a trump card was also noted by Dickens (Dickens, 2006).

In all three Areas, practice generally accorded with the formal position that decisions to apply for EPOs were made by social work managers on the basis of information provided by social workers and their team managers and advice from the legal department. Each had some power but none could make an application without some support from the others. Case workers felt their responsibilities acutely, and this could translate into feelings of powerlessness if they were not supported when they thought an order should be obtained. Local authority lawyers were dependent on social workers and managers for information about cases, but once their advice had been sought they had considerable power over the decision to take or not to take an EPO. Although almost all lawyers formally accepted the traditional position of lawyers acting on social worker's instructions, none gave examples of being asked to seek EPOs in circumstances where they thought this to be inappropriate. They could not make a manager agree to such action and routinely advised on alternatives when questions about EPOs were raised. The deference to legal advice and lawyers' knowledge of, and reference to, the expectations of the court gave them considerable power over the use of EPOs.

ALTERNATIVE PROTECTIVE ACTION – AVOIDING THE USE OF EPOS

An EPO is only one of a number of possible responses to a child protection crisis. Instead of applying for an EPO, the social worker may agree arrangements for the child's protection with the parents, request the police to exercise their powers to take the child into police protection or apply, on notice, for an interim care order. The use of police protection was only a very temporary measure; where matters were not swiftly resolved it was followed by an EPO or an agreement for the child's protection. The reasons why local authorities asked the police to take a child into police protection were discussed in Chapter 4, and the influence of court practice on this issue is considered in Chapter 7. Key factors in social services' reliance on police protection were the need for immediate intervention and the lack of access to the court. Occasionally, police assistance was sought because of a refusal by local authority management or the courts to allow an application to be made.

The focus here is on avoiding compulsory intervention by making agreements with parents. Protective arrangements might involve an alleged perpetrator leaving the family home or the child being accommodated by the authority under Children Act 1989 (s.20) with relatives or foster carers. Farmer and Owen noted that the pressure to make 'safe' decisions meant that where there was a high degree of uncertainty and risks were unpredictable, children were more likely to be separated at the point of investigation. They suggested that these factors meant that families who were not known to social services were more likely to be subject to such action and, combined with social workers' lack of familiarity with black and minority ethnic families, this could explain the over-representation of children from these families in the looked-after population. In their sample, EPOs were used in respect of 7 out of 11 children who were removed during investigations, including some where there was no attempt to make an agreement with parents or to explore offers of help from relatives (Farmer and Owen, 1995). Similarly, O'Hagan (1997) found that, despite agency policy which stressed the importance of alternatives to compulsory removal, there had been no discussion about alternatives with the majority of the 15 families whose children had been removed by EPO. He suggested that the crisis nature of emergency intervention 'precludes the implementation of parental participation in any meaningful sense' and that social workers did not involve parents because they found it too difficult or believed that this was not in the interests of the children (O'Hagan, 1997, 40).

The decision-making processes were the same in all six local authorities but lawyers from local authorities and private practice commented on variations *within* authorities in social workers' willingness to resort to EPOs rather than accept that children could be protected by agreements between the social services department and the parents. It was not suggested that EPOs were sought without reason rather that different social workers appeared to feel more able to manage risk without a court order. A very experienced child care lawyer in private practice reflected:

> I think that the use of EPOs is very varied [in this authority]. Sometimes they're knee jerk reactions to a situation. Sometimes they're used where clearly there had not been enough time to consider and institute care proceedings . . . I had one case where an EPO was applied for after the police refused to do a police protection. The decision whether to go for an EPO, whether to go for a written agreement, whether to go for an interim care order does seem to vary according to the team that's dealing with the individual case . . . It doesn't feel that [authority] are doing too many EPOs. If they were used as a matter of routine as the first way in for care proceedings that would be upsetting and more worrying. So at least at the moment, it does feel, whether the criteria are right, they are actually being tailored to the individual cases. (Solicitor, Area J)

However, as later comments about the use of agreements make clear, tailoring action to individual cases could be about using agreements to test parents' co-operation, to assess the need for an order or to get evidence for future proceedings.

A range of factors – the views of the team manager, the experience of the social worker, knowledge of and past dealings with the family, the nature of the incident and the time it occurred all contributed to the efforts put into obtaining agreements with parents before resorting to court proceedings. The power given by the order was seen as coming at a substantial cost both in relation to immediate and future handling of the case. Social workers were concerned to avoid court proceedings, especially EPO cases because of the stress they caused for all concerned and the consequent greater difficulty in working with parents in partnership. There was also recognition (discussed below) of the additional work an EPO created for the social worker and the legal department, all of which had to be done in a very short time. The slightly longer timescale allowed where care proceedings were used was less disruptive for the other work, which could not just be abandoned because of a crisis in one case.

> I think first of all going into the court arena, it raises the stress levels, it raises the ante really on the case . . . you've got time constraints the court will place on you. (Social worker, Area E)

> I think it's always a traumatic occasion for everybody because it's an emergency, and adrenaline is flowing on everybody's part, so it's quite daunting for everybody, and tiring. At the end of the day after you've done something like an EPO or police protection you feel absolutely shattered physically, emotionally and mentally. And parents . . . you're a professional worker used to working in this sort of an arena, how parents must feel particularly when it's meant that their children are taken away from them, it must be awful. (Social worker, Area J)

Solicitors in private practice also recognised that there could be some benefits for their clients of trying to work with social services and make an agreement rather than being subject to proceedings. This could help the social worker to view the parent more positively and also reduce the trauma for children. Consequently, they might try to forestall an application by encouraging parents to agree to their child's accommodation:

> ... it's about trying to convince the parent that actually she can take some control of the situation and she can arrange for her children to be accommodated. She can go with them, she can settle them in, the children can see that they've got their mother's approval, as opposed to you know ... (Solicitor, Area J)

Local authority lawyers had two further reasons for preferring agreements rather than EPOs, wherever possible. First, the court would only grant an order if it were required, and would therefore expect that appropriate attempts had been made to reach an agreement with the parents. For this reason, lawyers from all areas stressed the need for social workers to explore the possibility of agreements with parents.

> If you've said to them, 'Have you been out and spoken to the mother? Is the mother prepared to agree to accommodate the child?' If they haven't done that ... then there would be difficulties, I think. Then the first thing that would happen if you get to court, the bench would want to know is, 'Have you spoken to mother about this?' If [the social workers] haven't been able to do that initial thing then there can be problems. (Local Authority Lawyer, Area E)

There were 6 out of 86 cases where an agreement was made at court and the EPO application was withdrawn, and in one other case, after the court had a agreed to arrange a hearing, the mother agreed to go with her child to a refuge so the application was not pursued (**case 59**).

Secondly, agreements could provide additional evidence of (lack of) parental care and co-operation, and show that the local authority had tried to work in partnership, if it became necessary to bring proceedings. Lawyers in all Areas referred to 'breach of agreement' as providing evidence of the need for an EPO. In 10 out of 86 cases the EPO was sought after a protective agreement had been breached.

> We often advise about the use of written agreements partly as evidence gathering, partly to show we have done everything we can to work in partnership, demonstrated we have tried everything. (Local Authority Lawyer, Area M)

Although parents could be pressed to agree to their child being placed elsewhere, they would not necessarily agree. In such cases, protective action could only be pursued with the police or through the courts. The decision not to try to reach an agreement was not simply a matter of the parent's co-operation, it also involved considering whether it was safe to forewarn the parents of possible intervention and whether the parent could be relied on to keep the agreement. In **case 44**, the mother had failed to collect her child from infant school on two previous occasions in the same week. Despite a discussion with her social worker, there was a third incident. The team manager considered that there was no alternative but to seek an EPO.

> And then mother abandoned her in school and it became very clear that week that mum was going to go on abandoning her in school. So we had no alternative then it forced the hand. So that is how that one came about. (Social work team manager, Area M)

There was general agreement in all six authorities, and amongst other social workers and lawyers spoken to in the course of the project, that agreements should be used in preference to emergency proceedings. It was better for parents (and more compliant with human rights law) if the first court hearing was an interim care application where they had been given sufficient notice to obtain representation. This was better for the local authority because it meant that both social work and legal proceedings could be planned rather than rushed. There was less stress on workers, work on other cases was not displaced, and the cost of a further set of applications (and legal representation at them) could be avoided. Even though it might be necessary to bring care proceeding, initial protection by way of an agreement was seen by both social workers and lawyers as the approach to use 'if at all possible'.

CRITERIA FOR USING EPOS

> It's an understood thing that you only go for emergency protection orders in an emergency. It's not a decision you'd take lightly. (Social worker Area J)

Legal Criteria Threshold, Immediacy and the Need for an Order

The threshold conditions for an EPO were not considered to be hard to establish. A local authority lawyer noted, 'It's a very low threshold' and a private practice solicitor commented on the 'small evidential test'. Nevertheless, it might be difficult to justify seeking an emergency order where the family circumstances had been accepted for some time and nothing appeared to have changed apart from the social worker's feeling about the case. Social workers from all three areas recounted instances where they had been told that an EPO could not be sought:

> On 1ˢᵗ May I rang legal up and explained the situation and said, 'I don't want the kids to be with mum anymore, they are not safe. Have we got the grounds for proceedings if we need them?' And I think my advice at the time was that I did not have quite enough for an EPO but I certainly did have enough to go on notice for interim care orders. (Social worker Area J, **cases 5 and 6** (see p. 127))

Having 'enough for an EPO' usually meant being able to point to an incident, which justified immediate intervention, not merely that there were grounds for care proceedings. Neglect cases were a particular concern; EPOs were only sought in such cases where risks to children were very high, as in the case of young babies, or where the children's physical condition justified immediate removal, as in **case 12**, (above p. 121).

Although local authority lawyers checked whether the threshold criteria were met, they focused their advice and the social worker's attention on the need for an order, and on the 'immediacy' of the situation, that is whether the case justified emergency intervention or could be dealt with by applying for an ICO. If the case would 'hold for a few days' or temporary protective arrangements could be agreed, there was no need for an EPO. It might even be possible, at least in Area M, to get the court to agree to abridging notice to allow an earlier interim care order hearing.

> We have to ensure the grounds for an EPO, why is it an EPO? Why can't we simply deal with care proceedings? Everybody knows when the next [court] date is. Courts aren't rigid either about enforcing the three clear day service time so that enables you to get before the court quite quickly. (Local Authority Lawyer, Area M)

The volatility of cases might mean that even after proceedings had been issued it was no longer possible to wait for a hearing for an ICO which had already been timetabled. This depended on the perception by the social worker and the manager of the risk to the child following a further incident or a change in the parents' attitude, and the professionals' willingness to accept that level of risk. However, in the majority of cases children were already protected by agreements or hospital admission when the EPO was sought. Of the 47 cases where children were not subject to police protection prior to the EPO, only 18 (21% of the total sample) were living at home with their parents when the EPO was made. There were four other cases where the children were home alone (or had been left with unwilling or unsuitable, unrelated carers) and, in the remaining 25 cases, children were accommodated with foster carers, staying with friends or family by agreement or in hospital, immediately before the EPO. In these cases there might be anxiety that parents would demand the child's return, or if children were placed with relatives, a concern that relatives should legally be able to withstand claims by parents to remove children. Similarly, where children were in hospital, it was important for health service staff to know that parents access to, or removal of, their child was controlled.

Risk, Urgency and Seriousness of Harm

Despite the fact that social services were already involved with most of the families, the decision to take emergency action was not usually made as a result of an assessment of the child's circumstances but in response to the latest incident in a series that had raised concerns about the parents' ability to provide adequate care. The view of the front-line social worker was crucial, as was his or her ability to communicate this to the manager and the local authority lawyer.

> I mean when you think about it, it's about our perception as a field so-cial worker, we see the dangers and [others] may not see what we see. I think if it's not assessed properly, or written up properly, or conveyed to the other parties properly, that sometimes they look at it and think, 'Oh well it doesn't warrant intervention.' I think that's quite a problem. (Social worker, Area E)

Risks were seen to be higher where children's care could not be monitored. Despite the common perception of those interviewed in both studies, use of police protection and applications for EPOs did not appear to be more common on Fridays. However, the fact that the school holidays were about to start was crucial in precipitating an EPO for a six-year-old boy whose mother was known to be having difficulty coping.

> The head teacher stated that in her opinion the bruises looked like finger marks, she expressed grave concerns about [the child's] welfare, expressed her worries that school was breaking up for the summer in 2 days time and there would be no way of monitoring him. (Social worker, Area J, **case 14**, (below p. 190))

The seriousness of the circumstances as identified by the social worker (or a doctor) could also be a factor. Some workers considered that cases where there were serious injuries or death to a sibling could not be dealt with by an agreement with parents, but others were satisfied that children could be protected without an order.

What we did do, and this was one of the things that fuelled [mother's] anger... At the hospital we were writing up a written agreement, which you will see on the file. But... we received the news about the sexual abuse... just minutes later and that meant we changed our tack. And that is when we made a decision to go for the EPO, and I felt extremely uncomfortable about having reached an agreement with her and then having to change in the light of having fresh information. (Social worker Area J, **case 4** (above p. 124))

We try and keep to a minimum the number of applications, specifically EPO applications. But if at all possible, we try and hold the situation by getting a written contract pending an application by summons, then we would do that. I mean we've got a baby in Great Ormond Street at the moment with a severe head injury, but we've got a written agreement with the parents prepared because the child's not going anywhere and the other children are being looked after by extended family. That's all subject to written agreement – the parents' contact is supervised. So we are actually planning to make an application for a summons rather than an EPO. (Social work team manager Area E)

Three of the cases where EPO applications were withdrawn because of agreements made at court concerned cases where the use of agreements had been rejected by social workers because of the seriousness of the harm. **Case 4** was one of these. Where social workers were already concerned about children's safety, parental threats to disappear with the children could tip the balance in favour of action. This was also an issue in decisions whether to inform parents before obtaining an order, leading to the use of police protection or an application for an EPO without notice. **Case 1** discussed in Chapter 5 is an example.

Parental Co-operation

If parents would co-operate with protection plans, this obviated the need for an order. Where social workers could discuss with parents ways of securing their children's immediate safety without applying for an EPO, their managers, local authority lawyers and magistrates' legal advisers all expected them to try and get parental agreement to such an arrangement. Similarly, solicitors in private practice regarded applications for EPOs made without discussion of alternatives as reflecting a 'poor relationship' between the social worker and the parents. Wherever possible they too would seek to persuade their clients to reach an agreement with social services, and use their client's willingness to agree to deflect suggestions that proceedings were required, or to convince the court that an order was not required. However, few parents had access to legal advice before proceedings were started, and in none of the areas was there an advocacy service which might have helped parents to negotiate with social services.

The context for agreed arrangements was not a shared understanding about the family's problems and the child's need for protection based on the ideals of partnership. Rather it reflected the imbalance of power between the social worker and the parents. The alternative to an 'agreement' was an application to court. Agreements were often not negotiated but achieved in response to threats.

> Most families can be persuaded and it may be that it is a bit of an arm up the job. 'You work with us or we will go for an order.' (Social worker, Area M)

Solicitors who acted for parents were understandably concerned about such practices. Parents were misled, and might not understand what they had agreed to, getting into more difficulty with social services because they then failed to comply with the agreement. Also, by avoiding proceedings the local authority avoided external scrutiny of their actions. If proceedings were brought, the time between the first separation and the final hearing could be far longer than if proceedings had been brought initially.

> The other strategy that is used more commonly is to persuade the parent to agree to the child being accommodated in inverted commas voluntarily, on the basis that if the child is not accommodated voluntarily, the case will have to go to court and it will take a long time, and the child will remain in care for the whole of the court proceedings . . . I see a lot of parents who . . . describe this having happened within the last day or two and [they are] under the impression that the child will be returned to them shortly, when it was quite clear that there was no plan whatsoever for that and that they had not been told that. (Solicitor, Area E)

Agreements could not only secure the child's protection with minimal intervention, they could also change the way the case was viewed. Where parents co-operated, risk would be seen to diminish. In contrast, in the sample cases, breach of an agreement was taken to demand an urgent response through court proceedings. Where children were admitted to s.20 accommodation, the parents' statutory rights to remove them whenever they wanted were nullified through this process. In the words of a local authority lawyer from Area E, the case 'becomes an emergency because the parents are demanding the child.' Similarly, breaches of other terms of protection agreements could be viewed as creating unacceptable risks.

> I have attended a case conference . . . we haven't necessarily got enough [to bring proceedings], but I suggest that we need a pretty tight written agreement, and parents are co-operative, but failure to comply, or removing the child could result in immediate action. And that could be by an EPO. (Local Authority Lawyer, Area J)

Breach of an agreement necessitated social services considering again how the risk to the child should be managed. This generally meant immediately consulting the legal department. An application for an EPO would not necessarily result from a breach of an agreement, this depended on the seriousness of the breach, when it occurred, what it indicated about parental understanding and co-operation, and what had been said to the parent in the past. However, considering an event on the basis that it was also a breach of an agreement for the child's protection could mean that it was viewed more harshly, effectively the threshold for intervention was reduced. **Case 10** is one example where this occurred.

> The grandmother signed the agreement. It was either that or baby went to accommodation. So what we were saying was, 'OK let us see if we could sort this out.' The written agreement with the grandmother was that she would be the sole carer for [the baby]. The social worker called that evening to take some money round or some nappies or something like that and ... she found mum and baby in the house unsupervised at 8pm ... they had broken [the agreement] straight away. (Social worker, Area J, **case 10**)

In **case 10**, the social worker acknowledged that the one-year-old child appeared safe and well when she visited and that the breach was 'technical'. Nevertheless, because it occurred so soon after the agreement had been made and in a family where there was a history of alcohol abuse, violence and neglect, and where relationships between the adults were volatile, the matter could not be left. The following day she visited with the team manager with a view to getting an agreement for the child to go to foster care. However, 'nobody would agree with anything at this point' and the grandmother was 'quite threatening and intimidating' so an application was made to the court for an EPO on short notice. The order was made but was not followed by care proceedings (see below Chapter 8). The child was placed with her father who had recently been released from prison and who had left with the couple's other child to live near relatives in another part of the country. There had been no assessment of the father, but because both children were on the child protection register a formal transfer was made to the other authority.

This was not the only example of breach of an agreement leading to an EPO in circumstances where there was little evidence of immediate danger. A solicitor in Area M recalled a recent case (not in the sample) where the grandmother's breach of an agreement not to allow her partner, who had convictions for offences against children, into the home led to a decision to remove her children and her baby grandchild. The children were at home on care orders and could therefore be removed without further proceedings; an EPO was obtained without notice in respect of the baby. What made this action all the more extraordinary was that the local authority took it without any consultation with the family, during a case conference, attended by the grandmother and her lawyer.

There were 35 cases (41 per cent of the sample) where lack of co-operation with social services provoked an EPO application. In 10 of these cases, the families had breached their agreement, in another 13 they had refused to agree to the local authority's proposals and, in 12, the local authority wanted the order to secure the child's care because parents had threatened to remove him or her from s.20 accommodation. The possibility of obtaining a powerful court order had a major impact on the provision of s.20 accommodation. Where there were significant child protection concerns, accommodation could not be regarded as a service for families to choose if the local authority considered that children required it. Rather it was provision that parents could not refuse. The focus of the research on cases where EPOs had been sought mean that it was not possible to examine what happened in cases where agreements were made and not breached, or where breach was followed by care proceedings rather than an EPO. The practices identified nevertheless raise concerns that parents might be pressured into agreeing to out of home placement for their children in circumstances where alternative means of safeguarding children and supporting parents would have been appropriate and there was not a good case for bringing proceedings. Also, that out of home placements might continue without proper plans being made for contact and children's rehabilitation.

THE CIRCUMSTANCES IN WHICH EPOS WERE USED

In the majority of cases where EPOs were sought, they were intended to prevent children being removed *by* their parents, not to enable the local authority to take children from their homes. EPOs were used to remove children from the home where they were being cared for by parents in only a small minority of cases (see Figure 6.1). More commonly, initial protection had been secured, either by police protection or by an agreement with the parents. These could ensure a quicker response than applying to the court (see Chapter 7). Police protection lasted only 72 hours, insufficient time for the local authority to give notice of an application for an ICO, even where it was clear that care proceedings should be started. Where police protection had been used by the police independently, or the family were not previously known to social services, deciding whether care proceedings should be started could take a considerable time. Therefore, if the child continued to be at risk, the local authority needed to take further action to secure protection after the power to hold the child under police protection expired. Such protection could be arranged either by an agreement with the parents or an EPO. It was clear that both social workers and local authority lawyers generally preferred agreements.

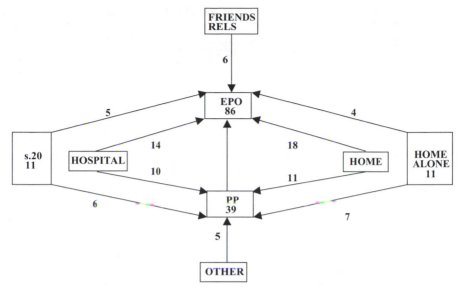

Figure 6.1   Location of child when protective measures taken

However, EPOs were required if parents would not agree, could not be relied on, broke the agreement, or where circumstances were such that the social workers considered that it was necessary to take action without informing the parents. Consequently, a study of EPOs is to a large extent a study of the failure or inadequacy of agreements between parents and social services.

Location of Children when Emergency Intervention was Used

Figure 6.1 illustrates where children were staying at the point when protective action was taken, whether by police protection or EPO.

Although 60 families (70 per cent of the sample) had their children living with them when protective action was initiated, by the time the application was made for an EPO this had declined to just 18 (21 per cent of the sample). Children had been removed from 39 families (45 per cent) by police protection and children in the remaining families were either in hospital, with relatives or accommodated under s.20.

Incidents Leading to the Use of EPO

As reviewed in Chapter 5, all but five families (6 per cent of the sample) were known to social services before the incident that led to the application for an EPO and over 80 per cent had been known to social services for six months

Table 6.1   Circumstances of the EPO application

Circumstances	Families	%	Children	%
Removal at birth	16	18.6	16	12.6
Home alone/no carer	9	10.5	19	15.0
From s.20 to EPO	12	14.0	20	15.7
Crisis	22	25.6	34	26.8
Non co-operation	23	26.7	32	25.2
Other	4	4.7	6	4.7
TOTAL	86	100	127	100

or more. Just less than half the children (59) were on the child protection register, and another 10 had previously been registered. Thus, in almost all cases the decision to remove the child was made against a background of prior knowledge about the family and concerns for the child's well-being. Table 6.1 groups the circumstances that led to the use of an EPO.

The cases where the child was already accommodated under s.20 included cases where the parents had threatened to remove the child, cases where they had breached agreements relating to contact, generally by failing to return the child, and cases where the local authority was no longer content to rely on the agreement. The crisis cases included 12 children who had experienced life-threatening events, mostly serious non-accidental injury, 13 with less serious injuries, 7 whose parent had been arrested and 2 whose sibling had died as a result of a suspected non-accidental injury. Cases where there was no co-operation from the parents included 11 children where parents had breached an agreement about keeping the child away from a specific person or providing appropriate care and 21 where the parents refused to enter into an agreement, usually for their child to be cared for by relatives or foster carers.

Neglect was a major feature in nearly half the families (39, 45 per cent of the sample); child abuse, in all but two cases, physical abuse rather than sexual abuse to a child in the family was the precipitating factor in 25 families (30 per cent). Domestic violence, drug or alcohol abuse and mental health difficulties featured in many cases. However, the incident that led to the EPO application was frequently no more serious than previous incidents in the family, which had been dealt with less forcefully by social services. In these cases, the last incident before proceedings amounted to a 'last straw', convincing social workers that informal working with the family was no longer adequate and therefore leading to a different response from them. In others, it was the family's refusal to co-operate at this point which led to formal intervention. Overall, neither the family circumstances nor the precipitating incident provide an adequate explanation for the use of EPOs. It was the interaction of the child's circumstances, the family's relationship with social services and the context in which the social worker was operating that determined whether an EPO application was made.

AFTER THE DECISION – PREPARING FOR THE EPO

The decision to seek an EPO was only the beginning of a process that involved the social worker, other social services staff and the local authority lawyer in considerable work, and, as discussed in Chapter 8, was generally expected to lead to care proceedings. In all three areas, social workers commented that they coped with the demands of emergency intervention through the support of other members of their team. 'The whole team was galvanised.' Casework responsibility was held by the social worker with his or her supervisor, but the preparation of the application for the EPO, and all the other work, such as finding placements for the children and liaising with carers was taken on by the team. Colleagues rallied round and so the extra work was managed as necessary.

> I think we always get good support because it's seen as an emergency. There's a lot of paper work that needs to be done. A lot of social workers come to-gether and one will do the chronology, one will do the care plan, one will do the statement; so everyone works together in getting all of it done. And there's always good advice from team leaders, service managers. (Social worker, Area E)

Nevertheless, this work was demanding. Worrying about whether an EPO should be sought was stressful, as was going to court when an application was made. All child protection work provoked anxiety, and working without an order could be equally stressful.

> No. I wouldn't say they [EPOs] are more stressful than any other work, I think sometimes trying to work in partnership with families can be equally stressful. (Social work team manager, Area E)

POWER AND PROTECTION

Social workers used power directly and indirectly to protect children, most commonly to prevent parents removing them from where they were currently being looked after but also so that social workers could determine how children would be cared for on discharge from hospital, to ensure care for children who had been left without care or to remove children from homes where they were being abused or neglected. Where this involved requesting the exercise of police powers or a court application it was a matter of last resort; the parents' lack of co-operation and the social workers' concern for the child's immediate situation meant that they considered that there was no alternative way of making the child safe. Children's safety was not just a matter of their physical care but also about avoiding disruption and risk from parents who were no longer trusted to provide care.

This separation of children from their parents necessarily involves an exercise of power. Social workers' identification with that power infects the professional relationships social workers have with families. Social workers are seen as people 'who take kids away'. This makes it difficult for them to establish relationships of trust that would allow parents to recognise the validity of their concerns and accept the need for action. Power is both a problem and a resource for social workers. Emergency powers can get in the way of partnership but they enable children to be protected when parents cannot or will not do so.

Although social workers, their managers and local authority lawyers are all engaged in child protection their priorities and immediate concerns may differ. This was reflected in their different thresholds for emergency intervention. Where intervention was planned, as in the case of babies who were expected by women who were considered incapable of providing satisfactory care, there was time to consider and review proposed action. Despite the very serious nature of the intervention, there was generally little evidence of disagreement but this could surface over the issue of expensive residential assessments. In other cases, the need for swift action precluded a thorough discussion between professionals. Power shifted within the professional group with managers and lawyers determining whether emergency action could be taken; support from both was usually essential for an application to court. This reflected other aspects of social work with children and families where the use of resources was subject to management control.

The existence of EPOs empowers social workers even where no order is sought. Despite agency requirements for management approval, the possibility of applying for an EPO means that social workers are not dependent on parental co-operation to protect children. They can apply to the court for power to remove or detain a child or ask the police to use their powers. The availability of EPOs is an important aspect of the context within which arrangements for child protection are discussed with parents, even if no application is made. Arrangements cannot really be *negotiated* when it is clear that any parental resistance will result in an application to court.

The possibility or even threat of an EPO can overcome the parents' reluctance to agree to the social worker's proposal and allow children to be protected without formal use of legal powers. Managers, local authority lawyers and the courts all supported this approach. The use of agreements (even forced ones) was viewed as minimising intervention in the family. It also allowed parents to retain parental responsibility and to demonstrate their co-operation with social services, a factor recognised by solicitors who represented parents. However, without advice about alternatives, a full understanding of what the local authority proposed, particularly how long protective arrangements were intended to last and how they could be renegotiated or ended, parents had no real power in their dealings with the local authority. Arrangements that might empower parents can be particularly disempowering where parents withdraw from the agreement; breach of agreement rather than the child's current circumstances could become the basis for an EPO.

7

COURT PROCESS IN EMERGENCY PROTECTION CASES

INTRODUCTION – THE BALANCE OF POWER BETWEEN THE COURTS AND THE LOCAL AUTHORITY

Emergency powers were reformed with the aim of increasing accountability and reducing their use (Parton, 1991; Cretney, 2003). The balance of power was shifted away from the local authority to the courts. Magistrates were given more powers but were also disciplined by working more closely with their legal adviser (formerly known as the magistrates' clerk), usually in pairs rather than alone, and by being required to give written reasons for their decisions. The question whether a child could be removed from their parents would no longer be decided by a single magistrate, acting alone, on the basis of a social worker's concern. The child's contact with their family, the need for medical assessments and the length of the order were all matters for the court to determine. Orders would still be granted in courts which were not open to the public, but the introduction of the adversarial process through the representation of parents and children meant that both the local authority's case and the court's actions would be open to scrutiny. In an emergency, an application could be heard *ex parte* (without notice to the respondents) and by a single magistrate, but only if the magistrates' legal adviser accepted that it was sufficiently urgent to justify this. And where orders were granted without notice, they were open to review after three days, in a hearing where parents could be represented.

This chapter explores how these provisions have operated in practice. It examines the balance of power between the local authority and the court, between the magistrates and their legal adviser, and between the local authority and the other parties to the proceedings. The various players change and their influence shifts at the different stages of the proceedings. Whether the application is heard on notice is a matter for the magistrates' legal adviser; local authority lawyers seek to influence this decision, which has a major impact on the conduct of the proceedings. Power and influence in the hearing depends on whether the application is heard on notice, and if it is, on the attendance and representation of the parties. An *on notice* hearing may involve parents' lawyers, the child's lawyer, the children's guardian in addition to the social worker and local authority lawyer, all of whom may try to influence the magistrates. In contrast, in *ex parte* proceedings, the magistrate will hear only the local authority's case. In either circumstance, the decision and responsibility for securing the child's protection is a matter for the magistrates, acting on legal advice.

THE APPLICATION

The decision whether a case can be heard without full notice is made by the magistrates' legal adviser (Family Proceedings Courts (Children Act) Rules 1991, r.4(4)(b)). Local authority solicitors wanting to make an application for an EPO usually telephoned in advance to warn the court of the need to prepare for a hearing, or if the local authority wanted to have the case heard without notice, to discuss the case with a legal adviser. Calls relating to the arrangements for hearings were generally handled by clerical staff with responsibility for listing, but legal issues were directed to a legal adviser.

The National Survey indicated that there were considerable differences between magistrates' courts areas in the legal advisers' willingness to allow EPO applications to proceed without notice to parents (see Table 7.1). Local authority lawyers in some parts of the country had more or less difficulty than others working elsewhere in obtaining EPOs quickly. Just over a third of the advisers indicated that in their courts it was unusual to have an EPO application heard without notice. This conflicts with the Children Act guidance, which states that such applications 'will usually be heard *ex parte*' (Department of

Table 7.1   Court response to without notice EPO cases (National Survey)

Response to without notice EPOs	N	%
Rarely allowed	15	36.6
Prefer to abridge notice	8	19.5
Usually hear cases without notice	13	31.7
No on notice EPOs	5	12.2
Total[1]	41	100

[1] For two large magistrates' courts areas two quite different policies and practices were identified.

Health, 1991a, para 4.46). Where EPOs were rarely heard without notice, legal advisers said that they emphasised the need for the local authority to convince them that it was a 'true emergency' or a 'dire emergency'. They operated a presumption that cases should be *on notice* and expected the local authority to justify why this should not be the case. Almost one-fifth of clerks said that they preferred to shorten the period of notice rather than to allow a case to be heard without notice. For some, this balanced the demands of the local authority and the rights of the parents; parents could be told of the application and attend court, but the local authority's intervention would not be much delayed. The 18 remaining clerks said that cases were usually heard without notice or that they were willing for them to be heard in that way. Five of these clerks said that EPO applications were *never* heard *on notice*. Indeed, they considered there to be a contradiction between providing an emergency response and giving notice. Although it is possible that these courts only ever received applications from local authorities in cases of exceptional urgency, this seems unlikely given the advantages of without notice hearings to local authorities. The automatic acceptance that an *ex parte* hearing is necessarily required appears to ignore the legal adviser's role as gate-keeper and to remove one of the safeguards in the process against oppressive action, a failure that also appeared to have occurred in *Re X.* (2006) (see p. 11).

Almost all of the legal advisers commented that the Human Rights Act 1998 had had some impact on the way EPO applications were handled. Twenty-nine legal advisers said that they were concerned to ensure a fair trial (article 6) and 20 of these indicated that fewer applications were now being granted without notice, or that they were more questioning about the need for an application to be dealt with in that way.

> We rarely disagree [with the local authority] at the end of the day but the court clerk may say, 'Well actually is there need for this to be *ex parte*?' We have to have regard to the European Convention on Human Rights and in fact the domestic legislation . . . militates against *ex parte* applications but for exceptional circumstances. And as a result of that conversation the clerk may persuade the local authority that it will be an *inter partes* application. (Magistrates' legal adviser)

Others who mentioned fair trial noted that they had always taken a restrictive approach to EPOs.

In two of the three areas in the Court study, Area J and Area E, the magistrates' legal advisers took a very restrictive approach to without notice applications. There was a general policy in Area J that applications should be heard on notice unless there were very good reasons why they should not be. The local authority had ceased trying to have EPO applications heard without notice but frequently sought police assistance. During the study period, there was only one without notice application in Area J. After the mother had removed her daughter from her carer and disappeared, the local authority applied for an EPO at a directions hearing in the care proceedings (**case 5–6**; see p. 127). In Area E, the court heard applications without notice but would only consider doing so after it had received information in writing about the case. Disagreement between the court and the local authority over without notice hearings had led to the development of a system which allowed local authority lawyers to get a second opinion from a senior legal adviser if their request was turned down. Local authority lawyers still sought without notice hearings; a magistrates' legal adviser commented that approximately half the local authority's applications for these were refused. These preliminary steps increased the time taken to obtain an EPO in Area E and were a major factor in social services' reliance on police protection. Overall, the courts in Area E heard just over a quarter of all EPO applications without notice to the parents.

In Area M, the courts were more willing to hear EPO applications *ex parte*. Local authorities were not required to file the application beforehand but expected to have to convince the legal adviser by telephone of the need for the case to proceed without notice. Just under half of applications were dealt with in this way even though a magistrates' legal adviser noted that she 'worked on the principle that EPOs should be heard on notice.'

The differences between the areas appeared to depend on the approach of the Clerk to the Justices and/or the specialist legal adviser who dealt with Children Act cases. Their views were based on their notion of when they should be expected to set up an immediate court and the importance given to holding a hearing where parents could attend. Where parents rarely took part, the importance of giving them notice was downplayed. These views, spread through advice to colleagues on individual cases and through more general discussion established the court culture. In Area E, this was reinforced by the formal procedure, which allowed the local authority to ask for a second, more senior view if permission for a without notice hearing was refused, but in Area J the legal court's authority and approach to EPOs was no longer challenged.

The Need for Intervention Without Notice

There was general agreement amongst all the professionals involved – magistrates' legal advisers, magistrates, solicitors, social workers and children's guardians that intervention without notice was sometimes necessary. There were some cases where immediate action had to be taken to protect a child, some where notifying the parents before securing the child's protection created unacceptably high risks to the child's welfare, and others where it was impractical to notify one or both parents because their whereabouts were unknown. A local authority solicitor identified these cases thus:

> ... evidence that demonstrates a real and immediate risk ... I'm considering very, very serious risk, I'm talking about life threatening risks to a child. So the considerations are: Is there a risk in giving notice in itself, so do we have to act straightaway? Or can we really give the parents a chance to get their legal act together as well and do it properly in front of a bench of magistrates. (Local Authority Lawyer, Area E)

In relation to newborn babies, there was a further concern that mothers might avoid seeking medical attention when they went into labour. More generally, there was anxiety that some parents would disappear with their children once they were alerted to the social services department's plans. In **case 56**, where there were current care proceedings relating to a sibling, the local authority solicitor wrote to the solicitor for that child to forewarn him that the authority thought it would be necessary to seek an EPO in relation to the baby whose birth was expected within the week. The local authority's solicitor's letter stated.

> You may think it is appropriate to forewarn the parents' solicitor (unless for welfare reasons you think that by notifying the parents they may seek to conceal the birth) so that the parents are given the opportunity to argue the matter ...'

Although this helped to secure representation for the baby at the EPO, it seemed to pass the responsibility for informing the parents from the local authority to the children's guardian and the solicitor currently appointed to represent the older sibling.

Fears that children would be harmed if parents knew that the local authority planned to remove them were not groundless; in the sample of 86 cases there were three where parents of new babies had either moved or threatened not to attend hospital to avoid social services' attention, and another seven cases where action had to be taken to find children after the EPO had been obtained. Social workers might be concerned about a parents' disappearance because of what they knew about them – known links outside the area, previous moves and threats – or because they knew little about them, and therefore felt unable to predict their response or to trust that they would co-operate.

> I think my main concern as the key worker was the safety of the children. My main thing was to get them into a safe place, before either parent could try and remove them, because I believe, both parents had made veiled threats, or open threats, that if social services ever tried to remove the children, that they would remove them to another town, or even take them out of the country. So my main worry was about the children being removed before we could get them into a safe place ... (Social worker, Area J)

In some cases even the time taken to obtain an EPO without notice might seem too long. New babies were very vulnerable and even if they were in hospital, staff had no right to stop parents removing them. A social work manager in Area E where the court scrutinised applications closely before allowing an *ex parte* hearing explained his concerns for the child before the order was obtained:

> Occasionally we get one born at 10 o' clock in the morning; you can get into court that afternoon if you're lucky. The issues are though in the newborns, and they are issues we repeatedly have come up against – if we are going to do that, do we leave the baby with the mother all that time?... We are still talking several hours... If it's been a substance abusing mother or a hepatitis C mother, who prevents them trying to breast feed?... So to deal with the practical realities we have to seek an order there and then. (Social work team manager, Area E)

But a solicitor in Area M faced with the same issue commented that the local authority was 'over cautious' in taking immediate legal action. He and other solicitors who had experience of the removal of newborn babies thought that arrangements should be made for mothers and babies to stay in hospital until there was a hearing, on notice, for an interim care order. This was 'the civilised way'. These solicitors did not think there was any risk that mothers would try to leave the hospital with their babies.

Where children were already protected by the use of police protection, local authority lawyers usually had no concerns about giving parents notice of the EPO application, and magistrates' legal advisers agreed without notice applications were inappropriate in such cases. Only six of the 39 cases where police protection was used were followed by a without notice EPO application, and in three of these, police protection had been used without consultation with social services. Before deciding whether further action was necessary, the local authority preferred to make enquiries, even if this meant that it would not be able to give full notice for an EPO hearing if one were required.

Applications on Short Notice

Where the court refused permission for the application to be made without notice they were usually prepared to allow it to be heard on short notice. In each area, approximately one-third of cases were heard on short notice; that is, without the parents receiving one full day's notice of the hearing. Typically, the application was approved at the beginning of the working day, served on the parents during the morning, for a hearing at 2 pm. Abridged notice appeared to be seen by both legal advisers and local authority solicitors as a compromise solution, securing a speedy decision for the local authority whilst giving the parents the opportunity to participate in the hearing. In Area J, the local authority had switched to asking for abridged notice instead of seeking without notice hearings and, in Area E, they asked for this as an alternative to a without notice hearing. In Area M, the court was said to propose shortening the period of notice. A local authority lawyer commented that if notice could be given, the case could probably be dealt with by care proceedings. Courts in this area were also known to be willing to allow applications for interim care orders without the full period of notice.

> The court will very often suggest [short notice]. I think you have to give one day's notice, but generally if we are able to give one day's notice then we are bordering on to possibly making application for ICO rather than EPO. (Local Authority Lawyer, Area M)

The courts' willingness to shorten the notice for the EPO hearing had implications for the representation of both parents and children, which is discussed below.

Giving Notice

In all six local authorities, the social worker had the task of serving the papers on the parents if notice were given. This could provide another opportunity for trying to get the parent to accept a protective arrangement, but there was only one case in the sample where the application did not proceed because an agreement was made at this stage of the process (**case 59**). Also, where children were still at home when the EPO application was served, the social worker might offer to arrange temporary care for the child so the parent could focus on getting ready for the hearing. Such arrangements also removed concerns that parents would disappear with the child, or that the child would be at greater risk because of the stress on the parent. In **case 22**, the social worker made doubly sure that the child was protected by arranging for two police officers to accompany her and take the child into police protection if the parent rejected the offer of temporary accommodation for the child. The police presence was sufficient to obtain his co-operation and the child was made subject to an EPO later that day.

Serving the EPO papers gave the social workers a chance to emphasise to the parents the importance of obtaining legal advice and attending the hearing. A social worker in Area J recalled how she had persuaded the parents to attend court for the EPO:

> And they said they were not coming and I said it would be inadvisable for them not to come, 'You must really come because you've got – you're part of the hearing and you can have a solicitor if you like.' All the rest of it – so when we got to court, they did come. (Social worker, Area J)

In all six local authorities, social workers were generally expected by local authority lawyers to urge the parents to get representation. Some individual lawyers went further to ensure that the parents were represented by good child care lawyers, emphasising the importance of representation in a letter accompanying the documents and even providing names of specific firms or telling the social workers to show parents the listings for family lawyers in the Yellow Pages. This helped both the parents and the local authority.

> If it's on abridged notice then I'll do a covering letter with the papers and I'll stick in the usual clause at the bottom saying – 'urge you to get independent legal advice from a solicitor specialising in public law Children Act matters.' And [I] always try and ask the social worker to hand deliver the stuff . . . and to urge upon the parent that they should get representation. If someone pitches up at court unrepresented – I'll introduce myself and sort of say the same thing there and then. (Local Authority Lawyer, Area E)

Although most social workers thought that parents needed to be involved and should attend the hearing, some expressed concerns about the destructive effect of the proceedings on the parents and the problems of managing the process with the parents present. Stating the concerns about parenting openly could help the parents to understand their seriousness but made for a highly charged situation where parents might lose control.

> I mean obviously parents need to be involved you know straight from the off as much as possible and that's always the intention because this is their children's lives that we're talking about – that we're going to court for. I do feel for parents in the court situation because we find it confusing at times, we don't understand the language and it must be even worse for a lot of parents. It must be – feel very intimidated and frightened by the whole event. I don't think there is a disadvantage only in terms of that they probably just find it very confusing and don't understand and it can be quite frightening for them – a lot of parents because they don't know what to expect. But the advantage for them is that they need to be aware of what's going on straight from the beginning really. It's only fair. (Social worker, Area E)

One social worker had been attacked by a parent at an EPO hearing. Another social workers thought that it was inappropriate to serve the application on a parent who was mentally very unwell, and that it would have been better if the EPO had been heard without giving this parent notice.

> It was the court clerk who really got up my nose, he wanted me to serve papers, because they don't like doing *ex parte* EPOs these days because of the Human Rights Act and everything. He wanted me to go to the hospital casualty department and serve papers on the mother, while she was just recovering from a major seizure. (Social worker, Area J)

Such paternalistic views of the proceedings were uncommon, but social workers (and lawyers) were concerned that parents found it difficult to understand care proceedings, even the comparatively simple proceedings leading to an EPO.

REPRESENTATION IN EPO PROCEEDINGS

Taking Instructions from Parents

The short period of notice, particularly where notice was abridged, gave parents very little time to find a solicitor who could represent them at the hearing, and to give instructions. Solicitors recounted frantic phone calls shortly before the hearing, clients stumbling into the office or being contacted by the child's solicitor or the children's guardian and asked if they could help. Particularly in Area M, contact often came only *after* the EPO had been made. Even where firms had a policy of never turning anyone away they might not be able to attend court on such short notice but solicitors would try to arrange representation though a colleague (who might not be a specialist) or through counsel. Representing parents in EPO cases was difficult, 'not for the faint-hearted'. Parents frequently had a range of problems which undermined their capacity both to care for their children and to engage with the legal process. They were often distressed and scared, and their behaviour could be volatile, angry or tearful. Few were able to seek support from friends or family, partly because of the acute shame they felt at having their children removed.

Solicitors in all three areas felt that the notice period was abridged too readily. In Area J where use of abridged notice was most common, one solicitor said that magistrates' legal advisers did this 'because they did not want to take the risk of not listing cases quickly'. Abridged notice defeated the purpose of notice, which was to allow the parents to get representation. Courts granted it 'automatically', or were 'gung-ho' with the consequence that parents had difficulty obtaining representation; solicitors had 'insufficient time to take instructions' so that it was 'not possible to prepare the case.' In Area M, it was exceptional for solicitors to be instructed before the EPO had been granted unless they had been involved in earlier proceedings relating to a sibling. Solicitors in the other areas gave accounts of being asked by the magistrates' legal adviser if they could represent a parent when they were at court for another case, of only seeing a copy of the application when they arrived at court and having to prepare without any papers about the case.

> I got this phone call at half past five on the Thursday and I arrived cold at court the following morning and just got things thrown at me. I took the instructions from the client on the hoof and then I had this very thick wedge of paperwork give to me. That's right, she had had papers, the client had received papers and she had brought them to court and I went through them with one eye and listened to her with one ear and took it in that way. (Solicitor, Area E)

Indeed, some lawyers (including some working for local authorities) viewed without notice applications as 'fairer to parents' than abridged notice. Parents given a short period of notice could attend the hearing but were probably not able to participate in it fully. However, if they had notice and attended, they lost the opportunity to challenge the EPO after 72 hours (s.45(9), (10)).

> What I said about Article 6 was that sometimes if the court is going to give you on notice hearing but very abridged notice for an hour or something which they did in that particular case, I think it's actually less human rights compliant than dealing with an *ex parte*. Because you've got a mum who's in a distressed state who's got an hour to go and get a solicitor – well it's not very realistic and in that particular case there was no solicitor because there was no time. But what there was, was a mum in a distressed state trying to deal with a court process. It might have been better to have granted the order *ex parte* and you know to have the ICO subsequently and give her an opportunity. All it did was upset her I think. (Local Authority Lawyer, Area E)

Representation for Children, the Involvement of CAFCASS

Emergency protection order applications are 'specified' proceedings. Consequently the magistrates' legal adviser is required to appoint a children's guardian 'as soon as practicable' after proceedings have begun, unless they consider that this is 'not necessary to safeguard the interests of the child' (Family Proceedings Courts (Children Act) Rules 1991, r.10(1)). Prior to the establishment of CAFCASS, there were agreements in some areas to ensure that the children's guardian service was alerted when EPO applications were being made, even where no notice was given to the parents. Although the duty guardian schemes, which were established in some areas when the Children Act was implemented, had mostly been abandoned, some panel managers were able to identify children's guardians to attend EPO hearings. In six of the magistrates' courts areas in the National Survey, the legal adviser said that children's guardians were appointed even for *ex parte* EPO applications, but in 12 others a guardian was never appointed in such cases. Even where a guardian was appointed, he or she might have pressing commitments in other cases and be unavailable for the hearing. In these circumstances, guardians would try to instruct a solicitor for the child who was able to attend. Similarly, where there is delay in appointing a guardian, the courts may arrange the appointment of a solicitor so that the child is represented but in such a case this solicitor would not have any instructions.

The shortage of children's guardians after the establishment of CAFCASS undermined arrangements for children's representation in EPO cases. In many parts of the country it was not possible to appoint a guardian when proceedings were started (House of Commons, 2003, paras 59–63). No specific protocols were agreed between local authorities and CAFCASS to ensure early notification of EPO applications. There are areas where children's guardians are appointed for EPOs but the CAFCASS service standard – 80 per cent of public law appointments to be made within seven days (CAFCASS, 2003, 24) – means that EPO proceedings are likely to be completed before a guardian becomes available. In none of the cases where the High Court has criticised the use of *ex parte* EPOs has the court appointed a children's guardian for the EPO hearing. Even CAFCASS's proposals for early intervention will not ensure that children's guardian are routinely available for EPOs (CAFCASS, 2005).

The crisis in CAFCASS impacted on the representation in both Areas M and E. Children's guardians were only appointed for the EPO in three out of 31 cases and 16 out of 35 cases, respectively. In Area J, where more than half of the sample related to cases started before the creation of CAFCASS, a children's guardian was appointed in 15 out of 19 cases.

The impact of short notice or without notice proceedings on parents' and children's representation for EPOs is clear from Table 7.2. Overall, a parent was represented in only 38 cases (45 per cent of the sample) and in another five cases parents attended without representation. A similar proportion of children were represented but in only just over a quarter (24 cases) did children have the benefit of tandem representation from a children's guardian and a solicitor.

As might be expected, parents were far more likely to be represented where the EPO application was made on full notice than where notice was abridged. The parent was represented in 24 cases heard on notice (71 per cent of these applications) and 13 short notice cases (50 per cent of this sample), see Table 7.2. The single application heard without notice in the presence of the mother's lawyer was made at a directions hearing following an incident where the mother had removed one child and disappeared. The local authority then

Table 7.2   Attendance and representation of parents and children at EPO

EPO type	Without notice	Short notice	On notice	Total
Attendance at EPO: LA only	24	9	9	42
Parent	0	4	1	5
Parent and lawyer	0	12	18	30
Parent's lawyer	1	1	6	8
Percentage parent represented	**4%**	**50%**	**71%**	**45%**
Children's guardian	0	3	3	6
Child's solicitor	1	4	5	10
Children's guardian and solicitor	2	4	18	24
Percentage child represented	**12%**	**42%**	**76%**	**47%**
Total	25	26	34	85[1]

[1] Missing data in one case.

used the opportunity provided by the directions hearing to seek an EPO (**case 5–6**).

The courts' willingness to hear cases without notice also impacted on the availability of a children's guardian. In only three cases where no notice was given, was there representation for the child. These three cases all concerned children who were being removed by EPO in the course of existing proceedings relating to them or their siblings. In contrast, children were represented in almost three-quarters of all cases where notice was given (see Table 7.2). As might be expected, Area M, which had the highest rates of use of *without notice* EPOs, also had the lowest rates for attendance by parents, parents' lawyers, children's guardians and solicitors for children. Overall, proceedings in Area M were more like those for Place of Safety Orders prior to the Children Act than the EPO proceedings in the other two areas. The lack of representation for children in these proceedings resulted from a shortage of children's guardians, hearing EPOs without full notice and the lack of any system for early notification of CAFCASS by local authorities or the courts where EPO cases were expected. Although the appointment of a children's guardian had been established as one of the safeguards against making EPOs inappropriately, a combination of practices had undermined this.

THE HEARING

Despite encouragement from social workers, many parents who were given the opportunity to attend the EPO proceedings did not do so. Overall, a parent attended the hearing in only 35 cases (41 per cent of the sample). Out of 60 EPO applications heard on notice, there were 18 (30 per cent) where the parent neither attended nor was represented. In a further five cases (12 per cent) a parent attended, without representation (see Table 7.2). Only four of the 16 mothers whose babies were removed at birth attended the EPO hearing; in three of these cases, care proceedings were already under way in relation to the baby's older siblings. Another four mothers were represented but did not attend. Where only a lawyer attended this was because the mother was still in hospital or was not in a fit state to attend. There appeared to be no provision for hearing these cases at the hospital to allow the mother's participation, a practice that occurs when the High Court has to make decisions about the treatment of critically ill people. Even fewer fathers were involved where babies were removed. Only two attended the proceedings and three others had legal representation. There were only two cases where both parents attended with lawyers. In **case 1** (see p. 114 above), all the planning for the child's removal had taken place without the parents being told, police protection had been used to protect the child from birth and the hearing was on full notice. In **case 56**, the parents already had legal representation because there were care proceedings relating to their other children. The fathers in the two other cases with concurrent proceedings did not have parental responsibility and only became parties later.

Representing Parents

Representing parents in EPO cases was not easy. The lack of information, the limited time to prepare, which usually precluded obtaining other views about the children's care, and the low hurdle the legislation set for the local authority meant that the chances that the court would refuse the order were 'almost zero'. Although some solicitors noted that the evidence presented was 'overwhelming', others said that it was often unsatisfactory. This appeared to be a fair reflection of the cases. Local authorities had a lot of information about parental failings and inadequate care but social worker's gave second- and third-hand accounts of incidents and repeated doctor's opinions, which were sometimes not reflected in detailed reports that were only received much later. However, this evidence was sufficient to satisfy the court of the need for the order. The only possible counter-evidence came from parents but they were rarely in a fit state to marshal or present it.

> Realistically [parents] don't have much of a chance [to oppose an EPO] because often all the eggs are in the local authority's basket – they usually have reams of paper of evidence ... and to be able to go through that and get evidence to challenge that in [a] very short timeframe is very difficult. (Solicitor, Area M)

The way the case was handled from the beginning was regarded as funda- mental. It set the tone for the future relationship between the parent and the social worker; parents might begin to show that they had some insight into their difficulties and could work with social services or reveal a complete lack of understanding of their children's needs. One common strategy solicitors used was to discourage parents from contesting the EPO and to encourage them to co-operate with social services. Parents were bound to lose contests over EPOs and this might destroy any relationship with the social worker. Getting parents to accept this strategy was not easy; some clients wanted to fight even though it was hopeless.

> I sometimes see people seeking to fight EPO cases that are absolutely hopeless, that they have no prospect of winning and worse than that what you find is that a social worker is put in a witness box and challenged quite hopelessly in front of the mother and has to say all sorts of things about the mother at a key time when the best chance for the parents to be reunited with the child is to co-operate with the social services ... (Solicitor, Area E)

'Sensible' clients accepted advice. However, a few solicitors recounted examples of cases where, acting for parents, they had 'won' and managed to convince the court that an EPO was not required. These cases were exceptional and none related to cases in the sample. It was slightly easier to negotiate an agreement with the local authority, but that involved persuading the parents to agree to a protective arrangement, which usually meant placing or leaving their child in s.20 accommodation. There were seven cases in the sample where an agreement was reached after the local authority had begun proceedings for an EPO but in four of these, the agreement included the local authority starting care proceedings, so the parents were still possibly facing the loss of their child (see Figure 7.1). In addition, in **case 4** (see p. 124) where the social worker had withdrawn the offer of an agreed arrangement when medical staff informed her that the child had been seriously sexually abused, the mother's lawyer brokered an agreement for an ICO with the mother and child being placed at a residential assessment centre. This gave the mother the best chance of retaining care of her child.

In the opinion of many of the solicitors interviewed, once the parents and child were separated the case had been '*lost*', and that set the course of the case for many months. Although it was theoretically possible to re-contest the interim care order which would almost inevitably follow the EPO, some

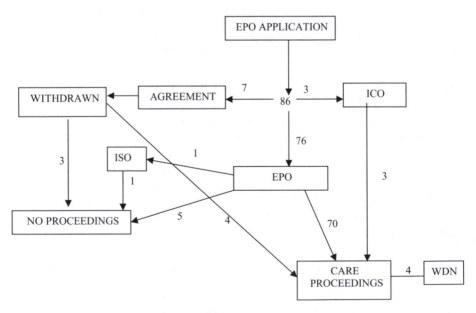

Figure 7.1   Overview of EPO applications (families)

solicitors considered this to be impractical where parent and child were already separated.

> And I suppose there's the thing that if you get an EPO wrong you're in a very difficult situation for the future of that family. When a child is removed inappropriately on an emergency basis, it's very hard to redress the balance. (Solicitor, Area J)

Fighting and losing could also 'sour' the solicitor's relationship with the clients. It was better to find out more about the circumstances and leave any contest to the interim care order application when evidence could be presented on behalf of the parent.

The majority of the cases were unopposed; in half of the cases parents were either unaware of the proceedings or did not attend even though they had been notified. Of the 43 cases where parents attended there were only seven where a parent was actively contesting the EPO application. In another eight cases the length of the hearing (two hours or more) suggested that there was likely to have been some discussion in the court between the parties. Even where cases were contested, it generally became apparent before the end of the hearing that the EPO was inevitable.

> And often what will happen is the afternoon will start off, 'This is contested.' And then after a couple of hours it is contested in name, but in reality it's left to the decision of the court. (Solicitor, Area J)

Conceding that there were grounds for concern which justified an EPO did not mean that there were no issues to be considered. Parents' lawyers wanted to ensure on behalf of their clients that proper plans had been made for children's care and for contact. Given the haste with which EPOs were sought, solicitors felt that sufficient attention was not always given to these matters. Contact was particularly important where babies had been removed if there was to be any chance of the mother regaining care.

Children's Representation

EPO cases also posed problems for the child's representatives. Children's guardians commented that their role was particularly difficult in EPOs; they had little or no time to make any enquiries before the hearing and might therefore only have the information which was presented to the court by the local authority. Sometimes they could speak to the parties at court and occasionally they had knowledge about the family from previous proceedings. Consequently, they generally felt unable to take a position about the application, but sought to ensure that local authority could justify the need for the order. Similarly, children's solicitors felt their role was very limited; most cases concerned very young children so if there was no children's guardian there was no one able to give instructions. In such circumstances, none of the solicitors was willing to oppose the making of the order outright but they might test the evidence by cross-examining the social worker.

The limited availability of representatives for children and the lack of time for any assessment of the child's circumstances meant that the court did not have an alternative professional view about the need for separation of parent and child. This was likely to be most crucial in cases involving newborn babies. However, children's guardians attended only three of the 16 EPO applications relating to babies and in one of these cases there were proceedings underway relating to siblings. It appeared that despite all the planning that had gone into arranging the child's safe birth and removal, proper representation for the baby at the hearing to authorise the removal was not part of the plan. Parents' solicitors were particularly concerned if there was no children's guardian in these cases. They felt that it was wrong for such a momentous decision to be taken without independent social work advice. The parents' best chance of regaining the care of their child was if there could be a placement in a residential family centre, or an agreement that the mother lived with relatives who fostered the child.

> Because if you have got a very strong guardian, particularly ... with newborn babies [the guardian] may say, 'Well, yes, I think there are concerns here but I think this needs to be [a placement at a] mother and baby unit ... ' And be able to put a lot of pressure. Whereas without a guardian ... (Solicitor, Area M)

A local authority solicitor also recalled a case involving a newborn baby where the service manager had refused to consider a residential placement for the mother and baby despite strong legal advice to do so. It now appears clear that the courts do not have the power to order assessments of parents and the decision whether to make such arrangements is a matter for the local authority (*Re G*, 2005).

COURT SCRUTINY OF THE DECISION TO REMOVE OR DETAIN A CHILD

The decision made by the magistrates' legal adviser about notice was crucial for the way the way the EPO application was dealt with in the court. Giving parents the full period of notice substantially increased the likelihood that they would be represented at the hearing, and gave their representative more opportunity to prepare the case. Similarly, a children's guardian was more

Table 7.3 Type of emergency action by area

Emergency action	Area			Total
	J	M	E	
PP at SSD request	9	4	14	27
EPO without notice	1	11	7	19
Short notice EPO	3	6	4	13
Full notice EPO	3	4	6	13
PP by police	1	7	2	10
Total	17	32	33	82[1]

[1]Excludes 4 cases with missing data.

likely to be appointed, to be able to appoint a solicitor and to attend the hearing. The guardian might also have some time for preliminary enquiries. However, more restrictive approaches to hearing EPOs without notice had very little effect on the court's involvement in decisions about emergency removal as Table 7.3 shows.

In Areas J and E where the courts took a restrictive approach to *ex parte* EPOs, local authorities relied on police protection to a considerable extent. Emergency protection was achieved in this way in over 50 per cent of cases in Area J and in over 40 per cent of cases in Area E. In these cases and those where the police acted independently, compulsory separation had already been achieved *before* the case came to court; in effect, the magistrates were being asked to accept that the police decision had been correct and separation should continue. It has been suggested that the process of 'sequentiality' precludes a court making independent decisions in cases where children have already been thought to need protection by another court (Cooper Davies & Barua, 1994). This process may equally prevent a proper assessment by the court of cases where the police have used their powers. The figure for Area M was much lower, only 12.5 per cent of cases started with local authority use of police protection, but more than a third of EPOs were heard there without notice. Overall, EPOs applications on full notice where children had not previously been removed by police protection were uncommon in all three areas, accounting for less than a sixth of the cases in the study.

CONTACT, MEDICAL EXAMINATION AND OTHER DIRECTIONS

Courts granting EPOs also have powers to make directions about contact with the child and medical examinations or other assessments (s.44). Courts were given these powers following concerns raised by Butler-Sloss J in the

Cleveland Inquiry. In Cleveland, many parents were prevented from seeing their children after they had been removed under a place of safety order; this 'caused great distress, much resentment and created great difficulties' and was 'a major ground of complaint' by parents to the Inquiry. The Inquiry considered that local authorities should not be able to restrict parental contact except where the child's safety demanded this but recognised that local authorities might need to control access to foster homes by unreasonable parents (Butler-Sloss, 1988). It recommended that there should be 'a presumption of access' when an EPO is made and that the local authority should be able to apply to the court for an order suspending access where it had good reasons for doing so (para 16.15). Where there is an EPO, the Children Act requires local authorities to allow the child reasonable contact with their family and friends subject to any directions from the court. If the local authority wants to restrict contact further, it can ask for a direction to this effect. Parents and others who want more contact than the local authority is prepared to arrange can also seek a court direction.

In relation to children's health and well-being, the Cleveland Inquiry recognised that local authorities needed to be able to consent to medical examinations and treatment for children subject to EPOs. However, it was concerned that children involved in legal proceedings should be protected from repeated examinations and assessments for forensic purposes. Consequently, it proposed that disputes about these should be referred to the court. An additional safeguard was included in the Court Rules; the court was given discretion to refuse to admit evidence from an assessment of the child where it had not given permission for that assessment (Family Proceedings Rules 1991, r. 4.18).

An EPO gives the local authority sufficient power to protect children in most cases. Requiring 'reasonable contact' permits the local authority to set limits, negotiate arrangements with parents and impose supervision. Similarly, the local authority can make sure that the child receives any medical care that appears necessary. The courts have been given further powers to deal with particular issues that do not routinely occur. They can exclude a person who poses a serious risk to the child from the child's home (s.44A) so that the child can be protected without being removed. Where the child's whereabouts are not known, the court can require a person to disclose information about this, authorise the local authority to search premises and grant a warrant to a police officer to allow entry by force (s.48).

Directions for matters other than contact were made in 22 of the 76 cases where an EPO was made. In 12 cases these concerned medical examinations, six the exclusion of an alleged perpetrator and five search and or entry to the home. None of the people excluded had been living full-time in the child's home, rather they were partners or former partners of the parent who was caring for the child. In all these cases, the directions were sought by local authorities in order to obtain additional formal authority, not merely to sidestep lack of co-operation. Local authorities wanted a direction for a medical examination because they expected to use the report in later care proceedings. For this reason, a magistrates' legal adviser from Area M (where parents were rarely represented at EPO hearings) thought that medical directions should generally be left until the first hearing in the care proceedings so that parents could argue against them.

> I've had applications where they want the child to be medically examined and more often that not I have refused that unless it's a particular reason because I think that sort of thing ought to be under an ICO when people can argue it. Unless there's a particular medical reason; the child suffers from a particular medical condition. But not as a general rule, we can't just have it as a general condition on the EPO. (Magistrates' legal adviser, Area M)

Elsewhere the magistrates' legal advisers did not regard directions for medical assessments as problematic.

Contact

Interviews from all professional groups remarked on the need for contact for children subject to EPOs. Solicitors recognised the importance of contact if parents were going to regain care of their child, and for reducing the stress and distress of the child's removal. Arguing for more contact could demonstrate to a parent client that the solicitor understood their plight and was on their side.

> What [the mother] was concerned about was contact; in fact my initial stance was that the application would be opposed unless the local authority made better, more satisfactory, proposals for contact. (Solicitor, Area J)

Opposing the EPO itself was generally regarded by solicitors as very difficult, unhelpful to parents and unlikely to be successful. Orders were almost always granted consequently, the main role for the parent's solicitor 'is to make sure [there are] proper contact arrangements.'

From the local authority's perspective this could mean that offers to agree to an EPO came with substantial demands for contact which local authority lawyers were reluctant to accept. Contact arrangements were generally considered to be social work matters, to be decided by the social worker and her manager and not brokered between the parents' solicitor and the legal department. Also, contact arrangements could put considerable pressure on carers and on local authority resources for transport or supervision.

> If an EPO is going to be granted, yes [the parents and their solicitor] will agree to it as long as they have evening contact and weekend contact for ten hours at a time; so yes contact's always a big issue. (Local Authority Lawyer, Area E)

Local authority lawyers preferred to leave contact to social workers. They wanted to make sure that contact was considered before the social worker went to court for the EPO because they knew that the magistrates were likely to ask questions about this.

> One of the main things in EPOs is of course to remember the contact – it's the first thing you forget. And try to encourage [the social worker] to set it up before they start and make you know make some comments to the magistrates about what the contact arrangements are. (Local Authority Lawyer, Area E)

Even where the social worker had been primed to think about contact plans, they could still face pressure in the court where the parents' solicitor was seeking to get more contact for his or her clients than the local authority had offered.

> [T]he magistrates were great. But it was drawn out, and it was allowed to go on. And the whole, in comes the cross-questioning for about an hour and a half, not about the application, but about contact, and that could have been dealt with much more quickly I felt. (Social worker, Area J)

Magistrates took it for granted that there would be contact. They expected that they would hear about it from one of the parties and might ask about it if they were not told.

> Certainly the local authority has a duty to promote reasonable contact, we would take that for granted in the first place, but it's a matter which might very easily be mentioned. Parents may be worried about contact and their representative will bring it up. And the normal thing will be that the local authority will accept that that is their responsibility, and an arrangement of some kind will be come to – very often then and there, round the table, that happens quite often. (Magistrate, Area J)

Although considering contact was a routine part of hearing an EPO application, this did not mean that the court commonly made directions for contact. In just over half cases where an EPO was granted were contact arrangements directed by the court, and, in over half of these, contact was stated to be 'at the discretion of the local authority'. Most specific directions were restrictions on contact, requested by the local authority rather than requirements on local authorities to arrange contact beyond what they had proposed. This reflected an understanding on the part of both social workers and magistrates about the arrangements that could and should be made.

There were particular concerns about contact for babies removed at birth, even where it was clear that the baby would be adopted. Contact arrangements were specified for at least one parent in eight cases and, in another four, contact was stated to be at the discretion of the local authority, including with permission to terminate it, in one case of very violent parents. In three other cases, the mother and child were placed together shortly after the EPO was granted. Five days a week contact, usually for 1–2 hours a day was initially allowed in three cases Over time, contact tended to decline; in four cases, at least one parent recorded as finding contact 'difficult' or 'too distressing', or not attending regularly, so contact was reduced but in two cases parents continued to have almost daily contact until the final order. These cases (which were all considered before the High Court raised concerns about separation of babies at birth, *Re M*, 2003; *Kirklees MBC v. S*, 2006) did not lead to major disputes between the local authority, the parents and the court. The magistrates appeared to operate on the principle that the local authority could be trusted in relation to contact, rather than on the basis that it needed to be controlled.

OUTCOME

The *Judicial Statistics* (Department for Constitutional Affairs, 2003) indicate that approximately 90 per cent of applications for an EPO result in an EPO being made (see Table 1.1). Figure 7.1 illustrates outcomes in the study on the basis of families rather than children. With one exception (**cases 53 and 54**, described in Chapter 5) the EPO application in relation to each child in the family was treated in the same way. Basing the data on families rather than children avoids the distortion that would otherwise occur due to the differing sizes of the families in the study. Out of applications in respect of 86 families (127 children), 76 (115 children) were made subject to an EPO. This amounts to a success rate of 90.5 per cent. However, no application was refused.

The 10 cases that did not result in orders were either withdrawn following agreements between the local authority and the parents (seven cases), or led directly to interim care orders (three cases). A closer look at the seven withdrawn cases suggests that the local authorities may have identified the risk to the children as lower in these cases. Three of these applications were made on full notice and two on short notice and these five were made without prior use of police protection. The other two cases started with police protection and were also heard on full notice. In all but one of the cases, which resulted in an agreement rather than an order, it was clear that either the parents were represented or there was a children's guardian. It is likely that these professionals were able to broker an agreement when the local authority had not tried to do so or had been refused by the parent. In **case 59**, the mother agreed to go to a refuge with her child, but it was not clear whether she had independent legal advice.

In all three cases where an ICO was made, parents were represented and their lawyers were involved in negotiating the agreement which resulted in an interim care order rather than an EPO. In one case there was a problem with fixing a hearing within eight days, the agreement for a nine day order (which had to be an ICO) solved this problem. This case provides an example of the lawyers reaching agreements that facilitate the working of the system rather than sticking to the formalities (which required three days notice for an ICO). In the other two cases, arrangements were made for the mother and child to go to a residential assessment centre. There was no advantage to any of the parties to return to court before a preliminary assessment had been completed. ICOs were made for three and four weeks in these cases, again without the notice period.

Length of EPOs

The National Survey indicated that across the country there were varying approaches to the length of EPOs. Although some magistrates' legal advisers were keen to stress that each case was considered individually, others indicated that this happened in the context of standard practices. Twelve stated that EPOs were always made for the 'shortest possible time', or 'as short as practicable', but did not indicate a length in days. Another eight said that the length of the order was fixed to fit in with the next court date, a response which was not inconsistent with the first, given that EPOs were generally followed by interim care order applications. There were five legal advisers who indicated a short period in days 'five days is as long as we go', 'never longer than four days if ex parte', 'three or four days, whatever the local authority wants', but the remaining 11 replied that orders always lasted for seven or eight days. One noted that 'longer orders may help sort out arrangements' for all the parties. Six legal advisers specifically said that the introduction of the Human Rights Act had led to shorter orders being granted, this was also said to be the case, initially, in Area E.

> Following the HRA, we revised our policy . . . because prior to the HRA I have to say generally whatever length of order the local authority were looking for we would consider to be acceptable bearing in mind it's up to eight day maximum anyway. Since the HRA came into force, it's less likely now that we will make them for the full eight day period . . . the magistrates are very aware now of the need to ensure that the order is proportionate and the length of time is absolutely necessary and what's going to happen within that period of time. (Magistrates' legal adviser)

Concern about the excessive length of Place of Safety Orders (maximum 28 days) was a major reason for the Children Act reform. EPOs last for a maximum of eight days and can be extended once for up to seven days. EPOs are usually followed by care proceedings. A key factor in determining the length of the EPO is allowing sufficient time for the local authority to prepare its interim care order application. In all three areas, magistrates' legal advisers said that it was usual to make the EPO for the full eight days. In practice, the availability of court time to hear the expected ICO application dictated the length of the order. As one magistrates' legal adviser put it:

> [The magistrates] make it the full eight days because [the local authority] don't put the ICO application with the EPO, that follows on. And of course you've got to give the three days' notice for the ICO, we do insist on that three days because otherwise the local authority get quite relaxed about it. They think the court will waive service, but we insist they give them the three days. (Magistrates' legal adviser, Area M)

A local authority lawyer in the same area gave a slightly different interpretation:

> It seems an almost total expectation that an EPO will run for eight days. The court will refine it according to when their next family [proceedings] day will be, they will expect that we are issuing proceedings for an ICO but commonly say if it was on a Friday they will make it for the next Wednesday, their family [proceedings] day. They will ask, 'Are you thinking of going for an ICO?' and then make it Wednesday. If we say, 'Don't know.' they may give it seven or eight days. (Local Authority Lawyer, Area M)

The practice of fitting the length of the EPO to fit with the days on which family proceedings were usually held was referred to by local authority solicitors in all three areas. But orders were most commonly for seven or eight days (see Table 7.4).

Despite the implementation of the Human Rights Act, at the time of the court study it appeared that a higher proportion of orders granted *without* notice were made for seven or eight days than those granted on notice (see Table 7.4). Differences between the three areas were not statistically significant. Where no notice is given, it is open for the parents to apply to have the order discharged after three days so there is an opportunity for parents to challenge these long orders. However, there were no instances of this having occurred in the sample. Indeed, such applications were very unusual; one adviser interviewed for the national survey recalled that a complaint had been made when time could not be found to hear such an application.

Table 7.4 Length of initial EPOs granted with and without notice

Order length	Without notice	%	With notice	%
Up to 4 days	2	7.7	6	11.3
5–6 days	3	11.5	11	20.8
7 days	4	15.4	13	24.5
8 days	17	65.4	20	37.7
ICO made			3	5.7
Total	26	100	53	100

As might be expected, local authority solicitors preferred longer orders, so that the social services department could consider thoroughly any future action and to prepare documents for care proceedings. This also gave parents who had not been represented at the EPO hearing time to obtain representation. The fact that the order was made for the maximum period was seen not to be a disadvantage to the parents or child because the child had to be returned if he or she was no longer at risk of significant harm.

> Generally we try and get them for the maximum amount of time, because I think you need, you need that period of time for the situation to calm down, for the parents as well. And to work out a meaningful plan. If you're going to go for care proceedings, [there is a] huge amount of work to do in terms of formulating a care plan, in terms of witness statements, social workers actually writing statements and getting all the evidence together, sorting out placements, sorting out assessments. So there's so much to do that you actually need that period of time in between, and even then if you get an eight day order, it's a rush to actually get it all done. (Local authority Lawyer, Area J)

Extensions of EPOs were not common, there were only 13 applications relating to 22 children and one of these (relating to two children) was withdrawn. Half of the renewals granted were for the maximum seven days, but a quarter were for only one day. Renewals occurred because the local authority wanted more time to plan its future action, or, in the case of very short renewals, because the court was unable to hear the ICO application when the EPO expired and formal arrangements were needed to secure the child's protection in the interim. In a contentious case, the EPO might be extended to facilitate transfer of the case so that the first interim care order application could be heard in the county court. Extensions were often agreed without any substantive hearing. The withdrawn extension application occurred because the parents' solicitor refused to agree; he sought to establish that his clients would co-operate by allowing their child to remain accommodated, thus beginning to build a case against a care order. Overall, 65 cases led to EPOs being made for eight days or less; of the remaining 14 cases, 11 were extended EPOs and three were ICOs. There were only three cases relating to six children where an initial EPO of eight days was followed by an extension of seven days.

Perspectives on the High Success Rate of EPO Applications

There are four possible explanations for the high success rate in applications. Each may operate individually or in combination with the others. First, the law may provide the court with no alternative but to make the order. Second, the conservative approach of applicants (local authorities) and their lawyers may ensure that only strong cases are presented to the court. Third, respondents and their lawyers may be ineffective in challenging applications. Fourth, the court may fail to scrutinise applications sufficiently, routinely favouring the applicants, regardless of the case they present or that of the respondents. Interviews with those concerned with EPOs supported all these explanations, whilst generally accepting that most orders were appropriately made.

Solicitors in private practice, local authority lawyers and magistrates' legal advisers agreed that the test for an EPO was easily satisfied. 'The balance weighs in the favour of the local authority heavily for obvious, reasons.' Unless the parents would agree to an alternative protective arrangement the court had no real options. It had to choose between making the order and protecting the child, or refusing it and leaving the child at risk. A solicitor in private practice reflected on the dilemma for the court:

> the court is placed in a difficult situation – 'Does it do absolutely nothing or does it step in?' By the time everyone's arrived in court, etc., usually speaking, people are thinking, 'If we've got here, something must be pretty serious...' (Solicitor, Area J)

And where applications were heard *ex parte*, all the court had to do was decide whether the local authority had made out its case.

> There is no one there you see; it is not opposed usually. I have never had an opposed one; I have never even had an EPO where the parents have been there. So there is no [reason] for [the magistrates] to go away and ... the facts are what I've written. The social worker's just given her evidence – those are the facts. They are not disputed because there's no one there to dispute them and the reasons are if they don't make the order, the child is likely to suffer significant harm because of abuse, neglect, abandonment. It's simple; they don't make a meal of it. (Magistrates' legal adviser, Area M)

It was also clear that the local authorities in the study each took care to ensure that there was a case in law and a social work need for seeking an EPO before an EPO application was made. Magistrates trusted local authorities only to bring cases where EPOs were warranted. A local authority solicitor summed up the position acknowledging that both proper applications should not be refused and the courts tended to assume that where an application had been made the children needed protection:

> I think once you get there, unless you really are up the creek on your criteria, then the court is going to probably be minded to grant your order. They tend to think there's no smoke without a fire and usually the evidence is sound enough. (Local Authority Lawyer, Area E)

Although solicitors in private practice occasionally challenged applications this was a difficult course of action. The evidence presented by the local authority was 'overwhelming'; lack of time and information meant that solicitors had nothing to set against it. In these circumstances, contest was impracticable and 'bound to fail'. And in many cases, contest at this early stage was not a strategy that would assist their clients to secure the care of their children for the future.

Lawyers thought that magistrates 'tend to take the safe option' and would not want to risk refusing an order if this mean the parent having care of the child. This view was reflected in comments from magistrates in all three areas. The damage to the child of a short-term removal was slight compared with the risk of leaving him or her in a dangerous situation. The anxiety provoked by allowing a child to remain at risk was profound.

> If the child was going to be at harm, at any risk, then one's not prepared to take [the responsibility for refusing]. You know you can be appealed. You can't go home if you think that you've left a child at risk. (Magistrate, Area E)

THE BALANCE OF POWER IN EPO PROCEEDINGS

Child protection provokes anxiety in all who have responsibility for it, the more so because of community expectations that children will be safe and the climate of blame that has followed public exposure of failures. Sharing responsibility may reduce anxiety but professionals may still feel personally responsible for the decisions they take. In this context, a power that can be exercised to protect children effectively operates as a duty which allows for no alternative course of action.

Emergency protection orders are sought for the protection of children but this action is taken for them, not with them. Children caught up in EPO proceedings are powerless; their young age means that they cannot influence the decisions taken directly, and most have no access to independent professionals who can represent their interests to the court. Parents have only slightly more power. They may be able to avoid compulsory intervention by agreeing a protective arrangement for their children, but have little opportunity to negotiate its terms. Such agreements may be more disadvantageous to their future as parents than court orders. Agreements are not time limited; unless parents retain good contact and have help to improve their situation, there is a real danger that the relationships with their children will be irrevocably damaged. Representation by a specialist child care lawyer gives parents access to a partisan professional who understands how the system works and can help them to achieve the best resolution in their circumstances. However, parents have no opportunity to obtain such support if the order is obtained without notice, and even when notice is given, they have very little time to do so. Representation provides little power when the representative has no time to prepare the case. In most EPO cases, parents' representatives can only ensure that the process is explained to parents and their contact with their children is properly considered.

Jurisdiction over EPOs is mostly exercised by those who are on the lowest rung of the judicial hierarchy. Most magistrates who do this work do so only part-time and have no professional qualification in law. They depend on their clerk for advice about the law. The key decisions whether the parents are notified and whether a children's guardian is available are also made by the magistrates' legal adviser and by CAFCASS. Unless the local authority's evidence is tested and alternative views are presented to the court, there is no option for the magistrates but to make the order requested. As a magistrate reflected,

> It has usually gone through the clerks and they have sorted it for want of a better word, whether it is *ex parte* and the legal side of it is sorted so that by the time it comes to us it is reasonably cut and dried. (Magistrate, Area M)

Although magistrates decide whether the order is granted this is a matter of formal responsibility rather than the exercise of power.

Social services' action to separate parent and child before the court hearing, either through requesting police protection or by forced accommodation (Department of Health, 2001) effectively removes the crucial decision of intervention in the family from the scrutiny of the court. In addition, the fact that the police have seen fit to remove the child and the legal adviser has allowed a hearing *ex parte* or on short notice indicates the action the magistrates are expected to take. Although local authority decisions on emergency intervention are formally subject to court control, local authorities have considerable influence over the way cases are presented to the courts, both in terms of decisions taken before proceedings and the information provided. As regular users of the courts they are 'repeat players' (Blumberg, 1967) who can both respond to the court's expectations and influence court practice. By turning to the police rather than disputing court decisions about giving notice, local authority lawyers can maintain the confidence of the courts in their standards and ensure that the local authority can secure children's protection whenever it thinks this is required.

Social workers' decisions to seek emergency powers are (as indicated in Chapter 6) subject to internal controls. Cases that emerge from this process are almost certain to result in orders. Local authority lawyers and magistrates' legal advisers have substantial influence on the progress of cases but even they can only change their course, not usually their outcome. Overall, the power the court appears to have over the local authority is illusory, alternatives are rarely open to the court and concern to protect overrides other considerations.

8

THE EPO AND AFTERWARDS

INTRODUCTION

This chapter reviews the EPO proceedings and what happened afterwards. The cases in the study were tracked through their court records to the final hearing of any care application; interviews with social workers and lawyers generally took place after the proceedings had finished. The combination of court records and practitioner interviews provide a picture of care proceedings in a sample of cases, which started with an application for an EPO between 2000 and 2002, in the three areas.

The closure that the end of the care proceedings appeared to achieve occurred only for the courts and the lawyers, not for the children, their families and the social workers. The end of legal proceedings meant that the children's legal position was clarified, not that their care arrangements were settled and satisfactory. The legal process produces formal decisions but these may not reflect arrangements in practice. Just as the application for the EPO marked the start of the legal process, but not usually the families' involvement with social services, the ending of proceedings did not resolve all the issues about the children's care. Consequently, the view provided here is quite limited; it focuses on the proceedings and the plans but cannot indicate how children fared in the long term. Nevertheless, the information it provides about proceedings extends knowledge and understanding about the role of emergency intervention.

FROM EPO APPLICATION TO CARE PROCEEDINGS

There was a general expectation amongst all the professionals involved in EPO cases that most orders would be followed by care proceedings and, usually, with an application for an interim care order (ICO). This expectation was reflected in practices in local authority legal departments and the courts. Some local authority lawyers prepared the care application forms at the same time as the EPO forms, using the same information, or asked the social worker to do so. This allowed the lawyer to lodge the ICO application when they were at court for the EPO hearing, and occasionally to get agreement from the other parties and the court for an ICO instead of an EPO, as happened in three cases in the study. It also meant that, after the EPO had been obtained, attention could be focused on the plan for the child's future care rather than the basis for the order.

> I've asked social workers to [complete the C1, C11 and the C13] before. To prepare them all because it is actually possible to then – while you're at the court – to issue the ICO application. If you know it's going to be an ICO . . . (Local Authority Lawyer, Area E)

Courts generally fixed the length of EPOs so that cases would easily fit with their timetabled 'family days' and the subsequent ICO application could be listed for a hearing when family magistrates would be available at court. Even though the same magistrates rarely heard both the EPO application and the first ICO hearing, they too expected that most EPOs would lead on to care proceedings.

> Unless you actually pick it up again at the ICO stage you never really know what happened in that particular case. I'm sure it's quite possible for an EPO to be made but for it not to go onto ICO because social services use some other intervention. I don't know what statistics are but I would – my gut feeling – my guess would be that probably the vast majority of EPOs [children] go on into care. (Magistrate, Area E)

Indeed, one magistrates' legal adviser took the view that most of the EPO applications should really have been started with an ICO application, often long before the EPO had finally been sought.

> What concerns me most that it's not really an application for an EPO, that a lot of the cases that come in really should be on for a first time ICO, and for whatever reason that hasn't happened, and then presumably somebody is in panic and decides that . . . it should be an EPO hearing, so that's a concern. There is also a concern that a lot of the cases there is a long history of involvement with the family, so question mark why hasn't something been done before, when I say a long history I mean years' worth, not just a few months. (Magistrates' legal adviser, Area E)

Social workers, local authority lawyers and solicitors who acted for parents or children explained the normal progress of EPO cases to care proceedings in terms of the types of cases where EPOs were sought and the problems of parents whose children were removed or detained using emergency orders. Care proceedings were used in cases where there were chronic concerns; in these cases a crisis might result in an EPO but it was un-usual for the problems, or the difficulties in obtaining parental co-operation, to resolve quickly.

> [T]here was no doubt that we met the criteria for the risk of significant harm, that we would be in court the next week if we got [the EPO] for interim care orders ... because we were going to initiate care proceedings as a result of that. (Social worker, Area M)

> I don't know why this might be but most cases that start with an EPO do tend to go into interim care orders, as opposed to cases that you might think we'll apply for an interim care order, but end up coming away from court with no order, but just an agreement and the care proceedings continuing by agreement. I think an EPO because of the nature of why you sought one, tends to more naturally lead into interim care orders. (Local Authority Lawyer, Area E)

> Normally an EPO is on the basis that ... because the care ... by one or both parents is of such concern that [the local authority] have to remove a child. So then it must follow because of the level of concern often ICOs are issued. (Solicitor, Area J)

Where there had been no recent social work involvement, as in some of the cases where non-accidental injuries had been identified at a hospital Accident and Emergency Department, the local authority had to consider whether care proceedings were required. In these cases, the short duration of the EPO provided too little time to complete assessments so an ICO was required unless the co-operation of the family could be relied on.

> Well obviously we needed time to assess the parents anyway and obviously there were a lot of issues; cannot be done in a very short time. EPO lasts eight days and obviously there's no way that we could have done anything significantly in eight days. So we needed an ICO that gives us time to do assessments. And it was obvious that this family needed to be assessed in respect of their capability. (Social worker, Area E) (**case 92**, see Chapter 5)

> In true emergency situations social services don't actually know whether they're going to have to issue care proceedings. That's the whole point about the EPO, it's a holding order while social services get their evidence together and do their initial investigations to see whether there actually has to be care proceedings. It may be there are other members of the family that can come forward and care ... (Local Authority Lawyer, Area E)

It was not usually possible to carry out enquiries or assessments in the short time provided by an EPO, and for this reason Hunt suggested that a longer or-der could be useful (Hunt, 1998). However, providing for these investigations to take place whilst an ICO is in place allows the parents and the children's guardian to make representations about them, and the court to supervise the instruction of experts and the timetabling of reports.

Overall, 77 out of the 86 EPO applications were followed by care proceedings (see Figure 7.1). Out of the 127 children originally made the subject of an EPO application, 115 were included in a care application. The 77 cases included three where the application for an EPO had resulted in an ICO and four where the EPO application was withdrawn following an agreement with the parents on the basis that proceedings would be started. There were only five cases where an EPO was granted, but it was not followed by care proceedings, and three where the EPO application was withdrawn and no subsequent public law proceedings involving the child were started during the study. There was one case where the local authority obtained an interim supervision order (ISO) following the EPO and did not pursue further legal action once this expired.

CASES NOT FOLLOWED BY CARE PROCEEDINGS

It was unusual for an EPO application not to be followed by care proceedings. This could happen where the conflict between the family and social services over the care of the child was resolved by an agreement for the child's protection; where a closer examination of the circumstances indicated that the child was not at risk of significant harm or where the crisis quickly resolved, for example through new arrangements for the child's care. Although the local authority's decision not to continue proceedings might suggest that the application had been precipitous or inappropriate, it might equally indicate that social workers had managed to gain parental co-operation or had worked with parents to achieve resolution of a crisis.

There were only eight cases involving nine children without any care proceedings; in addition, three children from one family were made the subject of an interim supervision order for 56 days (the maximum period). These proceedings were not continued apparently because the very limited co-operation from the family suggested that further intervention was unlikely to achieve improvement in the children's well-being. These eight cases included three of the seven cases where the EPO application had also been withdrawn. In these three cases, the commencement of proceedings with strong possibility that the children would be removed appeared to have led at least one parent to agree to an arrangement that secured sufficient protection for their child. One mother, who was a victim of repeated and severe domestic violence, moved to a refuge to protect herself and her child from the perpetrator (**case 59**). At the instigation of social services, a father obtained a prohibited steps order at the EPO hearing. This barred the mother, a drug user whom the father had asked to care for the child, from unsupervised contact with their child (**case 13**). In the third case, the only one relating to a family completely unknown to social services before the incident, the parents had removed the child from hospital and disappeared after non-accidental injuries were diagnosed. The child was located following a police search and taken into police protection. The parents and social services reached agreement at the court door; further proceedings appeared to be contemplated but had not been started within six months; the professionals involved were not interviewed and it was unclear how the child was protected (**case 11**).

In the remaining five cases, an EPO was granted but the local authority did not then seek a care order. In **case 35** (see Chapter 5), the EPO had been obtained with a recovery order so that Corinne, who had run away from her children's home and was becoming involved with sex and drugs, could be returned and placed in secure accommodation. Her mother agreed with this plan, so there was no need for a care order. In **case 23**, the local authority appeared to be quite indecisive whether the child needed to be protected. There were longstanding problems about the lone father's co-operation with professionals over the care and treatment of his children who had health and behaviour problems. The EPO application was made in response to concerns that the father was in a relationship with a woman who had previously harmed her own children. The father denied this but the woman was seen with his child on a number of occasions. Following the granting of the EPO, an ICO application was completed but never issued. A year later, in similar circumstances, a second EPO application was granted and followed by an ICO. A supervision order was made at the final hearing of the care proceedings. The other three cases all resulted in a change of carer from mother to father. The procedures followed in two of these cases raise concerns about the use of EPOs and role and responsibility of local authorities in disputes between parents.

Parents who cannot agree about the care of their children when they separate can apply to the court for a residence order. If the dispute remains unresolved, the court determines residence, applying the welfare principle. In order to do this the court usually hears from the parties and any witnesses, and obtains a report from the Children and Family Court Advisory and Support Service (CAFCASS) or occasionally from a local authority that has been working with the family. Parents have opportunities to put their case to the court and to cross-examine the other parent's witnesses and the CAFCASS officer. The judge must give reasons for the decision. This process was followed in **case 119**. The father applied for residence of his children because he was concerned that their mother was neglecting them. The mother was granted interim residence on condition that she lived with her own father. However, she moved away and continued to leave the children unattended while she went in search of drugs. The children were found alone and taken into police protection; the father was contacted. The local authority did not think it appropriate to place the children with the father as he did not have parental responsibility and there was a court order granting residence to the mother. The children were placed in temporary foster care whilst the father renewed his application for residence. As soon as the father obtained an interim residence order the children were placed in his care. The local authority made no further applications.

In contrast, in both **cases 10** and **14** (see Chapter 6), the local authority removed the children and transferred their care from their mothers to their fathers without any assessment or proceedings. In both these cases, the circumstances in which the EPO was obtained were questionable. **Case 10** involved no harm to the child but a breach by the grandmother of an agreement that the mother would not be left alone with the child. The father's behaviour also gave cause for concern. There was a long history of domestic violence in the family and the father had a recent conviction for 'aggravated something'. Nevertheless, the local authority arranged for him to collect the child after the EPO had been granted. In **case 14**, the child had bruises which he said had been caused by his brother during contact at his father's house. He was taken into police protection and, with his father's consent, to hospital for a medical examination. The medical examination found that this explanation was consistent with the injuries. Although the parents were already involved in residence and contact proceedings, the local authority obtained an EPO rather than leaving the father to seek an interim residence order. The social worker explained this decision:

> [Y]ou could argue that maybe the father could have gone and applied for an interim residence order because they were already in private proceedings, hence then we wouldn't have to have had an EPO. I don't know the thinking behind it, what people were thinking at the time, but we obviously felt we needed to share parental responsibility with an EPO. (Social worker, Area J)

Six of these nine cases (including the ISO) came from Area J, there were two cases from Area M (**cases 35** and **59**) and one from Area E (**case 119**). It appears from the detailed examination of these cases that care proceedings were avoided largely because issues had been resolved. Transfer of care or separation from the perpetrator had ended crises in five of the cases and in three others court orders had achieved this. However, there were three cases where it was not clear that EPO proceedings had been required. Although relationships appeared fraught in **case 14**, the dispute between the parents could have been placed before the court with the local authority providing evidence about the child's care in each household. In **case 59**, the application appeared precipitous and was withdrawn before the hearing after the mother agreed to go to a refuge. In **case 10**, it was far from clear that the child was safer in the care of the father than with the mother and grandmother. The local authority certainly did not have sufficient information to establish this. It did however, inform the social services department for the area where the father went to live so that it was aware of the previous concerns.

Although almost a third of applications for EPOs in Area J were either withdrawn or did not result in care proceedings (or both) there was nothing specific in the way applications were handled in the local authority which distinguished it from the other local authorities in the study. Social workers needed the agreement of their managers and of the legal department to seek an EPO, and approaches to this decision appeared similarly rigorous. However, a recent highly publicised child abuse inquiry may have made lawyers and social workers more willing to take compulsory action in cases of doubt. In contrast, a local authority lawyer from Area E noted that the practice of lawyers attending case conferences had helped avoid proceedings.

THE IMPACT OF THE EPO ON SOCIAL WORKERS' RELATIONS WITH PARENTS

For most families and most social workers the EPO was only an incident (albeit a major one) in a continuing relationship that was already likely to be poor. In over half the cases (46) social services had intervened, through the courts or with the assistance of the police, without giving prior notice to parents, and in another 10 the police had taken action independently. In some of these cases, the parents could not be contacted but, in most, the seriousness of the concerns and difficult relationships with parents meant that social workers dismissed the possibility of negotiating with them. Where parents had been consulted, either they had been unwilling to agree arrangements for the child's care with social services or had failed to comply with them. Social workers recognised that legal intervention was likely to make matters worse; this was not a reason for not intervening but a matter where their skills could make a difference. Also, there could be a positive result if parents realised the need for change and were able to work with the department to achieve this.

> For some parents it makes it worse and for some they can become quite abusive. And all you can say is, 'You need to talk to your solicitor about that', rather than get embroiled in discussions or arguments with parents. Some parents will work with us. Some ... not. Some do recognise the seriousness of the situation ... Parents, always have been anti social services and especially close knit communities like here. They still call us 'welfare' 'Oh look the welfare are here.' 'Child snatchers' and 'All you have ever wanted to do is to take my child off me.' (Social work manager, Area M)

> Sometimes – in the initial onset you know which is understandable, they've been very angry and they see you as the enemy and I think it's about your ability as a person and a professional worker, and you work through that. And I've been pretty lucky; I've always managed to work through that and I've managed to engage the parents ... (Social worker, Area E)

Half the local authority lawyers commented that legal proceedings usually made social work relationships with parents worse. The EPO was 'such a draconian measure it has such a phenomenal impact to destroy any relationship [with] social services.' This was not just due to the polarising effects of litigation but the emotional impact of the intervention, where action had been taken suddenly, often without warning and sometimes with the involvement of the police.

> I suppose it ups the ante for a temporary period. Cases go on for months of course and it's rare for a case to last less than a year. Sometimes people never get over the trauma that the beginning of a case caused but to say that was the result of the legal order made would be a bit of a misapprehension. I think the intervention and how it occurs often . . . has the emotional impact. I mean if the child's removed under police protection or if there's an emergency meeting with social services, all those things I suspect are going to be what's foremost in someone's mind. I think – I have to say EPOs do erode the opportunity for working together in partnership but then one can say the same largely about any situation where you had to go to court. Cynical but I think you could say that once you go to court it's often hard to see how you can build that bridge again. Sometimes you can but people get very polarised and entrenched if they're involved in litigation even litigation of this nature, which is not supposed to be like that but it seems like that. (Local Authority Lawyer, Area E)

Other local authority lawyers reflected that there was little difference between removing a child by EPO or by ICO. It was the fact of the removal rather than the type of order.

There were a few cases where the intervention secured change in the parents; the support of their family (and their solicitor), assistance from social services and the involvement of a children's guardian together produced the necessary improvements in parenting. Care proceedings meant that 'more money was thrown at the cases and there were more in-depth assessments', which could be helpful. In others, for example most of the cases where babies were removed at birth, siblings had been killed or children seriously injured, the outcome of permanent separation of parent and child seemed inevitable.

The use of EPOs also had a major impact on the local authority, particularly on social services. Despite the fact that there had been prolonged involvement by social workers in many cases, with the exception of the cases involving the removal of new babies, most applications were unplanned.

PROCESS OF THE CARE PROCEEDINGS

Transfer

Care proceedings are started in the family proceedings court but, with the agreement of the court, cases can be transferred to the county court or the

High Court if they are complex, the final hearing will last more than five days, or to allow them to be heard with other applications relating to the family. It was initially intended that the majority of care cases would be heard in the family proceedings court but an increasing proportion of cases is transferred with less than a third remaining there (Department for Constitutional Affairs, 2006b). Emphasis on avoiding delay encourages transfer at the earliest stage (Lord Chancellor's Department, 2002) when issues of complexity and hearing length are unlikely to be clear. The legal process is designed to identify common views between the parties and achieve agreement on matters that are incontrovertible. Consequently, some cases that have been transferred to the county court are uncontested at their final hearing.

Both local authority lawyers and solicitors in private practice generally preferred cases to be transferred to the county court. Although most lawyers were positive about the quality of the local magistrates and their legal advisers and noted that the family proceedings court could be less intimidating for parents and social workers, they thought that care cases were generally better dealt with in the county court. Professional judges had more experience and could get to grips with the issues more quickly so that hearings tended to be shorter. Judges tended to manage cases more closely and would deal robustly with local authority failure to take action or to submit material on time. However, in all three areas, there were major problems of delay in the county court; cases had to wait substantially longer to be heard at this level.

> I think it's much easier for a single judge to control the evidence; it's very difficult for three magistrates to be controlling the nature of the evidence. I think the magistracy has a problem as a result. I think a lot of hearings can be shortened by the control and direction that a single judge can give but a bench of magistrates struggles because to have a debate is very difficult between three people. (Solicitor, Area M)

> There are advantages in the county court. There's no messing around there, a district judge will get hold of it. He won't allow cases to just drag, he'll sort out assessments quickly; he'll make sure that timetables are kept on top of. There are occasions where it needs to go up there, to have that firm hand to keep hold of things. And obviously I think there are occasions where there are issues which can only really be dealt with by county court judges, particularly around sexual abuse issues. (Local Authority Lawyer, Area J)

Overall, 31 cases (43 per cent of those with a final hearing) remained in the family proceedings court, 39 cases (54 per cent of this sample) were transferred to the county court and two cases (both involving child homicides) were transferred to the High Court. The most common reason for transfer was complexity (27 cases) but five cases were transferred so they could be heard with care proceedings in the higher court. Transfers were most frequent in Area E, where almost three-quarters of cases were transferred. In this area there was a local practice direction which required all applications to free a child for adoption to be heard in the county court; this and the preference of the solicitors in private practice made applications for transfer commonplace there. In contrast, in Area J, two-thirds of the cases remained in the family proceedings court and, in Area M, just under half the cases remained there.

The Length of Proceedings

'Cases go on for months of course and it's rare for a case to last less than a year' (Local Authority Lawyer, Area E).

The length of care proceedings has been a matter of serious concern since the mid-1990s; delay impacts on the cost of proceedings (Masson, 2003; Department for Constitutional Affairs, 2006b) and on the lives and life chances of children (Ward, Munro & Dearden, 2006). The length of time to complete care proceedings has continually increased in all types of court. Cases that have been transferred to the county court tend to take longer than those which remain in the family proceedings court, partly due to their complexity and reliance on expert witnesses but also because of a shortage of judges (Booth, 1996; Lord Chancellor's Department, 2002). In 2003, the *Protocol for Judicial Case Management* was introduced by the President of the Family Division with a view to ensuring cases were completed more quickly; a target was set for 70 per cent of cases to be completed within 40 weeks, but this was subsequently reduced to approximately 50 per cent (Department for Constitutional Affairs, 2005).

Of the 72 cases that were ended in a final care hearing before the end of the fieldwork, 30 (just under 42 per cent) were completed in the Protocol target time of 40 weeks. As expected, a higher proportion of cases was completed in the family proceedings court (17 out of 31) than in the county court (13 out of 39); both cases in the High Court took over a year, partly because they could not be heard until after the completion of the criminal case against the parents. Ten of the cases involving babies removed at birth were completed within 40 weeks but three took over a year. The longest of these cases involved the baby's eventual rehabilitation to her mother but the other two cases had plans for adoption yet the babies remained in temporary foster placements for well over a year. Changes in adoption law with the consequence that children cannot be placed until a placement order has been made, mean that, in future, more babies removed at birth are likely to wait longer for a secure placement.

Given the considerable variation in the length of care proceedings between courts and in different parts of the country, it is not possible to say whether these cases that started as EPOs took longer or shorter to resolve than other cases. However, these proceedings were generally not planned; in most cases the local authority had not determined that the children should be removed having completed a core assessment. Except in the case of newborn babies, the local authority generally did not have a plan for the children's long-term care before their removal. Both assessment and planning had to be started (and completed quickly) if the cases were to end within 40 weeks. Cases can proceed more quickly where parents and their lawyers actively engage in the proceedings, responding to letters promptly and filing evidence on time, or if parents withdraw completely. Cases can take longer if parents maintain only intermittent contact with their lawyers, or if relatives ask to be considered as children's carers late in the proceedings and then have to undergo a substantial assessment. There were examples both where parents withdrew very quickly (in one case within days of the EPO) and others where they remained involved with their child even though rehabilitation appeared impossible. In the case which had not had a final hearing at the end of the research (two years after the EPO application) the local authority was engaged in assessing the third set of potential carers from the child's family.

Contest and Hearing

There were 42 cases (just under 60 per cent of the cases with a final hearing) which were not disputed at the final hearing, a similar figure to that in Hunt and colleagues' study in the early 1990s (Hunt *et al.*, 1999, 366), but lower than Brophy *et al.*'s 2003 study (Brophy 2006, 95). The majority of the contested cases were heard in the county court; only six out of 31 cases were contested in the family proceedings court compared with 22 out of 39 in the county court. Both the High Court cases involved disputed final hearings. The threshold was contested in nine cases, including six where the care plan was also contested. Disputes about the care plan were more frequent; parents disputed this in 23 cases, children's guardians in four cases, relatives in three cases and the child in one case. Unsurprisingly, adoption plans were most frequently contested, in 17 out of 29 cases.

In just under half the cases, the final hearing lasted less than half a day. There were only nine cases, where the final hearing lasted more than two days; in five cases the hearing lasted between 5 and 10 days. Long hearings reflected contested cases, but not all contested cases were long, five took one day or less. This reflected weakness of the opposition and the strength of the local authority case, which was nearly always supported by the children's guardian. Four of the five longest cases were disputed by the parents, two in relation to the care plan, and two over both the grounds and the care plan. The other long case was contested by relatives. There were four children, paternal and maternal relatives and parents involved, but only the relatives contested the plan under which two of the children would live with their father.

OUTCOME OF THE CARE PROCEEDINGS

Four cases were withdrawn before the final hearing, one following the death of the child and three because an order was no longer considered necessary. In **case 2**, which involved an allegation of sexual abuse to a teenager by a relative, after initial disbelief, the family came to terms with the allegation and supported the young person. An agreement was made for her to be accommodated and the care application was withdrawn after she returned home. In **case 31**, a mother's care had caused longstanding concerns. The child had been taken into police protection at the instigation of the police after she was found home alone following the mother's arrest. After the local authority obtained an EPO the mother worked with the social services to regain care of her child. She was said to have made 'excellent progress' so proceedings could be withdrawn. In **case 76**, parental co-operation under an interim supervision order led the guardian to recommend no order, and the local authority to apply, successfully, to withdraw the proceedings.

The information available from the court files allows the outcome of care proceedings to be described in a number of ways, which together provide a simple account of the arrangements for the child. The court file includes information about the care plan that was approved by the court; the child's current placement and whether this is with the same carer who looked after the child before the proceedings; and the order made (if any) by the court. The file does not make it possible to know whether the planned arrangements were actually achieved, or whether they lasted. Research on the implementation of care plans indicates that some types of plan are less likely to be implemented, or to survive, than others (Hunt & Macleod, 1999; Harwin, Owen, Locke & Forrester, 2003). Whereas plans for care by relatives were usually achieved, rehabilitation was much less likely to occur. Adoption plans were achieved in just under 60 per cent of cases where it was the plan in the study by Harwin and colleagues, and all the adoption placements made in Hunt and Macleod's study (23 per cent of the sample) were continuing at the end of the research period.

Out of the 109 children in the sample whose cases were considered at a final hearing in care proceedings, 89 experienced a change of their long-term carer (see Figure 8.1). Almost all of the children experienced some change of carer following the emergency intervention, either being placed in foster care (and often experiencing more than one foster home) or being cared for by their relatives. For the 20 who did not experience a change in their long-term carer, four remained with relatives or foster carers and 16 stayed with or returned to their parents. For the four children living with relatives or foster carers, the EPO had been taken to prevent a parent removing them; at the final hearing, care orders were made for two children and supervision orders for the other two children. No order was made in respect of five of the

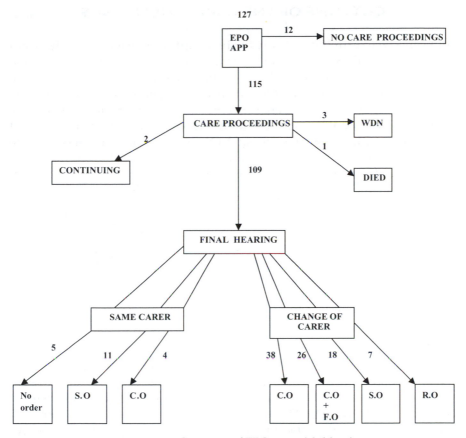

Figure 8.1 Outcome of EPO cases (children)
Abbreviations: EPO APP EPO application; WDN, application withdrawn; S.O, supervision order; C.O, care order; F.O, order freeing the child for adoption (now replaced by a placement order); R.O, residence order (Children Act 1989, s.8)

children who were in the care of the parent who had cared for them before the proceedings were started; supervision orders were made in respect of nine children and care orders for the remaining two. Amongst the children who did not experience a change of carer, despite the emergency intervention, and were made subject to a supervision order at the final hearing was **case 4**, the two-year-old child whose involvement with the child protection system was outlined in Chapter 5, above. Not all the children in the same family were the subject of the same order. For example, in **cases 111–114**, where EPOs where taken in respect of all four children after the father broke his son's arm for failing to do a chore, a supervision order was made in respect of this child but there was no order in relation to any of his siblings.

Of the 89 children whose long-term carer changed as a result of the intervention, 15 went to live with their other parent, 24 with relatives and 49 local authority carers. One child who was very disturbed after years of neglect and abuse was placed in a therapeutic residential unit. Many of these children faced further moves; the court approved an adoption plan for 27 children but only eight were placed with their prospective adoptive parents at the date of the final hearing. Care orders were the most common orders where the intervention had led to a change of carer; care orders were made in respect of 64 children and for 26 of these the court also made an order freeing them for adoption.

Peter and his sisters (**cases 60–63**, see Chapter 5) were unable to stay with the relatives who cared for them after they had been found home alone. A further family placement was considered for them but these relatives changed their minds about offering care. A plan for adoption was made in relation to Peter's sisters, and despite opposition from their grandmother, care orders and freeing orders were made. The final hearing of Peter's case was delayed for two months so that plans for his care could be clarified. The local authority agreed that he could remain with his current foster carers with whom he appeared to have a good relationship and he was finally made the subject of a care order a year and a half after the EPO application.

Eighteen children who changed carer were made the subject of supervision orders; these included Linda and Joe Martin (**cases 5 and 6**, see Chapter 5), who returned to live with their mother when her mental health improved, and were both made the subject to supervision orders for three years. Twelve children moved to live with their other parent and six were cared for by relatives. Residence orders were made for the other seven children, four living with relatives and three with their other parent.

Adoption was planned for all but four of the 16 babies removed at birth. Two children were rehabilitated with their mothers, **case 43** where a care order was made and the mother was living with her parents who were helping her to care for her baby. A supervision order was made in respect of Bobby, **case 110** (see Chapter 5). After a period in foster care he and his mother and brother went to a residential assessment centre. However, concerns about the children's care had not completely disappeared. The mother was still in contact with the father whose domestic violence had undermined her ability to cope and had a major impact on Bobby's elder brother. Two other babies, **case 9** and Tammy, **case 73** (see Chapter 5) were made the subject of residence orders and cared for by their grandparents. Freeing orders had been made for 11 out of the 12 babies whose adoption was planned, including baby Bates, **case 1** and Sarah, **case 54**.

There were another 20 children who were less than one year old when the EPO was made, for whom final orders were made in care proceedings. Adoption was planned for 11 of these children, four were placed with relatives and rehabilitation with parents was planned for the other five. Katie, **case 92**, who had been shaken, returned to her parents under a supervision order after a period in foster care. Christine, **case 12**, did not return to her parents and was freed for adoption.

Does Starting a Case with an EPO Lead to a Different Outcome?

A question that arises is the extent to which cases that start with an EPO differ in outcome from those where there has been no emergency intervention. Even if they did, this may not relate to the way they were started, for example if the problems in the family were more intractable, they might necessitate both emergency intervention and (independently) lead to a high rate of permanent placement outside the family. Indeed, the EPO sample appeared to include more very young children, and these children are more likely to be placed for adoption. The data on the families, and the interviews with social workers and local authority solicitors suggested that the majority of the cases where EPO applications were made were just serious child protection cases, which required compulsory intervention. In some cases the EPO was planned, in others it was at least, expected. Very few cases were 'real emergencies' in the sense of occurring suddenly and unexpectedly in a family where there was no current involvement in relation to the children. That being the case, the outcomes might be expected to be similar to those observed in other studies of child protection proceedings.

Comparisons are difficult because practices change over time, for example there has been a substantial growth of the use of kinship care since the mid-1990s (Broad, Hayes & Rushforth, 2001). Also, different local authorities have different cultures and pressures, which lead to more or less emphasis being given to adoption and foster care. Further, previous studies that have considered the outcome of care proceedings have included cases that started by EPO in their samples. Table 8.1 compares the orders made in the EPO study with those from Hunt and Macleod's care plan study (Hunt & Macleod, 1999) and Brophy and colleagues study of care proceedings (Brophy et al., 2003).

It is clear from Table 8.1 that similar outcomes in terms of orders were found in all three studies. The main difference was in the percentage of cases without an order, but the numbers are small. However, there were differences between the care plans in the studies. A far higher proportion of cases in the EPO study had a plan of adoption (36 per cent compared with 20 per cent in Hunt and Macleod's study). However, adoption was achieved for over

Table 8.1 Final orders in care proceedings compared with other studies

Final order	EPO N	EPO %	Hunt & Macleod Range %	Hunt & Macleod Av %	Brophy et al. %
Care order	68	62.4	52–59	57	70
Supervision order	20	18.3	9–17	17	19*
Residence order	7	6.4	5–9	7	11*
SO and RO	9	8.3	4–9	6	NA
No order	5	4.6	9–19	14	0
TOTAL	109	100	N = 131	101	N = 165

* Brophy and her colleagues (2003) used slightly different categories for orders. Residence order cases include those with contact or family assistance orders; cases with residence orders and supervision orders were not separately listed.

30 per cent of Hunt and Macleod's sample. If plans for adoption and fostering are taken together there was almost no difference between the two studies. Rehabilitation plans were substantially lower in the EPO study (27 per cent compared with 46 per cent). Conversely kinship placements were higher (24 per cent compared with 12 per cent). This may reflect a change in practice over the 1990s with greater emphasis on both adoption and kinship care. Overall, it appears that the similarity in the orders made masked considerable difference in what was planned for the children, with fewer children from the emergency intervention study returning to their parents and more living with relatives.

CONCLUSION

At the early stages of the process considerable pressure was put on all the professionals to work quickly. The rapid initiation of proceedings was not matched by speedy progress through the system; fewer than two in five of the cases where there were care proceedings ending with a final order in less than 40 weeks. However, there was no evidence that the use of emergency intervention made the cases take longer. The factors that contributed to long proceedings, the time taken for assessments of parents and carers and the availability of court time for a final hearing similarly impact on other cases. Neither the process nor the outcome of cases which started with an EPO indicated that they were substantially different from other care proceedings, except in the way that they began. Given the family circumstances, and the fact that EPOs were mostly not 'real emergencies', this is not surprising. Once the care proceedings were underway these cases followed the same course as others.

9

EMERGENCY INTERVENTION — REASSESSMENT AND REFORM

THE NATURE OF EMERGENCY POWERS

Emergency intervention by social services, separating parents and children, has three distinct forms. First, social workers seek to persuade parents to agree to their children being placed away from home, either with relatives or in foster care. Arrangements are forced rather than voluntary (Department of Health, 2001; Brandon, Lewis & Thoburn, 1996); direct threats that refusal to agree will result in proceedings are sometimes used. Where parents cannot be found, refuse to agree or are not trusted to maintain their agreement, social workers have to resort to legal powers but agreements are generally preferred. Most children are accommodated (Children Act 1989, s.20) but arrangements with relatives are sometimes informal; accommodation is frequently an emergency (unplanned) response to a crisis, accounting for about half of the occasions when it is used (Packman & Hall, 1998). Second, local authorities apply to a magistrates' court for authority to remove or detain children under emergency protection order. EPO applications are made to secure the protection of children whose parents might remove them from accommodation or hospital, to extend the protection of children originally removed or detained under police protection and in other cases where the child's need for protection is not so urgent as to put them at risk of further harm whilst proceedings are brought. If children are not already safe, and sometimes where they are, applications are made without notice to parents. Third, where immediate protection is required, during the evening or at weekends when it is not possible to arrange a court hearing or if the court is unwilling to hear the case quickly, social workers approach the police and request that children are taken into police protection. Such requests are rarely denied. Although police protection is easier, most local authority lawyers and social workers believe that they should apply for a court order where this is possible, a point which is reinforced in government guidance (Department of Health et al., 1999; Home Office, 2003; Department for Education and Skills, 2006).

Emergency intervention by social services is linked to a crisis in care for a child and a lack of parental co-operation (actual or presumed) with arrangements for the child's protection. In the majority of cases, social services were involved with the child's family prior to the emergency intervention. The crisis and non-co-operation reflected a breakdown of the relationship between parents and workers; psychiatric illness, substance abuse and violent relationships with male partners were common factors impairing parents' ability to care and willingness to work with social workers. Where co-operation with social workers or health professionals was poor, incidents where children were injured, placed at risk or left without adequate care could precipitate emergency intervention without being life-threatening. Emergency intervention often triggered court action, which had previously been avoided through agreements with parents. There were very few cases where the identification of a child with serious non-accidental injuries about whom there had been no earlier concerns resulted in an emergency order. Serious child protection concerns were sometimes identified during pregnancy, most commonly because children had been removed from, or killed by, the parents previously. In these cases, emergency intervention was commonly planned during the pregnancy and taken shortly after the birth in order to prevent the mother removing the baby from hospital. The problems that provoked emergency intervention were rarely resolved quickly; social services use of emergency powers was almost always followed by care proceedings and the overwhelming majority of these cases continued for many months until the final hearing of these proceedings.

Independent action by the police to protect children is rather different. Police protection provides a means of temporarily removing or detaining children who would otherwise be at risk of significant harm because they lack adequate care or control, or because care arrangements for them have broken down. It has a 'catch all' quality, covering children believed to be at risk in public places or in their own homes, and because of abuse, neglect or their own behaviour. Police officers use the power when they are faced with 'children problems', often bringing children to the police station whilst they and/or their supervisor establish how the problem can be resolved.

Emergency intervention powers allowed the parents' (and the young persons') lack of agreement to the proposed course of action to be overridden. They protected children because they controlled parents' exercise of parental responsibility in circumstances where what parents had done, or failed to do, caused children significant harm or placed them at risk of it. Children's well-being was therefore not dependent on their parents' care or co-operation but could be secured by police action or a court order. Access to these powers meant that when parents would not accept their proposals, social workers did not have to leave children with very inadequate care or in fraught situations until they could obtain a hearing for an interim care order application (at least three days). Also, social workers did not have to allow parents to take their children from their current foster carers and obtain an interim care order in order to re-establish protection. By enabling action to be taken quickly to protect children, the powers also created an expectation that they should be used when parents would not agree to protective arrangements. Both social workers and police officers felt that they risked criticism if they failed to do what they could for children's protection.

Child protection work is stressful and some parents are intimidating (Littlechild, 2005). The high profile that has been given to social workers' actions in cases where children have been harmed by their parents or carers adds to workers' anxiety and creates a climate that encourages intervention to remove children. Emergency powers are used. Limited professional and managerial support left some social workers struggling to manage the risks they had identified. In this context, and despite general support for working with families, social workers sometimes felt the need to rescue children – to remove them from circumstances where care or neglect was causing children to suffer. Where children were in very neglectful conditions or had been injured, social workers were uncomfortable leaving children with their families, even for a few days (see Chapter 6). High levels of anxiety were not confined to front-line social workers, local authority lawyers were also concerned that action should be taken quickly. The risks to children of neglectful and abusive parents were a major concern to magistrates who heard EPO applications (see Chapter 7). Their concerns meant that they were very unlikely to consider refusing an order unless it was clear that the child would be kept safe through other arrangements, such as a voluntary placement with a relative. Being blamed if children were harmed was also important for police officers' decisions to take children into police protection (see Chapter 3).

The Last Resort

Joan Hunt and colleagues entitled their study of care proceedings under the Children Act 1989, *The Last Resort*, reflecting the view that local authorities only turned to the courts after 'lesser alternatives' had been explored (Hunt *et al.*, 1999, 388). Making care proceedings a last resort is also linked to delaying intervention, risking greater harm to children and making it less likely that parents will be able to make the changes necessary for children's well-being. When it comes to the use of emergency powers, the idea that compulsory intervention is a 'last resort' is even clearer. Within the local authorities in the EPO study, the practice was always to consider whether children could be protected by agreements, an approach which was reinforced by the expectations of the courts (see Chapter 6). If the parents would not agree, or the risk of asking them was considered to be too great, social workers' attention turned to police powers and court orders, depending on how urgent the case was considered to be. Solicitors in private practice also noted that local authorities generally turned to emergency powers only where parents would not or could not agree. Emergency powers were widely regarded as draconian, and for that reason there was a general emphasis on limiting their use to cases where they provided the only legal means of securing the protection that the social worker and their managers thought necessary.

Similarly, the police used their police protection powers where they had to remove or detain a child and could not solve a problem informally. Officers sometimes resolved a situation just by bringing a child to the police station; this action was identified by their supervisor as *police protection* because there were no other powers which could have been used. The only power was the last resort. Any other action could only have been informal, a use of the officer's authority rather than any power given by law.

Where action which is considered to be 'the last resort' is viewed as appropriate, it becomes more difficult to identify alternative ways of approaching the problem. There is nothing else that can be done; work becomes focused on achieving what is viewed as the only possible solution as quickly as possible. Social workers who considered that this point had been reached focused on convincing their managers and the local authority lawyer that action had to be taken. And lawyers and managers who accepted the social worker's account sought to get an order as soon as the court would allow. Once the order was obtained, little consideration was given to whether it should be executed despite the express provision in the statute (Children Act 1989, s.44(5)(a)). The view that compulsory emergency intervention was the 'last resort' therefore served both to limit its use to serious cases and to prevent a detailed consideration of whether immediate intervention was required.

In this context, it is crucial to ensure that services are available to families before a crisis point is reached, that proper consideration is given to any alternative ways of securing children's well-being, and that there are always checks to establish that intervention, particularly in its most coercive forms, is necessary before powers are exercised. The use of emergency powers cannot be justified as a routine response where children are in need of some protection.

Defining Emergencies

Emergencies are generally regarded as incidents that require a quick response, just how quick and what sort of response depends on the nature of the emergency, and of other competing emergencies occurring at the same time. Child protection emergencies are similar. Any child who is suffering significant harm needs a quick response but that does not mean that EPOs or police protection have to be used in every case, or even in every case where parents will not agree to children being placed or kept away from home. However, if there is to be agreement about those cases where such intervention should be used, more consideration has to be given to defining emergencies by identifying features which can or cannot justify immediate, coercive action. Without a common understanding of when this action is appropriate, the individuals who operate it can only draw on their own understandings. These are likely to be heavily influenced by their experience and the context within which they are working. Those who have little support in this anxious task are likely to find assessments more difficult and may be less willing to take risks. Unless more direction is given about the appropriate use of powers and greater support in making these judgements, workers cannot be criticised for the lawful decisions they make. Difficulties will remain even if it is possible to agree the basis for emergency intervention. The lack of information about families and the impossibility of accurate prediction of behaviour will always leave uncertain the questions whether the criteria are met and whether this action is required. Account also has to be taken of the risks for children, parents and professionals of making mistakes which are very different depending whether the mistake is over- or under-intervention.

The *Child Care Law Review* rejected the suggestion that emergency intervention should be limited to cases where risk to the child was 'imminent' because it was concerned that this would be 'too narrow' and prevent action where risk is 'continual' (Department of Health and Social Security, 1985, para 13.9). Some jurisdictions do seek to limit immediate intervention by requiring 'imminent danger' or 'substantial risk' (Masson, 2004a) but the emergency/non-emergency distinction has also been rejected by others as both 'difficult and risky' (*KLW v Winnipeg*, 2000, para 106). Whether such distinctions are sustainable must depend on their effect. The more substantial the difference between the processes and the longer it takes to obtain 'non-emergency' orders, the wider the definition which must be given to *emergency* in order to ensure that children who need protection can be helped in time.

The Children Act 1989 provides no help in deciding whether emergency powers should be used. It does not define 'emergency' nor formally limit EPO applications to cases such as those suggested in *Working Together* 'where there is a risk to life or a likelihood of serious immediate harm' (Department for Education and Skills, 2006, 5.49). Guidance stresses that EPOs should only be used for 'genuine' emergencies (Department of Health, 1991a, 4.28), but gives no indication about what makes an emergency *genuine*. Rather, the Act uses the same standard – actual or likely significant harm – as the basis for all intervention but makes allowances for the more limited evidence available where action has to be taken without pre-planning, by requiring that the court has to find only that there is 'reasonable cause to believe' the standard is met, not that the significant harm is proved. Despite the wish to limit intervention by EPO, the test that has to be satisfied is no higher than that for an interim care order. Where access to the child is being refused it is lower – the applicant only has to 'suspect' the standard is met. Whether an EPO should be sought is effectively a matter for the judgement of the case responsible social worker with the supervision and guidance of their manager and a local authority lawyer. The decision whether to make the order is formally for the court. Neither local authority practitioners nor the courts are given direction by the statute.

In practice, social workers' reading of the latest incident of harm and their perception of the risk to the child were the key factors in the use of emergency powers. Risks are highest to young children because of their vulnerability, and in cases where parents are not trusted to keep to any agreement about the child's care away from home. Risk is not an objective matter where common agreement is easy to establish but is based on the individual worker's assessment, combined with gut feelings and (limited) knowledge of the family. Managers and local authority solicitors accepted that workers' ability to tolerate risks varied and tested their assessment but generally did not try to impose their own views.

An assessment tool that helped social workers to decide if emergency intervention is required could reduce the subjective element in decisions about emergency intervention but would not eliminate it. The development of such a tool would necessitate further research looking in detail at the circumstances preceding incidents where children have been harmed. The current studies indicate the circumstances in which police protection and EPOs were used but do not allow the wider comparisons that would be necessary. Analysis of cases where children have died or suffered serious injuries despite the involvement of child protection agencies suggest that prediction is problematic in even these most extreme cases (Reder and Duncan 1999; Sinclair & Bullock, 2002). An assessment tool could not be predictive but could highlight matters which should be considered. Such a tool would strengthen the position of social workers seeking to use emergency powers. Rather than just making their own judgement about the need to intervene to be tested by their manager, the local authority lawyer and ultimately by the court, they could be seen as making a professional judgement, supported by a recognised formal assessment, which should only be rejected if it has not been properly applied. It is not clear that it would lead to a more restrictive approach to emergency intervention.

The Effect of Emergency Powers

Social services' use of emergency powers had two main effects on the child and their family. First, the decision to separate parent and child was made without a full examination of the need for this as could occur with an interim care application. Second, some care proceedings were started earlier than would otherwise have been the case. It also impacted on the social worker is three distinct ways. First, social workers got more work and more support to do it. Colleagues rallied round and, at least in the authorities in the study, local authority lawyers took the lead in the proceedings, providing advice and securing representation. Second, they got power, which enabled them to impose protective arrangements. And third, where a court order was obtained, they also became subject to the control of the court, particularly to the court's timetable.

Initial separation was achieved by agreement, often coerced by threats of proceedings, by the use of police powers or, more rarely, by an EPO. Where police protection or agreements were used, parents had no opportunity to negotiate or to obtain advice about alternative action. And where parents and children were only separated as a result of court proceedings, cases were commonly heard without parents having an opportunity to counter the local authority's case. EPOs on full notice where children were currently in the care of their parents were exceptional; only four out of the 86 cases in the EPO study fitted this pattern. Nevertheless, local authorities did not take emergency action lightly; the children subject to EPO proceedings needed protection. In the overwhelming majority of cases, EPOs were followed by care proceedings that continued to a final hearing and resulted in a change of carer and/or a long-term protective order. The effect of the EPO was to initiate care proceedings that would otherwise have been delayed so long as parents continued to agree to their children's accommodation, or until the local authority decided that its plans or parental standards of care necessitated a care order. Although emergency intervention could be traumatic and deeply upsetting, bringing forward care proceedings could be advantageous to both parents and children. Representation, the external scrutiny of arrangements by the children's guardian and the court and the imposition of a timetable, focused attention on making decisions about the future and prevented drift. Through the engagement of a children's guardian, lawyers and the wider family, proceedings could promote greater efforts to re-unite the family or to find alternative long-term care for the child (Clark & Sinclair, 1999; Hunt et al., 1999).

The effect of police protection in cases where the police acted independently was more varied. Whereas many children were quickly re-united with their parents, a few were drawn into the child protection system and became the subject of care proceedings. Others, particularly adolescents, became accommodated and did not return to their families for a long time. Police officers focused on the problem that confronted them and rarely considered the longer term impact of their use of police protection. The effect of police protection on children, families and on social services was not a factor in their use of the power; making it so would require much higher levels of co-operation between police and social services.

PREVENTION AND EMERGENCY INTERVENTION

Prevention is the label given to a range of strategies and services designed to improve children's well-being by increasing the abilities of their carers, safeguarding them from harm and removing the need for more coercive action. In the case of emergency intervention, prevention can encompass both action to avoid the need for any compulsory intervention and planning so that proceedings are brought before a crisis occurs. These are forms of tertiary prevention, focused on families where there is the greatest risk of a breakdown of children's care (Hardiker, 1991). Considerable attention has been given in the refocusing debate to achieving a proper balance between safeguarding children and promoting their welfare, investigating the need for protection and supporting families to meet children's needs (Department of Health, 2001). Following the sharp reduction in the use of emergency powers under the Children Act 1989 and despite wide variation in practice, concerns about emergency intervention have largely focused on exhortations against the use of police protection instead of EPOs (Home Office, 2003; Department for Education and Skills, 2006, para 5.51) and against making court applications without notice (see Chapter 2, above) rather than on wider issues of prevention.

Avoiding the need for compulsory intervention is not necessarily positive; it could mean using social work power to coerce agreement from parents or delaying proceedings to the detriment of the child. However, work with, and services for, families in severe difficulty with the aim of developing higher levels of trust for social workers and increasing understanding and co-operation with plans are possible This was demonstrated in a few cases in the study where care proceedings were withdrawn or were completed without an order because of substantial improvements in parental care. Similarly, where parents have had previous children removed, counselling and support after removal to increase parents' ability to care for a child in the future, or to avoid a pregnancy that will inevitably result in another removal, could prevent the parents re-experiencing this trauma. It is not possible to eliminate the need for protective intervention, but earlier use of care proceedings where families are in severe difficulty could avoid the need for an emergency response to a crisis in some cases. Such action conflicts with the notion of compulsory intervention as a last resort and requires more attention to be given to the issue of child neglect. Intervention not in response to a crisis must be based on a comprehensive assessment, including the need for a court order. Such assessments require commitment and co-operation from both the family and the local authority; both may take the view that there is no need for this until things get worse. Moving away from emergency intervention thus demands change from families and from local authorities and social workers.

POLICING CHILD PROTECTION

The strongest case for the retention of police protection is that the existence of a formal power avoids informal action by officers which would be much more difficult to monitor and regulate (Reiner, 2000). The public, including children and young people themselves, assume that the police can and will take responsibility for children in crisis; officers will therefore continue to be drawn into this work. Officers assume that they can pick up children who need to be protected; the formal system with supervision by a designated officer serves to identify such action as police protection, to record it, and to ensure that incidents are resolved and children are looked after.

Police protection is about control as well as care. The breadth of the power creates the potential for oppressive action; more account needs to be taken of this through supervising individual decisions and monitoring use. Police protection forms can provide a framework which ensures that officers are reminded what action must be taken and for checking individual decisions. However, management responsibility and external scrutiny require more work by forces to collate and publish statistics. Police protection should not be invisible as it currently is in many forces (see Chapter 1). Information about the number of times it is used, the length of time children remain at the police station and where they go when they leave are important for decisions about officer training and for joint planning with local authorities.

The lack of refuge facilities for children means that the majority of children in police protection are taken to police stations, places that are not designed to be child-friendly and are potentially scary, imbued with police power. Instead of stressing the unsuitability of police stations and indicating that children should only be taken there 'exceptionally and for short periods' (Home Office, 1991, para 15; 2003, para 28), there is a need to recognise the reality of police protection and take action to safeguard children at police stations, even those taken there for their protection. The Children Act 2004 requires co-operation between local authorities and the police with a view to promoting children's well-being in accordance with the *Every Child Matters* agenda (Her Majesty's Treasury, 2003). Police authorities and chief constables must ensure that officers carry out their functions with regard to the need to safeguard and promote children's welfare and in accordance with guidance (s.11). Although this could provide the impetus for better collaboration in relation to the care of children in police protection, the guidance gives it little attention. Taking children into 'protective custody' is portrayed as just a contribution to safeguarding and promoting welfare, on a par with identifying children in domestic violence cases, work with child witnesses and drugs education. It appears to be assumed that the welfare of children in police protection is already well protected.

In practice, thousands of children are brought to police stations every year when they are taken into police protection, and an unknown number spend many hours there. Although the Home Office Circular (Home Office, 2003) stresses that the designated officer's responsibilities continue so long as the child remains in police protection, wherever the child is staying, and that the investigating officer has responsibility for explaining to the child what is happening (paras 11 and 35), no officer is identified as responsible for the child's well-being. Although the Circular states that 'every effort should be made to ensure that the child is physically safe' (para 29) and has access to food and drink, etc., in contrast to other children in custody there is no oversight or regular monitoring of the child's care. Consequently, children in police stations for their protection are less protected than those held in custody during the investigation of their offences. This is particularly unsatisfactory because the young people in police protection who are likely to spend longest in police stations are adolescents who have been brought there because of their behaviour. Rather than assuming that children in police protection are well protected in police stations, their care should be the subject of a Chief Inspectors' Safeguarding Review.

ACCOUNTABILITY IN CHILD PROTECTION

The Role of the Courts

The courts' exercise of their responsibilities to approve applications for emergency intervention orders has long been a matter of concern. In 1984, the Social Services Select Committee heard evidence from the Magistrates' Association about the high proportion of care proceedings that were started by a place of safety order. The Association of Directors of Social Services told the Committee that they 'were not aware of evidence of abuse' of these orders and 'quite correctly pointed out' that the order should not be made unless the applicant has established the case (Social Services Select Committee, 1984, para 123). The *Review of Child Care Law* sought to strengthen the protection of families by requiring that *the magistrate* be satisfied of the grounds for the order (Department of Health and Social Services, 1985, para 13.9), by requiring evidence to be given on oath and by limiting the power to grant orders to specialist magistrates (para 13.27). The role of magistrates in granting emergency orders was given little attention by the Cleveland Inquiry; the magistrates who made the orders that caused so much concern took no part in the Inquiry. However, in his evidence, the Director of Social Services for Cleveland pointed out that the orders had all been duly authorised by magistrates (Butler-Sloss, 1988). Similarly, following the Orkney Inquiry, John Chant, Director of Social Work for Lothian suggested that it was inappropriate to criticise social workers for decisions that had been made by the courts (Asquith, 1993, 77).

The reforms in the Children Act 1989 and in Scotland sought to increase the safeguards provided by the courts against misuse of emergency powers. In England and Wales, EPOs were either to be approved by the Clerk to the Justices as requiring an *ex parte* hearing and heard by a single magistrate, or heard on notice before at least two magistrates. Magistrates hearing EPO applications would be members of the specialist family panel and at least one of them would be qualified to chair the panel. In Scotland, the power to make CPOs was limited to sheriffs who are professional judges. Every order has to be referred immediately to the reporter, who has power to release the child and must arrange a children's hearing within two working days (Children (Scotland) Act 1995, s. 57; Scottish Office, 1997).

Elsewhere, less store has been placed in having these decisions made in the courts. In Canada, Mme L' Heureux-Dubé, giving the majority judgement in the Supreme Court in *KLW v Winnipeg*, noted that in the case of an *ex parte* application to protect a child:

> While review ... by the court will provide some protection against unjustified apprehensions, courts will tend to defer to the [child protection] agency's assessment given the highly particularized nature of child protection proceedings and the highly compelling purpose for state action in this context. This deference will be all the more warranted when the child protection worker's assessment has already been subject to an internal review process within the agency. (para 113)

For this reasons, and because of the additional risk to the child caused by the delay whilst court approval is obtained, the Supreme Court of Canada held that 'the principles of fundamental justice' did not require removals of children for their protection to be authorised by the courts, even where the law did not specifically limit such action to emergency cases. Sufficient protection was provided by a prompt review where parents were legally represented *after* the event. Even the dissenting judges accepted that the court had only a very limited capacity to assess *ex parte* applications:

> Even though ... on an *ex parte* application, a judge may have little choice but to defer somewhat to the presentation of the case by the applying agency, any concerns that the judge may have about the appropriateness of the initiative may result in further information being requested ... An independent judicial scrutiny of the appropriateness of the apprehension will also serve to ensure that child protection agencies act on reasonable and probable grounds, grounds that they can articulate, before initiating an apprehension in a non-emergency situation. (Arbour J at para 24)

Similarly, the European Court of Human Rights has accepted that the European Convention on Human Rights does not necessitate court authorisation before children are removed. Administrative mechanisms, including a review of the decision, could provide adequate protection for private and family life (Masson, 2004a, 2006a).

It has even been suggested that having court approval at an early stage where there is only limited evidence undermines the rights of parents and children. American academics have argued that the limited, initial review of an application is taken as establishing that the intervention was justified. This then colours the consideration of the case at later stages of the proceedings (Cooper Davies & Barua, 1994; Chill, 2004). Cases where there has been emergency intervention are assumed to be more serious and requiring compulsory action. For this reason, it has been proposed that there should be a presumption that the child will be released when the emergency period expires and that it should be necessary to satisfy a higher standard in order to maintain the separation of parent and child (Chill, 2004).

Scrutiny by the Courts in the Study

The research did not indicate that the courts were effective in scrutinising EPO applications. In the study areas, restrictions imposed by magistrates' legal advisers on access to *ex parte* hearings were easily by-passed by requests for the use of police protection. The notice period for *inter partes* hearings was frequently so short as to preclude meaningful representation for the parents, and representation for the child was not seen as a priority by the courts or by CAFCASS. In less than half of the *inter partes* EPO applications was the child represented by a children's guardian. Although the magistrates' legal advisers are required to appoint a children's guardian unless they are 'satisfied that it is not necessary to do so to safeguard the child's interests' (Children Act 1989, s. 41), the practical difficulties in appointing a guardian to act immediately and the limited time for any investigation meant that this requirement was frequently ignored. With little to contradict its case, the magistrates readily accepted that the local authority needed to use protective powers; they trusted that the local authority had good grounds and did not wish to be responsible if a child were harmed after an order had been refused. They routinely granted orders; rarely, parents who attended court were able to persuade magistrates that an agreement (usually also involving separation) would provide sufficient protection for the child. Magistrates made orders to fit the court timetable and frequently for the maximum available period, rather than to reflect the child's circumstances (see Chapter 7). Where they made contact orders these were frequently for contact 'at the discretion of the local authority' rather than to a schedule set by the court. Moreover, the national survey indicated that there were wide variations in court practice across the country, making it easier or more difficult to obtain an EPO without notice to parents depending on the location.

The general unavailability of courts out of office hours reflected the relative infrequency of applications and the costs of providing night-time cover from legal advisers and court security staff. It was simply not cost effective to ensure that courts could be held at any time, particularly because the police had a power that could provide the necessary protection for children. In addition, some legal advisers and lawyers recognised that it was not possible to provide instant justice at night. Parents had no access to lawyers and difficult decisions should not be made when people were exhausted.

Overall, the high expectations of the policy makers responsible for the Children Act 1989 about what could be achieved through court processes were not met. Courts could not evaluate local authority applications for EPOs; local authorities, not courts, decided to remove children from their homes. This was not a failing of individual courts but reflected the limitations of the judicial process in considering issues of child protection speedily and usually only with evidence presented by the applicant. Realistically, it was not possible for the court to form a balanced view of the need for an order when parents were unable to counter the information put forward by professionals with responsibility for protecting children. Even assuming a children's guardian were appointed, the very limited time between the application/appointment and the hearing usually precluded them from making a contribution to the decision. But even one day's notice was regarded as excessive where children were not already safe. In practice, EPO applications, particularly those heard *ex parte*, were treated little differently from properly considered place of safety orders made under the previous legislation.

Local Safeguarding Children Boards

Local Safeguarding Children Boards (LSCBs) were established under the Children Act 2004 to replace the non-statutory Area Child Protection Committees, which were themselves reconfigured from Area Review Committees by *Working Together* (Home Office *et al.*, 1991). Local Safeguarding Children Boards do not generally deliver services but are 'the key statutory mechanism' for securing agency co-operation about children's welfare in each area and for ensuring the effectiveness of safeguarding work undertaken by their member agencies (Department for Education and Skills, 2006, 3.2, 3.5). Their functions include developing policies and procedures relating to child protection investigations and the assessment of children in need. They are also responsible for monitoring and evaluating the work done to safeguard children, either directly or through self-evaluation within agencies, and they contribute to planning local services for children. Consequently, knowing about and influencing how police protection is used is important for the work of these boards. Child protection procedures should include arrangements for protecting children in emergencies, particularly outside normal office hours. By monitoring the use of police protection, LSCBs will be able to establish particular risks in the locality, for example high numbers of children running away from residential establishments, and help member agencies to address these. Knowledge of the use of emergency intervention could lead to the commissioning of new services, such as refuge facilities for children needing immediate protection.

The responsibilities of Local Safeguarding Children Boards provide a means of making police protection more visible. One role of these boards is to make agencies accountable for their work in child protection. 'Ensuring that work to protect children is properly co-ordinated and effective remains a key goal ... and they should not focus on their wider role if the standard of this core business is inadequate' (Department for Education and Skills, 2006, para 3.10). Monitoring agencies' work is crucial for identifying strengths and weaknesses, and improving practice. Boards should expect their local police force to provide information about its use of police emergency powers. Local child protection procedures should specifically provide for co-ordination between the police, local authorities and health services where police powers are used, so as to ensure that proper arrangements are available for children's care. Given that current police forces frequently cover the area of more than one LSCB and that the proposed, amalgamated forces will cover many, it will be important for LSCBs to work together so that force-wide procedures can be established. Collection of data by LSCBs will provide the basis for a nationwide picture of the use of police protection, comparisons between forces and the development of practice.

However, it should be noted that this work could have been undertaken by Area Child Protection Committees but generally was not. Local Safeguarding Children Boards have a wider remit, even though their functions in child protection remain the most important. The fact that police protection has not been viewed by police forces, the Inspectorate of Constabulary or the Home Office as a major police function may mean that it will continue to be ignored. And the emphasis given to not using it in *Working Together* (Department for Education and Skills, 2006) may make this more likely. If this happens, police protection will remain largely invisible and there will be little incentive to improve provision for the children it protects.

The use of police protection is not the only aspect of emergency intervention that Local Safeguarding Children Boards will need to consider. How care proceedings and EPOs are used is an indicator for understanding intervention thresholds, and the balance between intervention and support. LSCB monitoring of local authority emergency action will be more important if the courts cease to have a role in emergency intervention as is proposed below. LSCBs should be able to compare practice in their areas with that reported to other LSCBs. There is also a need to improve the arrangements made for protecting new babies so that separation of parent and child can be avoided until this issue is considered by a court.

REFORM OF EMERGENCY INTERVENTION LAWS

The Care Proceedings Review

A cross-Government review of the care proceedings system was set up in 2005 in order to examine how care proceedings could be improved by making the best use of resources (Department for Constitutional Affairs, 2005; Department for Education and Skills and Department for Constitutional Affairs, 2006). The context for the review was concerns about the increased costs of these proceedings falling on the legal aid budget, the lengthening duration of care proceedings and the pressure on CAFCASS caused by the increasing numbers and length of cases. The review proposed both immediate action and longer term strategic changes to reduce the use of proceedings, to improve the quality of initial applications, to cut legal aid expenditure and to improve outcomes for children. Particularly, it recommended changes with the aim of engaging parents in the child protection process in order to avoid the need for proceedings, and if this were not possible, to enable parents to understand (and therefore to address) the local authority's concerns. One element in this is a proposal for a pilot scheme to give parents access to legal advice (on a fixed fee basis) where they are at risk of care proceedings. Local authorities will be expected to prepare cases better before they bring proceedings. New guidance for local authorities will be issued; there will be an expectation that the local authority considers arranging a family group conference and completes its core assessment before it makes a care application to the court. The Review also proposed changes to care proceedings to streamline the process. It has suggested that the first hearing in the family proceedings court should occur three to four weeks after the initial application so that the children's guardian has time to review the local authority's assessments, the parents have had time to consider their lawyer's advice and the advocates have had time to prepare (Department for Education and Skills and Department for Constitutional Affairs, 2006, para 5.24–25).

The Review recognises that thorough pre-application consideration and preparation will not be possible in emergency situations and that the new procedure will create further distinctions between these and other cases. For example, the proposal for a later first hearing appears to delay substantially the court's consideration of the need to grant an interim care order and this may lead local authorities to resort to EPOs to secure the child's protection. However, the Review is also concerned that the new requirements should not create a 'perverse incentive' encouraging emergency applications. It therefore proposes that there should be more consistent use of orders for costs against local authorities where inappropriate EPO applications are sought (Department for Education and Skills and Department for Constitutional Affairs, 2006, para 5.20). This suggests either that local authorities will be penalised for daring to make an emergency application or alternatively, that despite the order being granted by the magistrates, a higher court may order costs against the local authority after the EPO has been obtained. Neither approach has any legal merit; both misunderstand the role of the court in scrutinising applications and the difficulties faced by courts and local authorities with responsibilities for children's immediate protection.

Changes to care proceedings will inevitably impact on emergency applications. If better information and advice to parents (and changes in social work practice) encourage parents to work with social workers and other professionals to provide good enough care for their children or to agree to care by others, it may be possible for parents to avoid the trauma of care proceedings and the family disruptions they bring. However, there is a danger that limited co-operation will discourage proceedings without improving care for children. Also, arrangements will be agreed that are acceptable to the parents and the local authority but fail to meet children's needs. In the context of pressure on local authorities to avoid court action, staffing difficulties and limited parental co-operation, it is likely that the unplanned use of court proceedings will increase not decrease as the Review Team intended.

Reforming Emergency Intervention Powers

Any reform of emergency intervention powers should seek to ensure that families are only subject to emergency intervention where this is clearly necessary to protect children, and that grounds and procedures are not so restrictive as to leave children unprotected where parents will not co-operate. Grounds and procedures should support good decision making so that workers can feel confident that their actions are appropriate and the public can have confidence in actions taken. Risk levels must be acceptable to workers with responsibility for these cases because without professionals who are able to handle the stress of these cases there can be no child protection system. A single system should operate for all cases involving social services; it should not be possible for social workers to avoid controls on their action by relying on the police. The system has to be workable with the levels of skill and experience that exists in the current workforce, and within the short timescales that apply where emergency action is required. The majority of the children who need emergency intervention for their protection are very young and completely dependent on adult care.

There is no need to retain the general power for any person to apply for an EPO. This has hardly ever been used. There is ample guidance advising professionals to refer their child protection concerns to the local authority (Department of Health *et al.*, 2003; Department for Education and Skills, 2006); local authorities all have systems in place for dealing with child protection referrals and are better able to assess such referrals than the courts. Members of the public also have good access to information about raising child protection concerns. It is most unlikely that a member of the public, who knew of a child needing protection, would apply to the court instead of contacting the NSPCC, the police or the local authority. If they did, they could easily be directed elsewhere. Where their concern is really a family dispute about a child's care or the child's abduction by a carer, this can be put before the court the by parent (Children Act 1989, ss. 8 and 10) or, in wardship, by anyone with an interest in the child's welfare.

Court Scrutiny

The system put in place by the Children Act 1989 does not allow for effective scrutiny of EPOs by the courts. Although most applications are justified, the system does not appear able to identify weak applications, particularly in the courts where *ex parte* proceedings are routinely held. Nor does the existence of the court process protect local authorities from criticism for taking emergency action. The requirement to make a court application may inhibit intervention but local authorities have other much stronger reasons for wanting to avoid care proceedings, and these are likely to be strengthened as a result of the Care Proceedings Review.

Cases where emergency action may be warranted will always be difficult because of the limited information available, the risks of being wrong and the need to act quickly. Professional judges may be more able to form independent judgements than the magistrates appeared to be. Requiring EPO applications to be made to a judge would also indicate the seriousness of the decision and act as a further constraint on local authorities. However, it is far from clear that even the most senior judges would be able to be as robust if they were taking responsibility for the child's protection by considering an EPO application as they have sometimes been when reviewing decisions months later. Despite wide powers to deal with emergency applications, few family judges have experience in dealing with similar matters; even when care issues were routinely handled in the High Court in wardship, decisions about children's removal had generally already been made by magistrates issuing place of safety orders (Masson and Morton, 1989). Also, transferring jurisdiction over EPOs to the High Court or even the county court would make substantial demands for judge time and add to the pressures on already overburdened care judges.

Scrutiny within Children's Services Departments

If court scrutiny of initial emergency action is not effective there is no value in retaining it. Instead, Children's Services Departments could be required to establish more formal systems for internal scrutiny of immediate action to replace approval by a court. Authority for immediate protection could be placed in the hands of the Director of Children's Services (or a named nominee) who would have to approve (in writing) any such action. The Children Act 1989 already limits some decisions in this way; for example, the decision to place a child who is subject to a care order with their parents has to be authorised by the Director. This could be strengthened by a requirement for the Director to take legal advice. Given that two-thirds of Directors of Children's Services do not have a background in children's social care, delegation of this power to an assistant director with the appropriate experience would be expected. Such an approach would place responsibility for initial decisions to separate parents and children, or to retain children against the parents' wishes, clearly in the hands of the Director of Children's Services who would be accountable, through the ordinary processes, to parents and children, to elected members and the community, to their professional body and, in terms of the effectiveness of their child protection services, to the Local Safeguarding Children Board.

Authority to detain a child would continue to be time limited. The power needs to last long enough to ensure that the first hearing of any care proceedings could involve a thorough assessment of the preliminary issues of separating parent and child and controlling parental responsibility. Realistically, this cannot be done in less than eight days. Arrangements should ensure that there had been time for lawyers to be instructed and for the children's guardian to complete preliminary enquiries and form an independent view of the child's need for protection. Parents should have a right to legal aid for care proceedings and a children's guardian should be appointed no later than the time when the authority to remove or detain the child is served on them. If, after authority to detain had been granted, it became clear that the child could be placed safely with their family, the local authority would be required to do this but would retain some responsibility for the child until the power expired.

The system should operate on the presumption that authority to detain would be followed by court proceedings. This would reflect the current practice; it is rare for EPOs not to be followed by an application for a care order. There should be no suggestion that the standard for emergency intervention is lower than in other care cases, or any encouragement for the local authority to remove children without thinking about their future, long-term care. In most cases, the use of the Director's authority would be followed by an interim care order application but an interim residence order to transfer care of the child to their other parent or a relative might be appropriate. There might also be cases where following an emergency detention the local authority considered that the child could be protected by accommodation in foster care or with relatives and the parents agreed to this. Allowing the use of the Director's authority to be followed by arrangements that neither enabled the child to return home nor were subject to the scrutiny of the court could appear to give the local authority too much power with too little accountability. However, to require the local authority to start proceedings when the parents were willing to co-operate with a care plan, particularly where this involved the child's rehabilitation seems both oppressive to the parents and a waste of local authority and court resources. Rather than requiring the local authority to bring proceedings or return the child, sufficient safeguards for families and children could be provided through access to legal advice to parents in this position and close scrutiny of the care plan by the Independent Reviewing Officer. Monitoring the use of accommodation after detention could be used to check that parents were not being pressured to agree to accommodation by use of the power to detain.

Replacing court scrutiny with accountable, professional decision making acknowledges the limitations of the courts in assessing matters of child protection quickly and on limited evidence. Experienced child protection professionals are in a better position than magistrates or judges to question staff and assess the risk presented by a situation. This is a matter of professional responsibility and should not depend, as the court process does, on prompting from parents, their representatives or a children's guardian. The local authority decision maker can also direct staff to take other action or conduct further inquiries, which the court has no power to do. It therefore becomes possible to review whether action should be taken on the basis of additional knowledge rather than to 'err on the side of caution.' The formal aspects of decision making are reduced. Decisions can be made wherever the Director is, with legal advice provided over the telephone. Proper recording of the basis for making the decision is essential, but such a system can be operated wherever and whenever it is required. Part of the decision maker's responsibility will be to determine whether immediate action is required at night or the matter can be left until the next day.

Practice standards within local authorities could be strengthened by requiring monitoring and reporting of the number of times the Director's powers are used, and particularly the number of occasions where authority is given but proceedings are not brought. LSCBs should regularly consider this information and it could also be an element in quality audits of child protection and care proceedings activity. Internal monitoring would also help identify the circumstances where immediate action is most frequently relied on so that services could be commissioned to improve the response to such events, including by avoiding the need for compulsory intervention. None of the local authorities in the study were able to state how many EPOs they sought each year, or what proportion of their care proceedings were started in this way. Emergency proceedings could not therefore be considered when they planned services. Arrangements developed in response to the immediate need for intervention might include a protocol with the local maternity hospital to supervise new mothers at risk of having their children removed, or a policy on responding with the provision of accommodation to children left unattended.

At the end of the project, these proposals were discussed with focus groups of lawyers, social workers and policy makers. Some lawyers suggested that, having heard key findings of the study (see Chapter 7), they would routinely oppose applications in order to ensure higher standards in the courts. This approach could only work where applications are heard *inter partes* and parents are represented, arrangements that occurred in only a minority of cases (see Table 7.2). Social workers also said they preferred the current arrangements because they allowed them to tell parents who would not agree to protective action that 'the court would decide.' They were uncomfortable acknowledging the role they played by applying for an EPO, even though (or perhaps because) parents thought of them as 'taking kids away.' However, none of the social workers or managers interviewed in the study was willing to accept that the courts *should* refuse the local authority's EPO applications; where this happened, or the court refused to hear the application *ex parte*, they turned to the police. It appeared that social workers and their managers wanted to have power to be able to protect a child where they considered this to be necessary but not to be seen as having this responsibility. The proposed scheme would give the power and responsibility to the Director; individual social workers would continue to have the difficult task of engaging with parents and removing children when authority was given.

Restriction of Police Protection Powers

Once the local authority has the power to take immediate protective action, there is no need for it to rely on the police power. Indeed, if this were still possible, it would undermine the internal system for approving and monitoring immediate intervention. However, the existence of a local authority power will not remove the need for the police to have powers for child protection. Police require these so that their action can be limited and they can be held accountable; formal powers are a necessary safeguard when official bodies take responsibility for children. New powers for the local authority may mean that police protection does not need to last as long. It will no longer operate as a holding power until a court application can be made, only until the child can be returned home or the local authority makes other arrangements, either accommodating the child or obtaining the Director's authority for detention. A period of 24 hours – the length of police powers under Scots law – should be long enough.

PROVISION OF ACCOMMODATION IN CHILD PROTECTION CASES

Agreements between social services and parents about the protection of children can serve a useful purpose in avoiding the need to take compulsory action. It is clear that in very many cases social services have sought to reach agreements before bringing proceedings (Brandon *et al.*, 1999; Hunt *et al.*, 1999), but that parents often feel pressured and ill-informed in this process (Freeman & Hunt, 1998). Agreements were sometimes made alongside an explicit threat to bring court proceedings if parents did not agree, and breach of these agreements was a major factor precipitating emergency proceedings (see Chapter 6). Despite the statutory provisions allowing parents to remove their children from accommodation at any time, where accommodation was provided to protect children, parents effectively lost their power to reclaim their children against the local authority's wishes. Although agreements might be less disempowering than court proceedings, they often left parents with little control over the arrangements for their children's care (Packman and Hall, 1998).

There are good reasons for local authorities seeking to avoid proceedings wherever possible in terms of maintaining control over the case, focusing on the issues that concern the authority, working towards more speedy resolution, saving expenditure and, if proceedings have to be taken, ensuring that they are properly prepared (Department for Education and Skills and Department of Constitutional Affairs, 2006). Keeping cases out of court can also benefit parents who are likely to find the proceedings baffling, demeaning and excluding (Lindley, 1994; Freeman & Hunt 1998). However, forced agreements cannot successfully protect children nor avoid the need for proceedings, unless their terms assist parents to improve their relationship with, and care for, their children, and local authorities provide the services that families require. For these reasons, and particularly if breach is likely to lead to the local authority starting care proceedings, parents need independent advice and representation when the local authority proposes a child protection agreement.

A single form of agreement is not adequate to cover both non-contentious situations where a parent needs temporary assistance from the local authority to look after their child during the parent's hospital treatment, and other cases where accommodation replaces compulsory action. If parents are being required to agree to their children's accommodation in circumstances where they are not free to remove them, this should be explicit in the terms of the agreement. In such cases, a notice period, which is long enough to enable the local authority to secure the child's care whilst it starts proceedings, should be included in the agreement. This term should override the parent's right to reclaim the child for a specified and limited period. The question whether the child can continue to be looked after by the local authority should then be decided by the court like any other application for interim care order. Parents entering into such an agreement need to be properly informed about its effects. This underlines the importance of making independent advice available as the Care Proceedings Review has proposed (Department for Education and Skills and Department of Constitutional Affairs, 2006, para 5.11–12). Such a term would also emphasise to all involved with the child's care, particularly the Independent Reviewing Officer, that accommodating this child is a matter of his or her protection and that the plans for the child's care need to reflect this.

POWER AND CHILD PROTECTION

Child protection necessarily involves the re-alignment of relationships of power, within the family between parents and child, and often between parents themselves, and between the family and child protection agencies, including the police. Abusive power is replaced by protective power. When this shift occurs suddenly, as in the exercise of emergency powers, its effects can be traumatic for all concerned, especially for parents and children. Although this may serve to alert parents to the need for changes in the way they are bringing up their children, it can also have a paralysing effect, undermining their ability to do anything about this. Also, if local authority power is met with resistance, parents may reduce their opportunities for assistance to regain the care of their children. The local authority gains power but also comes under new constraints. Engaging in care proceedings imposes additional responsibilities and controls over the local authority's actions. Social workers may appear to have more powers once an EPO or ICO has been made but they too become subject to the power of the court that determines the steps they have to take and the speed and direction of travel. The court's powers are also limited; they can only choose between available options and in many cases they have no choice in the final orders they make in care proceedings.

EPOs are currently subject to only limited, ineffective, external controls. Recognition that such action 'is not taken lightly', and the general concerns within local authority legal departments and of social work managers about bringing care proceedings, serve to restrict their use. Although magistrates' legal advisers used their power to prevent *ex parte* applications, this was not effective either in controlling local authorities, who turned to the police, or in empowering parents. The short period of notice provided, particularly where notice was abridged was completely inadequate to secure effective representation for people faced with this major intervention, especially when they were already over burdened with the difficulties that had precipitated the application. Without a different view to present to the magistrates, parents' lawyers felt powerless to mount a serious challenge to the local authority's case. Magistrates had little alternative but to make the order requested and felt constrained to do so because of anxiety for the child and support for the social worker. In effect, the process established under the Children Act 1989 could not change the power balance in emergency intervention.

Reforming emergency intervention powers in the way outlined above will not have a major impact on the balance of power between families and local authorities. Empowering the Director to approve immediate intervention is unlikely to lead to greater use of these powers by local authorities, particularly if there is regular monitoring and a continued expectation that such intervention is a 'last resort'. Similarly, changes to the terms of child protection agreements and the provision of legal advice are unlikely to increase conflict between parents and local authorities and resort to the Director's powers or to the court. With advice, parents may be more willing to recognise their children's needs and be empowered to negotiate arrangements, which will both help them and satisfy the local authority. For a few families, this will avoid the need for immediate compulsory intervention, and for others it may even be possible to avoid care proceedings. Although these changes may contribute to the reduction of care proceedings, their main function is to replace the (misleading) appearance of externally controlled intervention with effective internal controls, and to ensure parents and children have a real opportunity to hold the local authority accountable through the courts.

CONCLUSION

Protecting children in emergencies necessitates the exercise of substantial powers in circumstances where only limited checks are possible and the risks to children of failure to intervene can be extreme. Tight controls on these powers can make them too difficult to access and unavailable for emergencies, but lax controls may allow inappropriate or oppressive use. The architects of the Children Act 1989 sought to create a balance between parental privacy and intervention in family life with a clear and accepted standard – the significant harm test – approved by the courts. The practicalities of this scheme – how children would be protected between application and hearing, how to ensure representation for parents and children (not just the legal aid to pay for it) and the effective testing of the local authority's case – were largely overlooked. There seems to have been an assumption that justice could be assured regardless of the context or content of decisions placed before the courts, also that the provision of a court process would automatically secure justice.

Close examination of the practice of considering EPO applications reveals limitations in the court process. Speed, an important factor where an emergency response is required, precludes thoroughness in either an adversarial or inquisitorial system. Although it may be possible to bring parents and representatives to court swiftly, this does not deliver representation that can challenge the local authority's case and allow the magistrates to test its strength. Similarly, a children's guardian may help the court to assess an application, but only if there has been time to investigate the child's need for protection. Controls within local authorities to limit resort to the courts, one-sided presentation and community expectations that systems can protect every child combine to present the magistrates with cases where there can only be one decision, and to reinforce the magistrates' expectation that applications will result in orders. In this way, the court is transformed from the place where cases are argued and decisions made to one where applications are processed into orders.

Far fewer safeguards were provided in the Children Act 1989 against misuse of police powers. Despite considerable concerns about police powers generally, police work in child protection was (and is) given little consideration. Formal control of police protection was limited to the length of time that the power lasted, but safeguards were added to ensure children would be looked after by local authorities and leave police protection once they were not at risk of harm. The separation of the two means of intervention and the peripheral role of the police in child protection meant that the interaction of these two mechanisms was not considered. However, the existence of two parallel powers with different controls has led to the use of the more readily accessible one. It is natural for lawyers to advise their clients how to achieve their aims and avoid controls. Where staff are under pressure and resources are stretched, there is even more incentive to take the simplest route.

Shedding light on the operation of emergency protection laws and their impact has highlighted limitations in the legal process that were ignored. Parliament, legislating 'in the dark', focused on how it wanted the law to function in an ideal world, rather than how it would operate in this imperfect one. For this reason, its expectations of the courts were unrealistic and the processes provided were ineffective to hold local authorities to account.

Appendix A

DETAILS OF RESEARCH METHODS

POLICE PROTECTION STUDY

Access and Ethics

Initially, permission for the study was obtained from Chief Constable Tony Butler, the Association of Chief Police Officers (ACPO) lead on child protection matters. The forces were selected by the researchers and approached by ACPO to identify an officer to liaise with the researchers directly. One force refused access at this stage, due to current research commitments. Access to the police protection forms for the second stage of the study was negotiated separately in each force via the Child Abuse Investigation Unit (CAIU), none refused. Individual police officers were approached directly by the researchers for interviews, some opted to seek permission/advice from a senior officer, none refused.

No names or addresses of children were collected. Only the age of the child was used to identify the case to officers, who were informed that they could talk more generally if they did not wish to discuss the case in question. All officers were willing to talk specifically about these cases, as well as others with which they had been involved. Any names used during the interview were deleted at transcription. Officers were also informed that neither they nor the force would be identified in any of the dissemination of the research.

Procedure – Stage 1: The Survey

The officers in charge of each CAIU were contacted by letter, with information about the study and its endorsement by the Association of Chief Police Officers (ACPO). They were re-contacted a few days later by telephone for an interview at that time or at a later date. Interviews were recorded with the consent of the interviewee and lasted between 30 and 60 minutes. Copies of relevant written policies/procedures and forms were requested and collected.

Stage 2: The Use of Police Protection

Eight forces were asked to participate in the second stage of the study. The second stage involved visits by the researchers to each CAIU and accessing records of police protection taken in the previous 6 months. Recording schedules and questionnaires were piloted in one force not otherwise participating in the study. For forces with high use, data collected was limited to a sample consisting of every police protection decision in the past 2 months, and 1 in 4 for the remaining 4 months.

For each force, officers involved in the most recent cases of police protection in each division or district were approached for interview. The investigating officer and the designated officer were both asked to participate; interviews were conducted either jointly (for ease of shift timing and travelling) or separately. At this stage, three officers agreed to be interviewed by telephone. All interviews were recorded with the consent of the interviewee and were transcribed using a voice recognition system. Interviews took place during a five month period, and lasted between 15 minutes and one and a half hours. Details of the samples and interviews are set out in table A1.

THE EPO STUDY

Only 3 court (police force) areas were selected to make the research manageable. They covered 3 shire counties in areas E, J and M and 3 unitary authorities, one in the area covered by force M and the other two in the area covered

Table A.1 The police protection sample and interviews

Force	PP'S taken	Case sample	N interviews		
			DO	IO	SSD
A	Not known	49 **(61)**	6	4	
D	293	56 **(75)**	9	5	2
E*	229	64 **(80)**	5	2	2
F	22	22 **(31)**	2	1	
I	30[5]	33 **(46)**	1 (CAIU)	2 CAIU)	4
J*	130	33 **(45)**	5	3	2
L	28	31 **(50)**	3	5	1
M*	78	23 **(32)**	2	2	2
Total	810	311**(420)**	33	24	13

Numbers relate to incidents, number in bold relates to number of children (where known).
* Area included in EPO study.

by force E. Social services staff from the shire counties had been interviewed in the police protection study; links had been made to facilitate access and the researchers already had some information about local practices. Piloting was undertaken through interviews with relevant professionals in a separate location to develop interviews for all the stages of the study.

Access and Ethics

Protracted negotiation with the Lord Chancellor's Department (now Department of Constitutional Affairs) resulted in a privileged access agreement which enabled the researchers to access records from magistrates' courts on condition of anonymity for the areas and the individuals concerned. This was later extended to allow files of cases which had been transferred to the higher courts to be read. Once permission had been obtained, arrangements to access records, and to speak to magistrates' legal advisers and magistrates were made locally with individual courts. Solicitors in private practice who were members of the Law Society Children Panel or known to act regularly in care proceedings were contacted by telephone to request an interview, none refused.

Access to local authorities was negotiated by a twin pronged approach – via links made during the police protection study and an application to the Association of Directors of Social Services (ADSS) seeking consent for the research. Within each local authority, contact was made separately to the legal department and the social services department.

Issues of data protection and confidentiality were crucial for this study because of the sensitive nature of the subject matter and concerns of local authorities about this. Plans were made which enabled data from the various parts of the study to be linked but names and other identifying information to be protected. Despite preliminary approval one local authority withdrew agreement for access to documentary information (social services and legal department files) during the study. Instead, the researchers were permitted to interview the social worker who could refresh her memory or clarify points by reference to the file. This lengthened the time taken for interviews, and reduced the detail obtained by the researchers. Overall, given the quality of the interviews and the other sources available, this did not have a major impact. Standard approaches to changing names, geographical references and some identifying facts have been used to maintain confidentiality.

Stage 1: The National Survey

The Clerk to the Justices in each Magistrates' Court Committee Area was contacted by letter with brief details of the research and asked to identify a magistrates' legal adviser with responsibility for public law Children Act cases who could take part in the study. Arrangements were made for a telephone interview lasting approximately 30 minutes with this person. Interviews were recorded and transcribed; key information was tabulated.

Stage 2: Court Study

Information provided to the researchers by the Her Majesty's Court Service statistician of the number of EPOs in each court was used to estimate the size of the fieldwork task and to check that the sample was complete. The sample of EPOs consisted of all applications made in the 12 months prior to the initial visit to the Area courts. In Area J, this was cases from September 2000 to September 2001 (19 cases); in Area M, cases from January to December 2001 (32 cases) and in Area E, cases from May 2001 to April 2002 (35 cases). Data on the EPO and any subsequent public law proceedings were collected from court files. All cases, except one which was still continuing at the end of the project, were followed to find the outcome of the final hearing. The total sample consisted of 86 cases involving 127 children where an application was made for an EPO.

Stage 3: Local Authority Decision Making

In each of the 6 local authorities, interviews were conducted with a sample of staff from the local authority's legal department who dealt with child care work, and a sample of social workers and team managers who had been involved in the cases identified through the Court Study. In almost all cases respondents agreed to tape recording; interviews were fully transcribed. Local authority legal department and social services files were examined for information about the EPO in 32 cases, legal department files were seen in a further 15 and social services files in a further 9. Local authority files were therefore examined in 56 out of 86 cases. Three further local authorities which appeared to be low users of EPOs were identified through court service and Department of Health data. Approaches were made to the children's services

Table A.2 Sources of information for cases in the EPO study

Sources information	N	%
Court files only (no interviews)	9	10.5
Legal services and/or social services files	56	65.1
At least 1 interview	38	44.2
2 interviews	19	22.1
3 or more interviews	14	16.3
Total Cases	86	100

Table A.3 EPO study interviews

Interviewees	Area			Total
	J	M	E	
Magistrates' legal advisers	3	1	2	6
Magistrates	3	2	2	7
Social workers	8	4	7	20
Social work managers	3	3	2	7
Local authority lawyers	3	3	8	14
Private practice solicitors	10	5	9	24
Total	30	18	30	78
+ 7 in low use areas				85

manager – all agreed to be interviewed; interviews were also arranged with child protection specialists and local authority lawyers. Table A2 gives details of sources on information available on the 86 cases and Table A3 on the numbers of interviews in each Area.

Appendix B

LIST OF CASES

Covezzi and Morselli v. Italy app No 52763/99 ECtHR

Essex County Council v. F [1993] 1 FLR 847 FD

Re F (in utero) [1988] Fam 122 FD

Re G (interim care order residential assessment) [2005] UKHL 68

Haase v. Germany [2004] 2 FLR 39 ECtHR

Haringey LBC v. C, E and another intervening [2005] 2 FLR 47 FD

Johansen v Norway (1996) 23 EHRR 33 ECtHR

K and T v. Finland [2000] 2 FLR 79; [2001] 2 FLR 707 ECtHR

KLW v. Winnipeg Child and Family Services and the A-Gs of Quebec, Manitoba and British Columbia [2000] SCC 48 Supreme Court of Canada

Kirklees MBC v. S (contact to newborn babies) [2006] 1 FLR 333 FD

Langley v. Liverpool City Council and the Chief Constable of Merseyside Police [2005] EWCA Civ 1173

Re M (care proceedings: judicial review) [2003] 2 FLR 171 FD

Nottingham County Council v. Q [1982] Fam 94 CA

Olsson v. Sweden (1988) 11 EHRR 259 ECtHR

P, C and S v. UK [2002] 2 FLR 631 ECtHR

R v. Lincoln (Kesteven) County Justices, ex parte M [1976] Q.B. 957 QBD

Re S (Habeas Corpus) [2004] 1 FLR 590 FD

Venema v. The Netherlands [2003] 1 FLR 552 ECtHR

Re X (Emergency Protection Orders) [2006] EWHC 510 (Fam)

X County Council v. B (Emergency Protection Orders) [2005 1 FLR 341 FD

BIBLIOGRAPHY

Abel R (1973) Law books and books about law. *Stanford Law Review*, **26**, 175–228.

Abrahams C & Mungall R (1992) *Runaways: Exploding the Myths*. London, NCH.

Asquith S (1993) *Protecting Children – Cleveland to Orkney More Lessons to Learn*. Edinburgh, HMSO.

Atkin B (2000) Child abuse in New Zealand. In Freeman MDA (ed.) *Overcoming Child Abuse: A Window on a World Problem*. Aldershot, Ashgate, 305–328.

Ayre P (2001) Child protection and the media: lessons from the last three decades. *British Journal of Social Work*, **31**, 887–901.

Banks S (2004) *Ethics, Accountability and the Social Professions*. Basingstoke, Palgrave Macmillan.

Barry G (1993) *Police Protection under s.46 of the Children Act 1989 A Study of its Use in the First Year of the Act*, unpublished dissertation for Diploma in Child Protection, London University.

Behlmer G (1982) *Child Abuse and Moral Reform in England 1872–1908*. Stanford, Stanford University Press.

Bell S (1988) *When Salem came to the Boro, The True Story of the Cleveland Child Abuse Crisis*. London, Pan.

Biehal N, Clayden J & Byford S (2000) *Home or Away? Supporting Young People and Families*. London, National Children's Bureau.

Bittner E (1966) Police discretion in emergency apprehension of mentally ill persons. *Social Problems*, **14**, 278–292.

Bittner E (1974) Florence Nightingale in pursuit of Willie Sutton: a theory of the police. In Jacob H (ed.) *Potential for Reform of Criminal Justice*. Beverly Hills, CA, Sage, 17–44.

Blackwell A & Dawe F (2003) Non-resident Parent Contact. London, DfES, available at http://www.dfes.gov.uk/childcontactsurvey/.

Blenner-Hassett D (2004) K.L.W. and warrantless child apprehensions: sanctioning gross interventions in private spheres. *Saskatchewan Law Review*, **67**, 161–204.

Blumberg A (1967) The practice of law as a confidence game. *Law and Society Review*, **1**(2), 15–39.

Booth M (1996) *Avoiding Delay in Children Act Cases*. London, Lord Chancellor's Department.

Booth T & Booth W (2004) *Parents with Learning Difficulties, Child Protection and the Courts – A Report to the Nuffield Foundation*. Sheffield, Department of Sociological Studies, University of Sheffield.

Brandon M, Lewis A & Thoburn J (1996) The Children Act definition of 'significant harm' – interpretations in practice. *Health and Social Care in the Community*, **4**(1), 11–20.

Brandon M, Thoburn J, Lewis A & Way A (1999) *Safeguarding Children under the Children Act 1989*. London, TSO.

Braye S & Preston-Shoot M (2006) The role of law in welfare reform: critical perspectives on the relationship between law and social work practice. *International Social Welfare*, **15**, 19–26.

Broad B, Hayes R & Rushforth C (2001) *Kith and Kin: Kinship Care for Vulnerable Young People*. London, National Children's Bureau.

Brophy, J (2006) *Research Review: Child Care Proceedings under the Children Act 1989*, DCA Research Series 5/06. London, Department for Constitutional Affairs.

Brophy J, Jhutti-Johal J & Owen C (2003) *Significant Harm: Child Protection Litigation in a Multi-cultural Setting*, LCD Research Series 1/03. London, Lord Chancellor's Department.

Buckley H (2003) *Child Protection Work: Beyond the Rhetoric*. London, Jessica Kingsley.

Bullock R, Little M & Millham S (1993) *Going Home*. Aldershot, Dartmouth.

Butler-Sloss E (1988) *Report of the Inquiry into Child Abuse in Cleveland 1987* (1988 Cm 412). London, HMSO. (The Cleveland Report.)

Campbell B (1988) *Unofficial Secrets*. London, Virago.

Campbell L, Jackson A, Cameron N, Goodman H & Smith S (2003) High risk infants in the children's court process in Australia: dilemmas and directions. *Journal of Social Welfare and Family Law*, **25**, 121–136.

Care Services Improvement Partnership (2006) *Who's holding the baby?*, available at http://www.bedsandhertswdc.nhs.uk/workforce_development/downloads/whb_final_report.pdf.

Children's Society (1999) *Still Running*. London, Children's Society.

CAFCASS (2003) *Corporate Plan 2003–2006*. London, CAFCASS.

CAFCASS (2005) *Every Day Matters*. London, CAFCASS.

CAPITA (2004) *Review of the Guardian ad litem Agency Final Report*. Belfast: Department of Social Services and Public Safety. Available from http://www.n-i.nhs.uk/nigalaweb/pdf/Capita%20Final%20Report_100305.pdf.

Chatterton M (1983) Police work and assault charges. In Punch M (ed.) *Control in the Police Organisation*. Cambridge, Mass, MIT Press, 194–221.

Children Order Advisory Committee (2005) *6th Annual Report 2004-5*. Belfast: Court Service of Northern Ireland. Available from www.courtsni.gov.uk/.

Chill P (2004) Burden of proof begone – the pernicious effect of emergency removal in child protection proceedings. *Family Court Review*, **42**, 540–548.

Clark A & Sinclair R (1999) *The Focus on the Child*. London, National Children's Bureau.

Cleaver H & Freeman P (1999) *Children's Needs – Parenting Capacity*. London, TSO.

Cleaver H & Walker S with Meadows P (2004) *Assessing Children's Needs and Circumstances the Impact of the Assessment Framework*. London, Jessica Kingsley.

Clyde J (1992) *The Report of the Inquiry into Removal of Children from Orkney in February 1991*. Edinburgh, HMSO.

Commission for Health Improvement *et al.* (2003) *The Victoria Climbié Report Key Findings from Self Audits of NHS Organisations, Social Services Departments and Police Forces*. Newcastle, Commission for Health Improvement.

Cooper Davis P & Barua G (1994) Custodial choices for children at risk: bias, sequentiality and the law. University of Chicago Roundtable, Symposium: Domestic violence, child abuse and the law. Available at http://www.law-roundtable.uchicago.edu/s02.html.

Cretney S (2003) *Family Law in the Twentieth Century, A History*. Oxford, Oxford University Press.

Cretney, S. & Masson J. (1990) *Principles of Family Law* 5th ed. London, Sweet and Maxwell.

Cretney S, Masson J & Bailey-Harris R (2003) *Principles of Family Law* 7th edn. London, Sweet & Maxwell.

Curtis M (1946) *Report of the Care of Children Committee* (1946 cmd. 6922). London, HMSO. (The Curtis Report.)

Dartington Research Unit (1985) *Place of Safety Orders.* Bristol, University of Bristol.

Dartington Research Unit (1995) *Child Protection: Messages from Research.* London, HMSO.

Department for Constitutional Affairs (2003) *Judicial Statistics.* London, TSO.

Department for Constitutional Affairs (2005) *Autumn Performance Report 2005* (Cm. 6718). London, TSO.

Department of Constitutional Affairs (2006a) *Confidence and Confidentiality Improving Tansparency and Privacy in Family Courts,* Consultation paper CP11/06 Cm 6886. London, TSO.

Department for Constitutional Affairs (2006b) *Review of the Care Proceedings System in England and Wales Desk Research Report.* London, DCA & DfES.

Department for Education and Skills (2003) *Children Act Report 2002.* London, TSO.

Department for Education and Skills (2004) *Children Looked after by Local Authorities* 2003. London, DfES. Available at http://www.dfes.gov.uk/rsgateway/contents.shtml.

Department for Education and Skills (2006) *Working Together to Safeguard Children.* London, DfES.

Department for Education and Skills and Department for Constitutional Affairs (2006) *Review of the Care Proceedings System in England and Wales.* London, DCA.

Department of Health (1991a) *The Children Act 1989 Guidance and Regulations, Volume 1, Court Orders.* London, HMSO.

Department of Health (1991b) *The Children Act 1989 Guidance and Regulations, Volume 2, Family support, day care and educational provision for young children.* London, HMSO.

Department of Health (1991c) *The Children Act 1989 Guidance and Regulations, Volume 7, Guardians ad litem and related issues.* London, HMSO.

Department of Health (1991d) *Child Abuse, A Study of Inquiry Reports 1980–1989.* London, HMSO.

Department of Health (1993) *The Children Act Report 1992* (Cm 2144). London, HMSO.

Department of Health (1994) *Children Act Report 1993* (Cm 2584). London, HMSO.

Department of Health (1995) *The Challenge of Partnership in Child Protection: Practice Guide.* London, HMSO.

Department of Health (1998a) *Modernising Social Services* (Cm 4129). London, TSO.

Department of Health (1998b) *Children Looked after by Local Authorities* A/F 02/12. London, Department of Health.

Department of Health (2000) *The Children Act Report 1995–1999* (Cm 4579). London, TSO.

Department of Health (2001) *Children Act Now.* London, TSO.

Department of Health (2002) *Children Act Report 2001.* London, TSO.

Department of Health (2003a) *Children Looked after by Local Authorities* A/F 02/12. London, TSO.

Department of Health et al. (1999) *Working Together to Safeguard Children.* London, TSO.

Department of Health et al. (2003) *What to do if You are Worried a Child is Being Abused.* London, Department of Health.

Department of Health & Social Security (1985) *Review of Child Care Law.* London, HMSO.

Department of Health & Social Security (1987) *The Law on Child Care and Family Services* (1987 Cm 62). London, HMSO.

Department of Health, Social Services and Public Safety (2002) *Children Order Statistics April 1 2001 – March 31 2002*. Belfast: DHSSPS.

Department of Health, Social Services and Public Safety (2003) *A Better Future: 50 Years of Child Care in Northern Ireland 1950–2000*. Belfast: DHSSPS.

Devaney J (2004) Relating outcomes to objectives in child protection. *Child and Family Social Work,* **9**, 27–38.

Dickens J (1993) Assessment and control in social work: an analysis of the non-use of the child assessment order. *Journal of Social Welfare and Family Law,* **15**, 88–100.

Dickens J (2004) Risks and responsibilities – the role of the local authority lawyer in child care cases. *Child and Family Law Quarterly,* **16**, 17–30.

Dickens J (2005) *Local Authority Social Workers, Managers and Lawyers in Child Care Cases,* PhD Thesis, University of East Anglia.

Dickens J (2006) Care, control and change in child care proceeding: dilemmas for social workers, managers and lawyers. *Child and Family Social Work,* **11**, 23–32.

Dickens J, Howell D, Thoburn J & Schofield G (2005) Children starting to be looked after by local authorities: an analysis of inter-authority variation and case-centred decision making. *British Journal of Social Work.* Advance access published on August 15, 2005 at http://www.bjsw.oxfordjournals.org/papbyrecent.dtl. doi:10.1093/bjsw/bch275.

Dingwall, R, Eekelaar, J. & Murray, T. (1984) Childhood as a social problem: A survey of the history of legal regulation. *Journal of Law and Society* 11, 207–232.

Dingwall R, Eekelaar J & Murray T (1995) *The Protection of Children: State Intervention and Family Life,* 2nd edn. Aldershot, Avebury.

Donaldson T & Harbison J (2006) The Children (Northern Ireland) Order 1995 10 years on: The resource demands of legislative change. *Child Care in Practice,* **12**, 299–308.

Dr Foster Intelligence (2006) *Keeping People out of Hospital – The Challenge of Reducing Emergency Admissions.* Available from www.drfoster.co.uk.

Farmer E & Owen M (1995) *Child Protection Practice: Private Risks and Public Remedies.* London, HMSO.

Ferguson H (1990) Re-thinking child protection practice: a case for history. In Violence against Children Study Group, *Taking Child Abuse Seriously.* London, Unwin Hyam, 121–142.

Ferguson H (1992) Cleveland in history: the abused child and child protection 1880–1914. In Cooter R (ed.), *In the Name of the Child: Health and Welfare 1880–1940.* London, Routledge, 146–173.

Ferguson H (2003) *Child Protection in Time.* Basingstoke, Palgrave Macmillan.

Fernandez E (1996) *Significant Harm.* Aldershot, Avebury.

Freeman P & Hunt J (1998) *Parental Perspectives on Care Proceedings.* London, HMSO.

Gibbons J & Bell C (1994) Variation in operation of English child protection registers. *British Journal of Social Work,* **24**, 701–714.

Gibbons J, Conroy S & Bell C (1995) *Operating the Child Protection System.* London, HMSO.

Glaser B & Strauss S (1967) *The Discovery of Grounded Theory: Strategies for Qualitative Research.* Chicago, Aldine.

Gordon D & Gibbons J (1998) Placing children on child protection registers: risk indicators and local authority differences. *British Journal of Social Work,* **28**, 423–436.

Grace C (1994) *Social Workers, Children and the Law.* Oxford, Oxford University Press.

Hallett C & Stevenson O (1992) *Co-ordination in child protection.* London, HMSO.

Hardiker P (1991) *Policies and practices in preventive child care.* Aldershot, Avebury.

Harwin J, Owen M, Locke R & Forrester D (2003) *Making Care Orders Work*. London, TSO.

Hendrick H (1994) *Child Welfare 1872–1989*. London, Routledge.

Her Majesty's Government (2005) *Statutory Guidance on Making Arrangements to Safeguard and Promote the Welfare of Children under Children Act 2004, s.11*. London, TSO.

Her Majesty's Inspectorate of Constabulary (1999) *Child Protection, Thematic Inspection*. London, Home Office.

Her Majesty's Inspectorate of Constabulary (2005) *Keeping Safe, Staying Safe*. London, Home Office.

Her Majesty's Treasury (2003) *Every Child Matters* (Cm 5860). London, TSO.

Hilgendorf L (1981) *Social Workers and Solicitors in Child Care Cases*. London, HMSO.

Hodgson J (1997) Vulnerable suspects and the appropriate adult. *Criminal Law Review*, 785–795.

Hodson L (2005) *Struggle for Rights: The Role of Non-Governmental Organisation in Litigation before the European Court of Human Rights*, PhD thesis, Warwick University.

Home Office (1991) *The Children Act 1989*, Circular HO 54/1991. London, Home Office.

Home Office (2003) *Duties and Powers of the Police under the Children Act 1989*, Circular HO 44/2003. London, Home Office.

Home Office *et al.* (1991) *Working Together under the Children Act 1989*. London, HMSO.

Home Office *et al.* (1992) *Memorandum of Good practice on Video Recorded Interviews with Child Witnesses*. London, HMSO.

Horwath J (2006) The missing assessment domain: personal professional and organisational factors influencing professional judgements when identifying and referring child neglect, *British Journal of Social Work*. Available at http://www.bjsw.oxfordjournals.org/papbyrecent.dtl. doi:10.1093/bjsw/bcl029. Advance Access published on May 4, 2006.

House of Commons (2003) Select Committee on the Lord Chancellor's Department, *Third Report 2002–3 CAFCASS* (2002–3 H.C. 614). London, TSO.

Hughes B, Parker H & Gallagher B (1996) *Policing Child Sexual Abuse*. London, Home Office (Police Research Group).

Hunt J (1998) A moving target – care proceedings as a dynamic process. *Child and Family Law Quarterly*, **10**, 281–290.

Hunt J & Macleod A (1999) *The Best-laid Plans*. London, TSO.

Hunt J, Macleod A & Thomas C (1999) *The Last Resort*. London, TSO.

Ingelby Report (1960) *Report of the Committee on Children and Young Persons* (1960 cmnd 1191). London, HMSO.

Kearney B (1992) *The Report of the Inquiry into Child Care Policies in Fife* (1991–2 H.C. 191). Edinburgh, HMSO.

Kemp C, Norris C & Fielding N (1992) *Negotiating Nothing: Police Decision-making in Disputes*. Aldershot, Avebury.

Kirkwood A (1993) *The Leicestershire Inquiry 1992*. Glenfield, Leicestershire County Council.

Laming H (2003) *The Victoria Climbié Inquiry Report* (2003 cm 5730). London, TSO.

Lavery R (1996) The child assessment order – a reassessment. *Child and Family Law Quarterly*, **8**, 41–56.

Law Commission (1992) *Report No 207, Domestic Violence and the Protection of the Family Home*. London, HMSO.

Lindley B (1994) *On the Receiving End*. London, Family Rights Group.

Lipsky M & Smith S (1989) When social problems are treated as emergencies. *Social Services Review*, **63**, 5–25.

Littlechild B (2005) The nature and effects of violence against child protection social workers: providing effective support. *British Journal of Social Work*, **35**, 387–401.

Lloyd S & Burman M (1996) 'Specialist police units and the joint investigation of child abuse'. *Child Abuse Review*, **5**, 4–17.

Local Government Association & the Association of Chief Police Officers (1997) *Missing from Care: Procedures and Practices in Caring for Missing Children*. London, Local Government Association.

Lord Chancellor's Department (2002) *Scoping Study on Delay in Children Act Cases*. London, Lord Chancellor's Department.

Magistrates Association of England and Wales (1983) *Memorandum to the House of Commons Inquiry, Children in Care* (1983–4 H.C.360 vol. II). London, HMSO.

Masson J (2002) Police protection – protecting whom? *Journal of Social Welfare and Family Law*, **24**, 157–174.

Masson J (2003) Factors which impact on the costs to the LSC in Public Law Children Act Proceedings. Unpublished paper for the Legal Services Commission.

Masson J (2004a) Human rights in child protection: emergency action and its impact. In Lodrup P & Modvar E (eds) *Family Life and Human Rights*. Oslo, Glydendal Akedemisk, 457–476.

Masson J (2004b) Emergency protection, good practice and human rights. *Family Law*, **34**, 882–887.

Masson J (2006a) Fair trials in child protection. *Journal of Social Welfare and Family Law*, **28**, 15–30.

Masson J (2006b) The Climbié Inquiry – context and critique. *Journal of Law and Society*, **33**, 221–243.

Masson J & Morton S (1989) The use of wardship by local authorities. *Modern Law Review*, **52**, 762–789.

Masson J, Harrison C & Pavlovic A (1999) *Lost and Found*. Aldershot, Ashgate.

Masson J, Winn Oakley M & Pick K (2004) *Emergency Protection Orders: Court orders for child protection crises*. Warwick, School of Law, Warwick University. Available from www.nspcc.org.uk/Inform/Research/NSPCCResearch/CompletedResearch/ChildAndFamilyLaw/Home_asp_ifega23683.html.

McGhee J & Francis J (2003) Protecting children in Scotland: examining the impact of the Children (Scotland) Act 1995. *Children and Family Social Work*, **8**, 133–142.

Müller J (2003) *A Dangerous Mind: Carl Schmitt in Post War European Thought*. Newhaven, Yale University Press.

NIGALA (2003) *Annual Report 2002-3*. Available from http://www.nigala.n-i.nhs.uk/pdf/reports/Annual%20Report%20%202002-2003.pdf.

Norris T & Parton N (1986) *The Administration of Place of Safety Orders*. Huddersfield, Huddersfield Polytechnic.

Northern Ireland Statistical and Research Agency (2005) *Children Order Statistical Bulletin 2005*. Belfast: DHSSPS.

O' Hagan K (1997) Parental participation in emergency protection. *Child Care in Practice*, **33**(3) 22–41.

Pack A (2001) 'Most efficacious in every case?' exclusion requirements – an overview. *Family Law*, **31**, 217–220.

Packman J & Hall C (1998) *From Care to Accommodation*. London, TSO.

Packman J, Randall J & Jacques N (1984) *Decision Making on Admissions to Local Authority Care*, Report to DHSS.

Packman J, Randall J & Jacques N (1986) *Who Needs Care?* Oxford, Blackwell.

Parton N (1991) *Governing the Family*. Basingstoke, Macmillan.

Parton N (1996) Current debates and future prospects. In Parton N (ed.) *Child Protection and Family Support*. London, Routledge.

Platt D. (2006a) Investigation or initial assessment of child concerns? The impact of the re-focusing initiative on social work practice. *British Journal of Social Work*, **36**, 267–281.

Platt D (2006b) Threshold decisions: how social workers prioritize referrals of child concern. *Child Abuse Review*, **15**, 4–18.

Police Service of Northern Ireland (2005) Child protection policy PD 06/05. Available from http://www.psni.police.uk/0605_policy_directive.pdf.

Power M (1997) *The Audit Society*. Oxford, Oxford University Press.

Poyser A (2005) What *is* the point of inspection? *Seen and Heard*, **15**, 4.

Pugh R (2006) Variations in registration on child protection registers. *British Journal of Social Work*, available at http://www.bjsw.oxfordjournals.org/papbyrecent.dtl. doi:10.1093/bjsw/bch422. Advance Access published on January 17, 2006.

Punch M (1979) The secret social service. In Holdaway S (ed.) *The British Police*. London, Edward Arnold.

Punch M & Naylor T (1973) The police: a social service. *New Society*, 17 May, 358–361.

Reder P & Duncan S (1999) *Lost Innocents? A follow up study of fatal child abuse*. London, Routledge.

Reder P, Duncan S & Gray M (1993) *Beyond Blame: Child abuse tragedies revisited*. London, Routledge.

Reiner R (2000) *The Politics of the Police*, 3rd edn. Oxford, Oxford University Press.

Review of Child Care Law (1985) *Discussion Paper 6, Place of Safety and Interim Care Orders*, Department of Health and Social Security.

Scottish Office (1990) *Review of Child Care Law in Scotland*. Edinburgh, Scottish Office.

Scottish Office (1997) *Scotland's Children. The Children (Scotland) Act 1995 Regulations and Guidance Volume 1: Support and Protection for Children and their Families*. Edinburgh, TSO.

Scourfield J (2003) *Gender and Child Protection*. Basingstoke, Palgrave Macmillan.

Shapland J & Vagg J (1988) *Policing by the Public*. London, Routledge.

Sheehan R (2001) *Magistrates' Decision-making in Child Protection*. Aldershot, Ashgate.

Simey M (1985) *Government by consent*. London, Bedford Square Press.

Sinclair R & Bullock R (2002) *Learning from Past Experience: A review of serious case reviews*. London, Department of Health.

Social Services Inspectorate (1999) *Open all Hours?* London, Department of Health.

Social Services Select Committee (1983–1984) *Second Report 1983–4, Children in care* (H.C. 360). The Short Report.

Stevenson O & Hallett C (1980) *Child Abuse – Aspects of Interprofessional Co-operation*. London, Allen & Owen.

Strauss A & Corbin J (1990) *Basics of Qualitative Research: Grounded Theory Procedures and Techniques*. Newbury Park, CA, Sage.

Thoburn J, Lewis A & Shemmings D (1995) *Paternalism or Partnership? Family Involvement in the Child Protection Process*. London, HMSO.

Thomas T (1994) *The Police and Social Workers*, 2nd edn. Aldershot, Arena.

Thomas C & Hunt J (nd) *The Care Workloads of the Civil Courts under the Children Act*. Bristol, Centre for Socio-legal Studies, University of Bristol.

Trinder L, Connolly J, Kellett J & Notley C (2005) *A Profile of Applicants and Respondents in Child Contact Cases in Essex*, DCA Research Series. London, DCA.

Utting W (1992) *Children in the Public Care*. London, HMSO.

Waddington P (1999) *Policing Citizens: Authority and Rights*. London, UCL Press.

Wade J, Biehal N, Clayden J & Stein M (1998) *Going Missing. Young People Absent from Care*. Chichester, Wiley.

Ward H, Munro E & Dearden C (2006) *Babies and Young Children in Care*. London, Jessica Kingsley.

Waterhouse R (1999) *Lost in Care. Report of the Tribunal of Inquiry into the abuse of children in care in the former county council areas of Gwynedd and Clwyd since 1974*, HC 201. London, TSO.

INDEX